Strategies in Teaching Anthropology

SECOND EDITION

edited by

Patricia C. Rice
West Virginia University

David W. McCurdy
Macalester College

Foreword by Conrad P. Kottak

Introduction by Yolanda T. Moses

Prentice Hall, Upper Saddle River, New Jersey 07458

©2002 by PEARSON EDUCATION, INC.
Upper Saddle River, New Jersey 07458

ISBN 0-13-034070-7

Printed in the United States of America

Table of Contents

iv

CONTRIBUTORS

Clifton Amsbury (formerly Contra Costa Community College)

Vicki K. Bentley-Condit (Grinnell College) bentleyc@pioneerserver.grinnell.edu

Susan Birns (Massachusetts College of Liberal Arts) sbirns3907@.aol.com

Anne E. Campbell (Washington State University) annec@mail.wsu.edu

John L. Caughey (University of Maryland) jc29@umail.umd.edu

John Coggeshall (Clemson University) raucus@clemson.edu

Jeffrey Cohen (Pennsylvania State University) jhcll@psu.edu

Lorenzo Covarrubias (University of California, Santa Barbara) covarrub@humanitas.uscb.edu

Marilynne Diggs-Thompson (Hunter College – CUNY)

Charles O. Ellenbaum (College of DuPage) ellenbau@cdnet.cod.edu

Carolyn Epple (Southern Illinois University at Edwardsville) cepple@siue.edu

Juliana Flinn (University of Arkansas at Little Rock) jbflinn@ulr.edu

Daniel M. Goldstein (College of the Holy Cross) dgoldste@holycross.edu

Robert Bates Graber (Truman State University) rgraber@pop.truman.edu

Harold D. Juli (Connecticut College) hdjul@conncoll.edu

Grace Keyes (St. Mary's University) keyeg@lake.ollusa.edu

Suzanne LaFont (CUNY, Kingsborough Community College) suzannelafont@hotmail.com

Scott A. Lukas (Lake Tahoe Community College) lukas@ltcc.cc.ca.us

David W. McCurdy (Macalester College) clorac@aol.com

Brent Metz (University of Kansas) bmetz@ukans.edu

Robin O'Brian (Elmira College) robrian@mcgraw.elmira.edu

Michael J. Oldani (Princeton University) moldani@princeton.edu

Sam Pack (Temple University)

Mark Pedelty (Miami University) pedeltmh@tc.umn.edu

Janet Pollak (William Paterson University) pollakj@wpunj.edu

Mary H. Pulford (Lake Superior College) m.pulford@lsc.cc.mn.us

Patricia C. Rice (West Virginia University) price@wvu.edu

Mary Riley (Columbia College -- Chicago) slabat1@uic.edi

Phillip Carl Salzman (McGill University) philip.carl.salzman@mcgill.ca

Michael Sheridan (University of Vermont) sheridan@together.net

Spyros Spyrou (Cyprus College) sspyrou@dial.cycollege.ac.cy

David Sutton (Southern Illinois University at Carbondale) dsutton@siu.edu

Susan Buck Sutton (Indiana University - Purdue University at Indianapolis) ssutton@iupui.edu

Charles F. Urbanowicz (California State University, Chico) curbanowicz@csuchico.edu

Peter Wogan (Willamette University) pwogan@willamette.edu

Dickie Wallace (University of Massachusetts) dk@anthro.umass.edu

Editor's Preface

Four years ago, *Strategies in Teaching Anthropology* was only a glimmer in our eyes. The AAA had finished its four year task force on teaching anthropology, and in 1997, a volume of pedagogy, the first in 35 years, titled *The Teaching of Anthropology: Problems, Issues, and Decisions* (edited by C. Kottak. J. White, R. Furlow, and P. Rice), was published by Mayfield Publishing Company. But the 1997 volume was "delinquent" in one area due to lack of space, and that was an absence of any articles of a "how to do it" nature. Members of the General Anthropology Division of the AAA and its permanent teaching committee COTA (Committee On Teaching Anthropology) mounted a Call For Papers in hopes of filling that void. We were extremely happy when Nancy Roberts, publisher at Prentice-Hall, agreed to publish the volume in 2000.

In this second edition, we are pleased to present 30 new strategies for teaching our discipline. Like the strategies in the first edition, some are "quick fix tricks" for a one-class session (or less), some take a week or so, and some continue through a term, though on an occasional basis. It is not our intent to present course outlines or syllabi, but rather strategies to use in teaching introductory-level courses. Some of the principles used in these strategies can be used in upper division courses (for example, in fieldwork courses or those doing role playing), but all are suitable, and indeed "invented" for use in introductory level courses where students normally get their first taste of anthropology. Some 10 of the strategies in this second edition were published in the first edition, but because of their general applicability and timeliness, they are republished here.

We have had many positive unsolicited comments about the first edition, with people telling us they have used many of the strategies and thanking us for putting the volume together because the strategies "worked." One of us (PCR) mentored Danelle Marable, a first-time instructor in a summer Introduction to Anthropology course for 50 students when the book was only in manuscript form and loaned it to her. She used 10 of the strategies, reporting on a weekly basis how well they all worked. She particularly liked her first day in class when she sat in the back, looking and acting "just like them." While doing all 40 strategies in a single class might prove to be a bit too unorganized for most students, in the case of instructor Marable choosing 10 of the strategies, her class evaluated her as an excellent instructor in her first time teaching role.

The articles in the second edition are organized by anthropological subfield, and pages vii through xiii give a quick look at each article by topic, (expected) learning outcomes, and student activity. The Contributor's list also contains email listings for the authors. Some authors have written in their articles that they would be happy to supply further information. Feel free to get in touch with authors directly about any questions you might have. We are again happy to have both Conrad Kottak and Yolanda Moses contribute to the volume, and thank Nancy Roberts and Sharon Chambliss at Prentice-Hall for not only seeing virtue in publishing a book that can only improve the teaching of anthropology, but for making our jobs seamless.

ANNOTATED INDEX: TOPICS, LEARNING OUTCOMES, AND STUDENT ACTIVITY

The Use of Bible "Stories" as a Discussion Point for Evolution Versus Creationism (Amsbury)

... Biblical stories and biological evolution;
... all Biblical stories about creation cannot be correct because they are contradictory;
... no student activity until after the instructor reads two stories from the Old Testament; then the class discusses the contradictions and biological evolution.

Hands-On Exercises for Four-Field Introduction to Anthropology (Bentley-Condit)

... skulls, burials, latrinealia, and HRAF exercises;
... hands-on exercises so students can "do" anthropology;
... students measure skull features, "excavate" burials, collect data on lavatory graffiti, and do cross-cultural analyis via HRAF files.

Culture as "The Rules of the Game:" Simulating Fieldwork While Playing Cards (Birns)

... culture as "the rules of the game;"
... culture and fieldwork are paradigms of rules that just seem arbitrary;
... by playing a card game, students discover the analogies with culture and fieldwork.

Using Values Orientation to Understand the Role of Culture in Cross-Cultural Communication (Campbell)

... cross-cultural values orientation;
... students learn their own values orientation, that of mainstream American culture, and that of one or more non-American cultures;
... students read, discuss, and do taxonomies on values orientations for self and other cultures.

How to Teach Self Ethnography (Caughey)

... ethnography of self;
... how to do field work and discover "hidden truths" about one's own culture;
... students choose an informant whose cultural background is significantly different from their own and through "field work" interviewing, compare the resultant life history with their own.

Nacirema Writing (Coggeshall)

... writing about the relationship between assigned readings and a related subject;
... the importance of writing skills and how to apply the specifics in a reading assignment to a

general theme;

... 12 times a term, students write a l0-minute in-class essay on an assigned reading as a prelude to class discussion launched by that reading.

Family Altars in Introductory Anthropology: Making Kinship Relevant (Cohen)

... the importance of the American family;

... how important family, friends, and pets are in our culture;

... students construct a family altar by "building" one on paper using photos and other graphics and then describing the importance of each person.

Dynamic Ethography, Methods, and Next-Door Anthropology (Covarrubias)

... local ethnography;

... how to do a focused ethnography in a near-by neighborhood;

... students choose an aspect of the group-assigned project and through class-taught methods, do a partial ethnography.

Building Student Interest, Input, and Engagement: Organizing Small Group Projects in Large Lecture Classes (Diggs-Thompson)

... term team projects;

... anthropology is the study of modern, technologically complex people, not just ancient, extinct, "primitive" cultures;

... in teams of 9-10, students make in-class presentations based on one of 60 randomly chosen topics gleaned from articles in *The New York Times*; the presentations can be reports or debates and can include data, slides, or charts.

Discussion Preparation Guides (Ellenbaum)

... discussion of articles or films;

... how to share information and views on articles or films;

... students sit in groups of 5, use their filled-in preparation guides, and discuss the main points of a reading or film.

Student Experiential Learning on Social Control, Class, and Gender (Epple)

... mini field-projects on social issues;

... many cultural constructs are anything but "natural;"

... students go to field sites and observe rules, then break one and make similar observations, or they go to both upscale and discount stores dressed down and dressed up and observe biased treatment, or they spend a day gender cross-dressing, noting behaviors suitable for the "new" gender.

Acting Out Anthropological Concepts (Flinn)

... acting out simple concepts;
... concepts such as consensus, distribution of goods and services, and postmarital residence patterns are learned by acting them out;
... after reading about cultural concepts, students are divided into groups and asked to design and perform specific examples of the concept.

Fieldwork and the Observer's Gaze: Teaching the Ups and Downs of Ethnographic Observation (Goldstein)

... elevator ethnography;
... how fieldwork can be done and how observers impact the fieldwork encounter;
... students spend time in an elevator, noting behavior before and after being objects of observation themselves.

Potlatching Classroom Participation: Using "Prestige" and "Shame" to Encourage Student Involvement (Goldstein)

... classroom participation;
... the principles of potlatching, reciprocal gift giving, and their associated shame and prestige;
... students must attempt to answer questions pertaining to recently presented class material on Durkheimian social theory in order to discharge their obligation for a gift given to each.

Coming of Age in Statistics (Graber)

... anthropological statistics;
... analysis of Mead's Samoa data using Yule's Q and Chi-square statistics;
... students put the data in the proper cells, calculate frequencies, and determine whether their findings are statistically positive.

The Trouble With the "Race" Concept: It's All in the Cards (Graber)

... the concept of "race;"
... the traits used to construct "races" are not concordant and therefore do not produce groups/ "races;"
... using two decks of manufactured cards, students easily sort one deck into two "races," but no matter how hard they try, cannot sort the second deck because more than one trait is used.

The Illegal Antiquities Trade, Looting, and Archaeological Ethics (Juli)

... archaeological illegalities;
... stereotypes in archaeology and illegalities/ethics;

... through film and reading, the instructor takes students through archaeological reality.

"TSM Cube:" Illustrating the Scientific Method (Keyes)

... the Scientific Method in action;
... all aspects of the Scientific Method: observation, hypothesis, evidence, conclusions, fact, inference;
... the instructor shows a cube with numbers on it and students must do the steps in the Scientific Method to infer what number is on the bottom of the cube.

Creating Cultures: Taking the Pain Out of Writing in Introductory Courses (LaFont)

... writing fictive culture;
... how to apply anthropological concepts to a fictive culture through writing;
... students "invent" and write up a culture, giving it a history and environment as well as social, political, economic and belief systems; then a new technology arrives and changes the culture.

Teaching Cultural Anthropology Through Mass and Popular Culture: Seven Pedagogical Methods for the Classroom (Lukas)

... hands-on exercises in popular culture;
... how "culture is us" by doing exercises;
... students do partial ethnographies on popular culture, demonstrate material culture in class, do cultural snapshots and focused collages, collect data on body images, and apply anthropological theories to contemporary news stories.

Teaching Culture Through Life History: The Spradley Approach (McCurdy)

... cultural life history;
... how to define and use culture as knowledge, as self-knowledge and as cultural knowledge;
... students write about their childhood in terms of cultural categories such as "primary turf maps," daily eating rules, and rewards and punishments from family.

Grounding the Culture Concept, or Pulling the Rug Out From Students (Metz)

... defining culture;
... culture is a social construction and as such, there are microcultures, main-stream American culture, self-reflecting culture, and metaculture;
... after discussing the various meanings and facets of culture, students apply the concept to critique TV commercials or write a mini ethnography as if they were a cultural Other.

Reading Textiles for Cultural Messages (O'Brian)

... textile "messages;"

... how items of material culture can give clues to social organization, gender systems, and even cosmology as well as technology;

... students view a collection of textiles, even trying them on, and hypothesize about their meaning and function.

Taking Students on a *Walkabout* (Oldani)

... use of a feature film to teach culture;

... through viewing and discussing, students learn about civilization, "primitive," "race," nature, cultural relativism, modernization;

... students see the film and then discuss the principles observed.

Familiarizing the Exotic in Ethnographic Film (Pack)

... viewing ethnographic film;

... how to critically examine the ethnographic films students see;

... with only their brains and eyes being active, students see films of "the primitive" from a non-ethnocentric perspective.

The Cultural Dialog Project (CDP): Approaching Ethnographic Texts Through Playwriting and Performance (Pedelty)

... writing cultural dialog;

... understanding readings;

... students write fictional dialog with plot, characters, and dialog concerning an ethnographic encounter from a text.

Ping-Pong Archaeology: A Non-Destructive Field and Lab Exercise (Pollak)

... simulated archaeology excavation;

... basic excavation techniques in archaeology from measuring to mapping to analyzing;

... students "excavate" ping pong balls that have been precisely set out by the instructor and analyze their symbols to find meaning and context.

"First Steps" in Hominid Evolution: A Lesson on Walking (Pollak)

... critical thinking about bipedalism;

... how to dissect a seemingly easy behavior – walking – and thus learn how anatomically and physiologically complex the behavior is;

... students write a paragraph for "an owner's manual" for standing/walking by either observing others or "practicing" the behavior; after reading a sample of the first drafts to the class, the instructor returns the papers for rewrites.

Critical Thinking in the Anthropology Classroom (Pulford)

... material culture and critical thinking skills;
... how to analyze material culture for answers to economic and social questions;
... students in pairs analyze lists of garbage and write reports answering above questions.

Strategies for Becoming an Outstanding Anthropology Teacher: From the Student Perspective (Rice)

... becoming an outstanding teacher;
... anthropology instructors learn what students claim to want and what they praise in teachers;
... students will be the recipients of selected strategies/activities to improve teacher teaching and student learning.

Getting Into the Act: Using Classroom Role-Playing as a Type of Participant Observation (Riley)

... role-playing cultural scenarios;
... individuals make individual and group decisions in all cultures, not just in ours;
... based on instructor-written cultural scenarios, students "become" others in a controlled case study.

Ethnography, Humanity, and Imagination: Seeing a Culture and Society Through the Eyes of an Individual (Salzman)

... individuals in culture;
... individuals have distinct roles in culture;
... students write a "sociobiography," which is a portrait of a fictional individual, based on a classic ethnography.

Linguistic Models in Anthropology 101: Give Me The Cup (Sheridan)

... politeness by gender in language;
... males and females use different forms of language having different meanings;
... students form groups in class and rank order politeness of one "request," then sort for likely male or female speakers with subsequent analysis of findings.

Using Ads to Teach Anthropology (Spyrou)

... the ubiquitous ad;
... ads tell students about stereotypes and everyday culture;
... students go through magazine ads that portray particular groups of people, discuss the implications in small groups, and then discuss the project as a class.

Introductory Fieldwork: the Meaning of the Gift (D. Sutton)

... the "anthropology of the gift;"
... how to analyze gifts and put them in anthropological context;
... students self interview and then interview a friend to categorize and then analyze gifts.

Reading Between the Lines: Representing Diversity, Conflict, and the Broader World in International News Stories (S. Sutton)

... anthropology and international events;
... the anthropological perspective makes a difference in our everyday lives relative to the world;
... a current newspaper article (and a set of questions) is used to provoke in-class discussion concerning a timely event that has anthropological overtones.

Teaching as Theater (Urbanowicz)

... dramatizing the persona of a famous anthropologist;
... insights about the life and times of an anthropologist not attainable through normal reading or lecture formats;
... students are not active, but the instructor is.

Gender and Language: A Fieldwork Project (Wogan)

... gender and compliments
... how to do fieldwork to collect data on one topic and then analyze the findings;
... students gather data, look for patterns, compare the findings to hypotheses laid out in the reading, concluding that both qualitative and quantitative data are important.

"Flags:" The Power of Patriotism and Nationalism; the Arbitrariness of Symbols and Significance: A Classroom Exercise that'll Wake'em Up (Wallace)

... symbols are arbitrary;
... that symbols such as flags are cultural and are emotionally charged;
... students do in-class activities that show the arbitrariness of symbols.

Pre-Class Fieldwork: Ethnographic Introductions (Wallace)

... an ethnography of the first day of class;
... field methods and the ethics of doing field work;
... no student activity. The instructor sits in the back of the room dressed as a student, takes notes and observes behavioral patterns as students come into the classroom the first day of class. This becomes the basis for an immediate discussion of field work and ethics.

Foreward

Conrad P. Kottak

We all have our teaching tricks and we sometimes share them anecdotally with colleagues. We may do this in meetings, conferences, or over lunch with a fellow faculty member. Usually, however, our focus at national meetings and professional conferences is the more exalted domain of research. As anthropologists, we don't talk about **how to teach** as much as we should. The second edition of this volume provides a welcome forum for another group of seasoned teaching anthropologists (some are repeat authors) to share 30 new pedagogical techniques, knowledge, and observations with their fellows. And in a sense, this is a sequel to the 1997 *The Teaching of Anthropology: Problems, Issues, and Decisions* that I co-edited with Jane White, Richard Furlow, and Patricia Rice. The two strategies "how to" volumes are the applied side of the pedagogical nature of teaching our discipline.

Anthropology's breadth supports an array of teaching strategies, and it is useful to have a number of these strategies assembled here in (another) single volume. A range of articles representing anthropology's sub-fields exposes numerous teaching "tricks." As teachers, we have discovered that some things work while others do not. Some of the strategies we use with undergraduates may not work with graduate students. One strategy that can work at both levels, when used properly, is the team project. In a large class, such projects can also reduce our workload, permitting us, say, to read fifteen papers instead of thirty. Teamwork, a tradition in archaeology and biological anthropology, is featured in several of the strategies discussed in this volume. Such joint work does pose a challenge to the lone ethnographer model that has long, and probably unfortunately, dominated cultural anthropology. But I have found that joint writing projects, especially involving teams of two students who are allowed to choose their own partner, enhances the quality of presentation. Students have to get their points across to each other before trying to explain them to me. Better, clearer writing, and higher grades result, along with a sense that even cultural anthropologists can learn to work in teams.

Often we develop special strategies for parts of the introductory course that our students find particularly challenging, such as statistics and kinship. The papers in this volume offer tricks for making comprehensible several of anthropology's "esoteric" topics. These range from the potlatch and economic exchange theory, to cross-cousin marriage and avunculocal residence. Other contributors describe strategies they use to demonstrate anthropological perspectives that contradict everyday experience and establish social categories, as in teaching about the social construction of race.

The book offers teaching tricks ranging from specific to very general applicability. Strategies involving interviewing, hypothesis testing, ethnographic film viewing, and role playing can be applied in a variety of courses. Others have more particular goals, such as using Mead's own research in Samoa to teach students the rudiments of anthropological statistics or playing cards as an analogy to culture and fieldwork (this one is diabolical!). Almost everyone who teaches introductory anthropology has learned the usefulness of using the familiar to illustrate the novel. Students appreciate American culture examples, whether we are teaching about kinship, genetics, race, gender, rituals, or values.

This volume enhances anthropological pedagogy by assembling tricks of the trade from anthropologists working in a variety of teaching settings. For those of us who value teaching, which after all most of us do for a living, this book, once read, should be placed on an easily reachable shelf right next to the first edition. Seventy-five percent of the second edition features new strategies. You need both editions.

Introduction

Yolanda T. Moses
President, American Association For Higher Education

The second edition of *Strategies in Teaching Anthropology* presents 30 new articles as well as revisits old favorites from the first edition that explore the teaching of anthropology across the four traditional sub-fields of anthropology. With the four sub-fields, Cultural-Social, Biological, Archaeology, and Linguistics, there are also two dimensions within anthropology: research and applied studies. One major problem with anthropology in the United States is that it is not usually taught in high schools, so the first time most students are exposed to the subject is at the college or university level. Consequently, the first exposure to anthropology and how it is taught is critical.

Anthropology professors, like most classically trained academicians, do not learn how to teach as part of their training. We learn our subject matter, often in great detail. In fact, we are often the only experts in our particular subject area in the entire world. There is, therefore, a huge gap between the student who is taking an anthropology class for the first time and faculty members who know their own "dense" subject matter, but do not know how to pitch it to their audience, to "engage" them in anthropological subject matter and its processes. I have found in my many years of teaching students (mostly non-anthropology majors), that they learn anthropology best by "doing it."

This second edition continues the tradition of focusing on the "how" of teaching anthropology across all of its sub-fields, with a wide array of learning outcomes and student activities. For example, in Part I, the general section, the authors recommend tried and true strategies to engage students in all sub-disciplines in learning about anthropology. These strategies are particularly appropriate for students first exposure to anthropology and college classrooms in general. For example, "Discussion Preparation Guides" by Ellenbaum and "Using Modern Material Culture (Garbage) to Teach Critical Thinking in Anthropology" by Pulford give tips on how to create student successes every time by reinforcing critical thinking skills.

In Part II, Archaeology and Biological Anthropology, "First Steps in Hominid Evolution: A Lesson on Walking" by Pollak provides the opportunity for students to develop critical thinking skills around the deceptively simple art of walking, which actually turns out to be an extremely complex phenomenon. Students then write about standing or walking by observing others or "practicing" themselves. Graber's article "The Trouble with the 'Race' Concept: Its All in the Cards" shows students that the traits used to construct "races" are not concordant and therefore do not actually produce biological "races." By using two decks of cards, the students easily sort one deck into two "races," but no matter how hard they try, they cannot sort the second deck into "races" because more than one trait is used. Both of these examples have the ability to engage students in understanding the complex issues of hominid evolution and "race" through activities and props very familiar to them.

Part III is a new section on Language and Culture and it features gender differences explored through language in "Gender and Language: A Fieldwork Project" by Wogan and "Linguistic Models in Anthropology: Give Me the Cup" by Sheridan.

Part IV has the largest number of teaching strategies, ranging from "Acting Out Anthropological Concepts" by Flinn to "Reading Between the Lines: The Representation of Diversity, Conflict, and the Broader World in International News Stories" by S. Sutton. These authors engage students in a series of activities that challenge the familiar and reveal that which is masked or often covert.

Fieldwork is emphasized in "Fieldwork and the Observers Gaze: Teaching the Ups and Downs of Ethnographic Observation" by Goldstein. In this article, students find a field site (such as an elevator) and observe behavior, taking notes on what they find. Class discussion regarding fieldwork as well as a written paper follow. In "The Rules of the Game: Simulating Fieldwork by Playing Cards," Birns plays cards with a group of students while the rest of the class watches. This exercise is used as an analogy to doing fieldwork.

The hallmark of cultural-social anthropology is ethnography. I am pleased to see that the second edition of this book also contains articles that directly teach ethnography. Wallace's "Pre-Class Fieldwork: Ethnographic Introductions" from the first edition is joined by "Ethnography, Humanity, and Imagination: Seeing a Culture and Society Through the Eyes of an Individual" by Salzman and "Dynamic Ethnography, Methods, and Next-Door Anthropology" by Covarrubias. These provide an opportunity for students to experience and write ethnographies from a communal as well as personal perspective.

Thank you again to the editors, Patricia Rice and David McCurdy, for bringing together another talented group of colleagues to share their best practices with other teachers, anthropologists, and non-anthropologists so that we can continue to provide our undergraduate students with the best experiences possible in their discovery of the wonder of anthropology, the discipline of the 21st century.

Hands-On Exercises for Four-Field Introduction to Anthropology

Vicki K. Bentley-Condit

I teach a four-field Introduction to Anthropology course at a small, liberal-arts college in the mid-west. I am fortunate in that our introductory level courses are always small, closing at 25 students, and our department has a good set of fossil casts, skeletons, ethnographic films, and other materials with which to work. As those of you who teach a four-field introductory course know, we tend not to spend much time on any given topic. Therefore, over the past few years I have been trying to develop some hands-on exercises or "labs" that can be done in class in one 50-minute class period or outside of class as a paper exercise. Note that we do not do any of these exercises in an actual lab facility; all are done in either a regular classroom with moveable desks or outside of class. The exercises are described in the order in which we do them in class and by field. In addition to the descriptions below, the complete instructions given to the students for the biological paper, linguistics lab, and cultural paper exercises can be accessed and printed from my course syllabus: http://www.grinnell.edu/courses/ant/s01/and10 4-01.

(1) Biological Anthropology – Skull/Fossil Cast Paper

In this exercise, each student is asked to take measurements on some aspect of two or more of the skulls/fossil casts and then present their methods, data, results, and a discussion of the possible implications in a short (2-3 pp.) paper. For example, students can measure the molars of *Australopithecus boisei* and *Australopithecus afarensis* and discuss their dietary implications. Another example would be to measure the canines of male and female primate species and discuss the implications of the degree of sexual dimorphism. Yet another example might be to measure the pelvis or femur of a chimpanzee and a hominid and discuss the implications for locomotion. This is not meant to be a large research paper; only a couple of sources are required and one can be our text, i.e., Lewin 1999. I also accept valid on-line sources. The goal is to give the students some real hands-on experience with the specimens and the use of calipers and to have them think about the behavioral implications of the various physiological traits. It is always a successful exercise. The down side is that it requires the students to have access to the specimens in order to take their measurements. Since we do not have an actual lab where the specimens can be made constantly available, this means scheduling individual appointments with each student. The exercise could easily be tailored to work with whichever specimens are available, with or without an actual lab facility, and with a graduate student in charge of the specimens instead of the instructor.

(2) Archaeology – Burial Lab

In this exercise, I construct two "burials," with assorted grave goods in the classroom, i.e., two complete disarticulated skeletons with various pieces of my daughter's 1980s jewelry, scattered seeds and nuts, and other objects made of wood, stone, or metal "buried" between two bed sheets. I then divide the students into two teams and their job is to carefully "excavate" their burial, noting the position of the body and the types and positioning of grave goods. Prior to this exercise, the students have read Kamp's *Life in the Pueblo* (1998) and are provided with some handouts on how to sex and age skeletons. Each team is to determine the approximate age and the sex of the individual and whatever else they can about either the individual's society or the individual him or herself, e.g., health or relative wealth. Each team is also to send an envoy to the other side to see if any useful information might be gained for comparison. For example, I generally split pairs of matching earrings so that each burial has one of the pair. Astute students should discover this. We then use the last 15 minutes or so of the 50-minute class for the teams to present their findings and interpretations. Again, this exercise could be easily modified to include more burials or different grave goods depending on the size of the class, the classroom, and available resources.

(3) Linguistics – Graffiti Lab

This exercise requires some work by the students outside of class and prior to the day on which the "lab" is done. One of the readings we do for the linguistics section is Maltz and Borker's *A Cultural Approach to Male-Female Miscommunication* (2001). We discuss some of the differences described in the article and the students' own experiences with this issue. For the lab, we then set out to determine if these supposed differences in communication might also be seen in male and female graffiti. I divide the students into five same-sex teams and choose a "team leader" at random for each. Each team then chooses their "research site" – usually either a male or female restroom from various on and off-campus locales. The library tends to offer particularly good "data" as do a couple of the local establishments. Each team is to copy all graffiti (some would call it "latrinealia")

available at their site. They usually divide the task by "stalls." They then bring their data to class and we decide on a few ways to categorize it by type or topic. The students write their own graffiti under the appropriate category title, and we look for patterns. The students are instructed not to use any complete names (initials will do) and that it is OK to abbreviate inappropriate language. The students enjoy this exercise, it is easily done in one 50-minute class period, and we always find some interesting female-male patterns. The exercise could be easily modified for more or fewer teams, as long as there is sufficient chalkboard space.

(4) Cultural – Cross-Cultural Research Paper

In this assignment, students are asked to formulate a hypothesis based upon something they have read or seen (for example in Heider's *Seeing Anthropology: Cultural Anthropology Through Film* [1997]). The hypothesis is to propose a correlation between two cultural factors and they then investigate these factors cross-culturally to determine if their hypothesis is supported. For example, the student might hypothesize from readings or various ethnographic films that societies that practice slash-and-burn horticulture tend to have animistic religious practices. The student would then conduct cross-cultural research to investigate this hypothesis. I demonstrate and have the students use the web-based electronic HRAF database to do their research. They are asked to examine at least 10 societies where one of the variables is present to see if the other variable is also present. While this is not a random sample, it is more productive than choosing 10 societies at random. The student is asked to present the data in a table format and to devote most of the five to seven page paper to an introduction explaining why this is an interesting topic and what others have had to say on this issue (i.e., a short literature review) and a discussion section outlining why the student found pattern(s). Ultimately, it does not matter whether their hypotheses are supported or how strongly they are supported. The point is to collect the data, see what if any pattern(s) emerge, and discuss why or why not the pattern or lack of pattern exists. In addition to gaining exposure to at least 10 different societies and the type of research that cultural anthropologists have conducted, students also learn that things are seldom as simple or straight-forward as they might think. Often, by the time the paper is finished, students have a very different interpretation of how cultural factors are linked than they did at the beginning of the exercise.

In sum, the four exercises presented above have all been effective in getting the introductory student to "do anthropology." They all work well with a relatively small class and they all could be easily modified depending on the instructor's needs, goals, and resources, and to accommodate larger class size.

References Cited

Heider, K.
2001. *Seeing Anthropology: Cultural Anthropology Through Film*, 2nd ed. Boston: Allyn and Bacon Publishers.

Kamp, K.
1998. *Life in the Pueblo: Understanding the Past Through Archaeology*. Prospect Heights IL: Waveland Press.

Lewin, R.
1999. *Human Evolution: An Illustrated Introduction, 4th edition*. Boston: Blackwell Science Press.

Maltz, D and R. Borker
2001. A Cultural Approach to Male-Female Miscommunication. In *Applying Anthropology: an Introductory Reader, 6th edition*. P. Brown and A Podolefsky, Mountain View CA: Mayfield Publishing Company, pp 162-173.

Critical Thinking in the Anthropology Classroom

Mary H. Pulford

Two factors have influenced the use of this project in my anthropology courses. First, critical thinking has been and continues to be a life-long skill that is both at the heart of a liberal arts education and a component of many colleges and universities' learning outcomes. As a result of accreditation and assessment needs, many higher education institutions put a strong emphasis on writing and critical thinking.

The second reason for including this project in my courses centers around the fact that introductory anthropology courses are often part of a college or university's general education component. Many of our introductory courses are broadly configured to cover four or five anthropology fields, while others are more specific.

Regardless of the content of an introductory course in anthropology, we find ourselves at a crossroads between subject matter (anthropology) and college outcomes and general education requirements. This intersection presents us with the opportunity to promote our discipline as a leader in developing critical thinking skills, thus giving anthropology another stronghold as a relevant general education component of a liberal arts education.

This project is designed to introduce critical thinking skills to undergraduate students in introductory anthropology courses. It can be used equally well in classes ranging in size from 15-75, and is equally usable in cultural anthropology or four/five field introductory courses.

Critical Thinking

Teaching anthropologists have the opportunity to introduce to their students the skills they use as professional anthropologists in the field, museum, or lab. Critical thinking is clearly one of those skills. We use critical thinking as a tool in ethnographic work, archaeological excavation, analysis of skeletal material, forensic work, and applied anthropology in the corporate world; the list is endless. One of the major recruiting tools of anthropology as a component of the general education curriculum in liberal arts education should be the skills that anthropologists bring to the table.

There are four major components of critical thinking: factual, rational, evaluative, imaginative. (See Figure 1 in appendix.) I spend a significant amount of time early in the term discussing these four aspects of critical thinking and then re-enforce the discussion throughout the term with examples from lectures, readings, films, and/or class discussions.

As anthropologists, we use all of these skills in our profession. While each of the four critical thinking areas is both valuable and valid, I emphasize the importance of Imaginative Thinking or Seeing the Big Picture. Of course this area of critical thinking is dependent on students being able to master the other areas as well.

Application

In my five field Introduction to Anthropology course as well as the introductory Cultural Anthropology and

Introductory Archaeology courses, students do a group project after we have discussed subsistence patterns and economic strategies. This exercise is called simply enough the "Group Garbage Project." It is not a very flashy title, but I have been doing this project in my courses for several years and new students look forward to this part of the course as they have heard through the college grape vine that it is an interesting project.

The project requires the instructor to have several case studies of household garbage in the form of lists to distribute to students. I generally offer an extra credit assignment in one of my courses that requires students to keep a detailed list of all of the garbage their household recycles, composts, disposes in a trash container, burns, or puts down the garbage disposal. This list must be detailed and kept for seven consecutive days and must be listed by day. The appendix contains three such lists. I then use these garbage lists the following term for the Group Garbage Project. Usually I have enough students who want extra credit that the garbage lists only have to be compiled every two years. Throw-aways are culturally timely, and since even two years will "date" garbage, it is best to keep it contemporary.

Student Assignment

This project is designed to be done as a group endeavor. Experience has shown that group work on the project enhances the individual learner's critical thinking skills. Students are given three case studies (Household Garbage Lists) as well as directions for completing the project.

The project has two sets of important goals. The first goal is to increase the individual's ability to work with a group, and the second is to develop and enhance critical thinking skills. Students are instructed to do the following in order to complete the project task:

Step 1: Before starting the project, students read "From Tikal to Tucson: Today's Garbage is Tomorrow's Artifact" (1981) and G.G. Harrison, W. Rathje, and W.W. Hughes "Food Waste Behavior in an Urban Population"(1975). Both of these articles can be found in a number of anthropology readers.

Step 2: Students are to read through the three case studies before meeting with their group.

Step 3: After completing Steps 1 and 2, groups meet to discuss and derive answers to the following questions for each case study:

... How many people live in this household?
... What are their ages?
... Can you determine the sex of the individuals living in this household?
... What is their general health?
... Can you determine their economic status?
... Do you have any additional comments about the group or their garbage?

Step 4: The groups must build a case for their answers to the questions in Step 3 using several areas of critical thinking. For example, an answer to the first question can not be only that two people live in a household, but how did the group determine that number? What is the evidence to support their assumption?

Step 5: Groups turn in a typed report that includes the answers to all of the Step 3 questions for each case study. Groups are encouraged to also include any dissenting opinions from group members.

Project Outcomes

This Group Garbage Project has been implemented in my anthropology courses for the past four years. The following are observable learner outcomes based on student performance:

... enhancement of critical thinking skills;
... better group communication skills;
... improved learner attitudes;
... student confidence in problem solving skills;
... increased environmental awareness.

References Cited

American Anthropological Association
   1981. From Tikal to Tucson: Today's Garbage is Tomorrow's Artifact. *Anthropology Newsletter* 22:3.

Harrison, G.G., W.L. Rathje, and W.W. Hughes
   1975. Food Waste Behavior in an Urban Population. *Journal of Nutrition Education* Vol 7:1, pp 13-16.

Peterson, J.
   2000. Diagram of Critical Thinking Skills. Personal Communication.

Note: the following Garbage Lists may be copied and used without written permission.

Figure 1: Critical Thinking Areas*

Thinking Concerning Facts	*Thinking Through Reasoning*
Factual clarity, accuracy, and fairness Observational detail, accuracy, and scope Pattern identification	Identifying structure and order Identifying hierarchies Argument identification and evaluation Rule manipulation Judging strength of evidence Awareness of thinking strategies
Thinking Concerned With Values	*Thinking Involving Imagination*
Sensitivity to values – individual and collective Applying values to problems Respect for individual and collective differences Willingness to risk and commit Valuing your individual and collective self	Seeking the larger context Seeking alternative perspectives Relating the known to the unknown Seeking alternative means of expression Using questions as probes

* Source: J. Peterson (2000)

Household Garbage List #1

Tuesday

tomato soup can
3 cheese slice wrappers
Taco Bell bag
envelope package
Subway bag
2 concentrated lemonade cans
Cub Food receipt
tuna can
3 paper towels
paper plate
3 beer cans
20oz Nestea bottle
pot pie package

Wednesday

Party Pizza box
10 beer cans
mustard bottle
OJ bottle
sour cream container
2 mouse trap pkgs
paper plate
sugar wafer package
½ gallon milk carton
light bulb package
bread bag
microwave popcorn bag

Thursday

10 slice cheese wrappers
ziploc baggie
3 egg shells
4 pieces moldy bread
2 paper plates
cream of chicken soup can
corn can
1 lb hamburger pkg
5 beer cans
piece of aluminum foil
paper towel

Friday

4 gum wrappers
empty bag from donut shop
taco salad leftovers

11 beer cans
2 paper towels
2 paper plates
cigarette pack
coffee cup
Hardee's cup

Saturday

4 paper towels
5 egg shells
concentrated OJ can
20 oz Mountain Dew bottle
1 beer bottle
ziploc bag
Tater Tot bag
onion ring bag
4 beer cans
Budget Gourmet box
tortilla chip bag
2 slice cheese wrappers
shredded cheese bag

Sunday

lunch meat wrapper
paper towel wrapper
burrito wrapper
corn dog package
8 paper towels
3 paper plates
pop bottle
Pasta Roni box
paper towel roll
cigarette pack

Monday

junk mail
Burger King wrapper
OJ bottle
granola bar box
corn dog package
Tater Tot bag
2 styrofoam plates
lettuce bag
hot dog package
granola bar wrapper
dryer sheet
1 egg shell

3 beer cans
paper towel
brownie mix box
video update receipt

8

Household Garbage List # 2

Friday

tissue
coffee grounds and filter
napkin
thread
cheese slice wrapper
beef scraps
beef wrapper
ketchup bottle
2 tea bags
paper towel
straw
cat food can
candy wrapper
cat litter

Saturday

tissues
plastic bag
coffee grounds and filter
junk mail
tissue box
margarine wrapper
3 egg shells
1 can diet no caffeine Coke
1 can Nestea
Alka Selzer wrapper
Q-tips
2 Dixie cups
Popsickle sticks
cat litter

Sunday

5 egg shells
vanilla bottle
coffee grounds and filter
2 tea bags
sales receipt
price tags
2 candy wrappers
cling wrap
4 paper towels
egg noodles
powdered sugar
popcorn cakes pkg
diet no caffeine Coke carton
bread wrapper

chicken noodle soup can
tissue
2 Old Gold Menthol Light packs
2 ice cream wrappers
cat litter
3 cans diet no caffeine Coke

Monday

2 paper bags
envelopes
cough drop box
cheese slice wrapper
3 tea bags
deli ham plastic bag
coffee grounds and filter
2 Old Gold Menthol Light packs
buillion cube wrapper
2 paper cups
cat food can
2 tangerine peels
tissues
candy wrapper
broccoli
green pepper
apple
instant potato wrapper/box
kielbasa wrapper
2 paper towels
can diet no caffeine Coke
2 cans cream soda

Tuesday

tissues
2 Old Gold Menthol Light packs
paper towel roll and wrapper
8 egg shells
egg carton
4 chocolate wrappers
Raisin Bran box
coffee grounds and filter
2 fabric softener sheets
dryer lint
2 cans diet no caffeine Coke
lunch meat wrapper
scrap paper
cookie wrapper
onion skin
cat litter

sandwich bag
margarine wrapper
straw
tangerine peel

Wednesday

tissue
coffee grounds and filter
dental floss container
6 paper towels
powdered sugar
3 packs Old Gold Menthol packs
cat litter
8 egg shells
margarine box/2 wrappers
2 tea bags
cling wrap
grocery receipt
2 tangerine peels
paper plate
waxed paper
egg carton
tuna can
gallon milk carton
straw
Q-tip
Alka Selzer wrapper
paper cup

Thursday

½ gal OJ carton
tissue
coffee grounds and filter
Old Gold Menthol Light pack
cat food can
bread crumbs
price tags
plant leaf
2 tea bags
candy wrapper
chicken rice soup can
paper cup
paper towel

Household Garbage List # 3

Wednesday

cardboard/Mountain Dew case
3 cans Mountain Dew
cinnamon gum wrapper
Roma Pizza package
Strawberry Pop Tart wrapping
old socks
Colgate toothpaste box
Kraft Grape Jelly jar
Kraft Free Salad Dressing, Italian
lettuce core
croutons box
carrot peels

Thursday

Kraft Macaroni and Cheese box
egg shell
Aunt Jemima pancake mix box
2% milk carton
2 cans Mountain Dew
Shamrock pizza
leftover fettuccini
Newport cigarette box
dill pickle chips bag
Top the Tater container
Inland Valley hashbrowns
cellular phone bill

Friday

egg shell
Nestle chocolate chip package
walnut package
chocolate cake mix box
cupcake papers
homemade dill pickle ends
Blue Bonnet margarine foil
Fruit Loops cereal
Coco Roos cereal bag
Kraft cheese slice wrapper
Health Choice wheat bread crust

Saturday

Old English 40 oz beer bottle
Special Reserve beer bottle
Newport cigarette box
Marlboro Light cigarette box

Kools cigarette box
Secret deodorant
Roma Pizza package
cherry Coke bottle
Barq's root beer bottle

Sunday

4 cans Mountain Dew
3 wild cherry Pepsi cans
Little Debbie Nutty bar wrapper
Little Debbie oatmeal pie wrapper
Newport cigarette box
kleenex
cinnamon gum wrapper
power ball tickets

Monday

Roma Pizza package
OJ container
Ramen noodle package
2 cans Mountain Dew
egg shell
Pillsbury blueberry muffin mix
bacon scraps
Two Peak bagel bags
napkin
Newport cigarette box

Tuesday

chicken bone
tin foil from chicken
corn cob
baked potato skin
5 cans Mountain Dew
1 can wild cherry Pepsi
Popweaver popcorn bag
bank statement
homemade pickle ends
Kleenex box
Popice freezer wrapper

Strategies for Becoming an Outstanding Anthropology Teacher: From the Student Perspective

Patricia C. Rice

There is nothing "wrong" with deciding to be an Outstanding Teacher. But, outstanding teaching doesn't just happen and outstanding teachers are not just born. Being an outstanding teacher takes considerable skill and hard work and often the altruism of friends and colleagues. Using some of the strategies for teaching anthropology as given in this book (and the first edition published in 2000) might be one step toward become an outstanding teacher, but it takes a larger set of principles and a wider image to make it happen. Perhaps this contribution can help.

About five years ago, I was asked to address the faculty at my university on the subject of what makes an outstanding teacher. Not having the slightest idea of how to begin, but being an inductive scientist, I decided to gather data on the subject before offering a single opinion or coming to a single conclusion on the subject. I chose to collect data from two sources: from students and from faculty who had been named "outstanding teachers." Right away I suspected there might be a connection between the findings of the two sets of data.

The student data came from asking 1400 students in 15 classes at my university to characterize an outstanding teacher. The question posed was: "what traits would you like to see in your teachers?" The question was open ended and 10 slots were provided on the questionnaire sheet. The questionnaire was given to students in courses in all three fields: natural science, social science, and humanities, and in three different colleges within the university: arts and sciences, engineering, and journalism. The questionnaire was not systematically administered nor were other colleges or universities used; rather I used faculty friends who would take 10 minutes of class time to help gather the data. It is, however, not unlikely that a similar response would have resulted under more systematic guidelines.

The data on outstanding teachers came from asking the recipients of the last 25 Outstanding Teaching Awards at my university to allow me to read the written statements by students on instructor evaluation forms for the question "what did you like about this teacher's instruction?" The already predigested questions were not used. I copied what students said about this group of teachers and collapsed the comments into categories.

The Data

The student-generated data from the open-ended questionnaires were separated into freshmen and upper classmen because it was initially thought that the two groups might have different expectations about their teachers, with upper classmen's wish lists being somewhat mitigated by the reality of their experiences. Chart 1 shows those findings. The only real difference between the freshmen and the upper classmen response frequency was that upper classmen hoped that their teachers would "be knowledgeable," whereas the freshmen did not cite that trait nearly as often; that category ranked second among the upper classmen but ranked near the bottom among freshmen. Perhaps freshmen merely assumed their teachers would be knowledgeable, or perhaps fear drove them to hope the teachers would care about them more than anything else. Otherwise, the rank orders were fairly similar. In the top three (of 16) ranks for all students were "cares about students/me," "good sense of humor," and "communicates well." Interestingly, not only did "cares about me" show up on more trait lists than any other single trait, it was listed **first** more often than any other trait. Assuming students write down what is most important to them first, this is particularly pertinent. The rest of the chart shows the rank order of frequency of the most commonly cited 16 traits.

Many of the traits listed in Chart 1 are interrelated, such as "is helpful" with "cares about me" and "is knowledgeable" with "is intelligent." Collapsed categories, therefore, may be more meaningful than individual phrases, and I collapsed the 16 categories into four "supercategories:" knowledge, skills, attitudes, and style. In order of frequency, what students list most often in their teacher wish-list is:

... **attitudes** (54% of total responses). They want us to care about them, be friendly, helpful, understanding, fair, nice and kind, and realistic.

... **skills** (21% of total responses). In our teaching, they want us to be able to communicate well, be well organized, and explain clearly.

... **knowledge** (14% of total responses). They want us to be knowledgeable and intelligent about what we teach.

... **style** (11% of total responses). They want us to have a good sense of humor as we teach, be interesting, enthusiastic, and to enjoy teaching.

Do students "get" what they hope for in their teachers? They do with the teachers who are judged by their peers to be "outstanding teachers;" some of that judgment comes of course from student evaluations. Looking only at the open ended answers to questions about what students liked about the teacher being evaluated, and restricting the data to those who received teaching awards, students praised the outstanding teachers for being knowledgeable, interesting, and caring about them. These were the three highest ranked traits and they show a pattern similar to the student wish lists.

It is just as interesting to **not** find certain traits listed on their wish list. No one wished for nor praised teachers for "being an easy grader," or one who would "give us no work to do," or one who "dismissed class a lot." This gave me some confidence that the students were serious about their education and serious about the questionnaire.

In general and without making any statistical claims, students do get from the recipients of Outstanding Teaching awards what they claim they want most in teachers.

An Outstanding Teacher

As a result of looking at these two sets of data, a characterization of an outstanding teacher might look like the following. Outstanding Teachers:

... care about their students, how well they do in the class they are in, and in their futures;
... are friendly, helpful, and understanding;
... have a good sense of humor and are not stodgy (I added the stodgy part);

... are effective in the classroom scene because they are well organized, explain well, and are effective at communicating about the subject matter;

... are smart.

And now that you are on your way toward being an outstanding teacher, try these on: always be on time to class (the better students grumble when instructors are consistently late); don't stick your nose behind notes but rather get out there in front of the desk or podium and talk **with** the class, not **to** it, at least as much as possible; enjoy yourself and they will too; and finally, be creative and make student learning an active experience. And that brings us back to using your friends and colleagues who are sharing successful strategies for teaching and learning anthropology. Try some of them out, modify them to suit your particular needs, and finally share some of **your** good teaching techniques with the rest of us.

Chart 1

Summary of Student Questionnaires and Evaluations on "Ideal/Outstanding Teachers"

Trait	Questionnaires			Evaluation statements
	All	Upper classmen	Freshmen	

All **rank orders** are done by total frequencies of responses

cares about students	1	1	2	3
good sense of humor	1	2	1	7
communicates well	3	2	3	4
is knowledgeable	4	2	12	1
is friendly	4	5	5	--
is understanding	4	6	3	--
is interesting	7	6	8	2
is helpful	7	10	8	--
is intelligent	7	8	6	13
is fair	10	8	8	7
is enthusiastic	11	10	11	6
is nice, kind	11	10	8	--
is trustworthy	13	13	14	--
enjoys teaching	14	13	14	13
is well organized	14	16	14	7
explains clearly	14	15	13	--
is realistic	14	16	14	--
is well prepared	--	--	--	4
is stimulating, informative	--	--	--	7
is challenging, encouraging, entertaining, professional, inspirational, stimulating				15

Data based on 1400 questionnaires and 25 sets of written evaluations.

-- indicates no responses.

"TSM Cube:" Illustrating the Scientific Method

Grace Keyes

Nearly all introductory courses in the social sciences, including anthropology, have a section on the scientific method (TSM). The TSM Cube exercise I describe here is a wonderfully easy and engaging way to illustrate the basics of the scientific method and the role of inference in science. I have taken the basic idea and activity plan from *Teaching About Evolution and the Nature of Science,* a 1998 book by the National Academy of Sciences.

Ask almost any freshman to describe the scientific method and he or she will almost mechanically tell you that it is "empirical," based on "facts," and tests "hypotheses." These are words they like to use because they seem to believe that using the correct terminology is sufficient or maybe they suspect this is what their instructor is expecting to hear. But when asked to clarify certain terms such as what they mean by "empirical," some students are stumped. Others quickly respond that it refers to something that is "observed." And yet, it has been my experience that if one probes a little deeper, most freshmen have some erroneous conceptions about how science works. This exercise not only illustrates the basics of the scientific method that most textbooks touch on, but it also demonstrates the role of inference in scientific studies. This is particularly important when teaching something like evolution. Indeed, it was in a course on human origins that I first realized the utility of this activity. Given the need to explain, re-explain, and apply concepts to different fields of study, this TSM Cube exercise is usable in archaeology and cultural anthropology classes as well as biological anthropology classes, for any size class, and at most any level.

Constructing the TSM Cube

I use a four inch cube that is just a simple cardboard box of the variety that can be collapsed or folded because it makes it easy to slip into my lecture notes folder. Write the numbers clearly with heavy pen or use paste-on already printed numbers, making sure the opposite sides add up to 7. Thus, the number 5 will be on the top and the number 2 on the bottom and the 4 on the opposite side of the 3, the 6 opposite 1. (For reasons given below, it might be best to just not put the number 2 on the bottom.) Underline the even numbers or write them in a different color (See illustration below.) You can make one fairly large cube that you hold in the palm of your hand and rotate so that students can see the numbers on all sides but **not** the number on the bottom. Alternately, you could make small cubes for students to work with in small groups. If done this way, be sure to give students strict instructions not to turn the cube to see what's at the bottom. (An option is to write number 2 but cover it with a taped piece of paper or write a question mark.) Rotate the cube so students can see all sides **except** the bottom. One large cube is preferable in a class of 30 or fewer students so the entire class can be involved with the instructor.

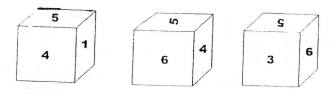

The TSM Cube Activity

This simple cube is used to get students to first make some simple **observations** and to begin asking **questions**. One of questions is then turned into a **hypothesis**, and then the class proceeds to find **evidence** to support or reject the hypothesis. As students begin to build the evidence, the hypothesis becomes stronger until after 3 or 4 pieces of evidence, we reach the **conclusion** supporting the hypothesis. It is at this point that some students have a little difficulty accepting the conclusion. Some argue that the hypothesis cannot be accepted because they cannot actually **observe** the last bit of evidence (the 2 on the bottom of the cube). These students seem to have the misconception that if something cannot be observed, then it cannot be a **fact** and, therefore is not scientific. They clearly have not pondered deeply about how science works and about the role of **inference** in scientific investigations. Indeed, I have noticed that most anthropology texts never mention anything about inference, so it is little wonder that students walk away with misconceptions. This exercise provides a good opportunity to discuss the significance of inference, deduction, and induction in the context of the scientific method.

I have found that it is important to steer students into thinking methodically and to point out when they are jumping to conclusions and giving interpretations too hastily. For instance, as soon as they see the cube with numbers on it, someone will invariably state that what they observe is a "die" – well, yes, it looks like a die, but this is more of an interpretation than an observation. As they make simple observations, they will notice patterns such as the observation that the even numbers on the box are underlined or are of a different color. The hypothesis they generally suggest is "The number 2 is at the bottom of the box." Now they are ready to start listing bits of evidence to support this statement. The evidence the students give generally follows this pattern:

... the box has numbers on all sides so there is probably a number on the bottom too;
... the numbers range from 12 to 6 and only 2 is missing, so it must be at the bottom;
... even numbers are underlined, so the bottom number is probably an even one;
... the sum of the numbers on opposite sides is 7, and the number on top is a 5, so 2 must be on the bottom. (Not many students make this observation right away, so usually this is the last and strongest bit of evidence they provide.)

Not many people will dispute that $5 + 2 = 7$, but in this exercise some students will remain skeptical because they cannot see the bottom of the cube to verify their hypothesis. Invariably, they will ask me to show them the bottom and invariably I refuse. I tell them that it would be wonderful if that were the way science worked but, alas, in many cases we simply cannot see first hand all of the evidence. For example, I have had staunch creationist students argue that since we cannot see directly the process of evolution we cannot accept it as scientific fact. While this exercise presents TSM in a rather simple manner, it opens a window of opportunity to discuss the nature of science and to try to clarify misconceptions about it.

Stephen Jay Gould addresses the topics of "fact," "theory," and "inference" in an article titled "Evolution as Fact and Theory" which I often assign to students in courses that cover human evolution. In that article, Gould is primarily demonstrating how the creationist attack on evolution fails, but it is also a good article for discussing the nature of TSM. Combining Gould's article with this TSM Cube activity can be very productive, especially in classes on human evolution.

Notes:

Even though the *Teaching About Evolution and the Nature of Science* (1998 Washington DC: National Academy Press) book is aimed mostly at pre-collegiate level teaching, there are many valuable ideas that can be modified for use in introductory college-level courses. See chapter l, pp 66-73. The book can also be read on line by going to www.nap.edu/readingroom/books/evolution98

The Gould article originally appeared in *Discover* 1981, but has been reproduced in John Chafee's *Thinking Critically (*4th edition. Boston: Houghton-Mifflin.)

Discussion Preparation Guides

Charles O. Ellenbaum

A Common Teaching Problem

Have you ever had the depressing experience of showing a provocative and exciting film to your students, asking for reactions after the credits have run, and getting virtually no response? Have you ever had large- or small-group discussion on an assigned article become the sharing of ignorance by students? Films and readings are necessary vehicles for teaching our visually exciting discipline, but there appears to be a problem common to all of us and that is getting students to properly discuss the materials.

One Way to Solve the Problem

At a National Institute for Staff and Organizational Development Conference on Excellence in 1992, I heard James Gonzales (El Paso Community College) speak about his problems in running class discussions. Knowing I was not alone was a relief. His solution was based on *Learning Through Discussion: Guide for Leaders and Members of Discussion Groups* by William Fawcett Hill (1982). Gonzales claims to have learned the technique through an earlier presentation by Laura Hodges and Jean Carlisle (Rice), and he modified it to fit certain specific needs.

I made anthropological modifications to the technique and tested them first in my Cultural Anthropology classes and later in Peoples and Cultures of the World. I now use them in my World and Comparative Religion classes as well because it works! I have used the technique in lower division undergraduate classes that range from 30-47 students, and in both honors and regular sections.

Almost any anthropology reader could be used in conjunction with this technique, from basic introductory to more specialized readers. In my Peoples and Cultures of the World course, for example, I use *Distant Mirrors: America as a Foreign Culture* (De Vita and Armstrong 1998); students are assigned readings and fill out a Discussion Preparation Guide for each reading (see appendix). Although the small-discussion group technique could be used for a small number of films during a term for any course, for my Cultural Anthropology course, I use Karl Heider's *Seeing Anthropology: Cultural Anthropology Through Film (2001)*. The students view film clips on their own time that are an integral part of the text. Using my modification of Heider's general questions about films, students meet in their small groups each week and discuss the film clips, having filled out a Film Discussion Preparation Guide during and immediately after seeing each film (see appendix). The guides are a basis for the small-group discussion. Given scheduling problems, sometimes an in-class film has to be shown one day and discussed the next day, but by filling out a guide, the student can recapture some of the immediacy of the film. The following process is used for small discussion groups that focus on either readings or films.

The Discussion Process

Assigning groups. Either divide up the class (e.g., count off by eight to divide a class of forty into groups of five) or have the students divide themselves into groups. In general, the groups maintain their integrity for the term, although individuals are allowed to switch groups every three to four weeks. A packet of guides should be given to each student, and they must be reminded to carefully read the instructions on the back of the guide before the first discussion group session.

Discussion days. There is at least one regularly scheduled discussion every week. Students are required to come to class on those days with their discussion guides filled out. At the beginning of the session, I check to see that they are completed, and assign a grade of 8 (top) to 0 (bottom) points based on how well their answers pertain to the reading or film; I take off points if the answers are blank, extremely brief or incomplete, or do not deal with the specific materials. Students are seated in their small groups in a circle or around a table. Occasionally, after small groups discuss an article or film, I ask each group to report the main points they discussed to the class as a whole, and the entire group becomes involved in a general discussion.

You need to convince one student in each group to volunteer to serve as discussion leader, a job that earns an additional eight points. Be sure to check to see that the discussion guides of the volunteers are filled in or they are not likely to be prepared. The leaders do not "play" instructors, but act as moderators to budget the time allotted for the day's discussion and to keep the discussion moving. The leader collects the Guides from the group members at the end of the discussion session and marks the total discussion points each person earned, initialing the score. The leader then returns the guides to the students before leaving that day. Leaders should not serve again in that capacity until every student in the group has had the job.

Once the discussion begins, the instructor should remain silent and sit away from the students. This is difficult and at first, I felt I was taking a lazy, unprofessional way out. I have since realized how important it is to keep my distance, and I now sit where I can see and be seen, and can listen to what is being said, but in an unobtrusive manner. Occasionally, I walk around the room. I found that once students got used to this format, discussion proceeded well.

Learning is taking place in a variety of styles during the discussions. The leader follows the discussion guide and calls on those wishing to speak. Since both content/task functions and process/maintenance functions of a group are valuable, points can be gained in several ways: by initiating discussion, giving information, asking for information, raising questions, answering questions, giving a restatement of another's contribution, asking for clarification, giving examples, encouraging others, or relieving group tension. Students are encouraged to make at least eight positive contributions to each discussion. The leader may call on any member of the group to offer an opinion or to ask a question even if the student has not raised his or her hand. The leader should not ask questions and then offer opinions, but rather should concentrate on drawing out contributions from the rest of the group, making sure that each item is adequately considered before moving on to a new item. The group should aim for a dynamic discussion with plenty of interaction among participants, and students should address their questions and remarks to the group rather than to the leader.

Unsupported opinions (e.g., "I didn't like it") do not gain points since they do not serve to illuminate the reading or film. Students may lose points for counter-productive behavior such as trying to dominate the discussion or mocking another group member. Students should use the discussion sheet itself to mark their contributions with stars next to the appropriate items and make additional brief notes to document responses to items not originally noted on the discussion guide. This identifies what they contributed to the discussion and helps the instructor resolve the rare grade dispute. If a student misses a discussion session, the group will determine the required make-up work, subject to approval by the instructor. Discussion guides are kept by students, once graded by the instructor and the discussion leader. The discussion guides can be turned in after each session or as a unit, depending on personal preference.

The points for each discussion guide and session are as follows: eight possible points for an appropriately filled-in discussion guide plus eight possible points for discussion equals a possible 16 points. The point and grade ranges are: 16-15 = A; 14-13 = B; 12-11 = C; 10-9 = D; 8-0 = F. At the end of the term, points can be totaled and divided by the number of readings/films, using the grade range, to give a final discussion grade. I always announce in the course outline how much of a student's final grade comes from this grade. How much of a student's grade comes from discussion depends on the relative amount of work done for this segment of the course.

Finally, there were two unintended consequences of this technique. First, unstructured discussion (not announced class discussion) also improved. For example, in one case I passed out copies of "Body Ritual of the Nacirema" for them to read and asked them to discuss two questions: What errors of fact did you find? What interpretations do you disagree with? After discussing these questions in their small groups, they reported to the class as a whole, leading to class-wide discussion. This has changed from groups sitting like lumps making few comments, to lively and probing discussions. After a few small-group discussions, more questions -- in general -- have been asked in class. A second unintended result was that the groups become a focal point for networking and support both inside and outside of class. My college is a commuter college where students come and go, often lacking primary group support while on campus. The people in the discussion groups become important to each other and I encourage the comradery by having the group assign make-up work if a student misses a discussion period.

The two guides in the Appendix that follow may be photocopied or modified to suit your particular needs. The two guides can be photocopied back to back on a single sheet.

References Cited

De Vita, P.R., and J.D. Armstrong
    1998. *Distant Mirrors: America as a Foreign Culture*, 2nd ed. Belmont, CA: West/Wadsworth.

Heider, K.
    2001. *Seeing Anthropology: Cultural Anthropology Through Film,* 2nd ed. Boston: Allyn and Bacon.

Hill, W. F.

    1982. *Learning Through Discussion: Guide for Leaders and Members of Discussion Groups*, 2nd ed. Walnut Creek, CA: Sage.

DISCUSSION PREPARATION GUIDE

Name _____   Date _____

Author/Title/Article/Chapter: _____

1. Note words that are unfamiliar or seem to be used in a special manner to create a particular impression. **Define the word in the context of the phrase where you found it.**

a.

b.

c.

d.

e.

2. What particulars seem especially significant or puzzling to you? These may include: a statement, the setting, a name, the title, the situation, a conflict, an irony, or anything of interest. Prepare questions about these items to ask in discussion. "How..." "Why..." questions are especially good.

a.

b.

c.

d.

3. State in one complete sentence, the theme of this work.

4. Sum up the reading in a motto, a bumper sticker, or in a T-shirt slogan.

5. How would you relate this material to other sources you have read, to materials you have studied in other courses, or to something you learned outside of school?

6. What is your opinion of this selection? Give a reason for your opinion.

7. What did you learn from the article? Be specific and concrete.

8. What is your personal reaction to the material you read? Be specific and concrete.

TO THE STUDENT

1. You must come to class on the day of the discussion with your discussion preparation guide filled out. Your instructor has graded it prior to the beginning of the class. They will not be counted if turned in ungraded with your exam. Completed discussion guides are worth eight points. You will be seated in a circle or at a table in groups or as one large group. Names can be displayed until everyone is acquainted.

2. One of you will volunteer to serve as discussion leader for this specific material that earns the discussion leader 8 points. You cannot volunteer if your discussion guide is not completely filled in prior to class. The discussion leader does not "play" teacher but acts as a moderator to budget the time allotted for the discussion and to move discussion along. The discussion leader will collect the guides, mark the total discussion points each person earned and initial the marked score. Return them to the group that day. You will not serve again as leader until all in the group have served as a discussion leader. Then you may serve again.

3. Once the discussion begins, **the instructor will remain silent and will sit away from your groups**. You are entrusted with the responsibility of discussing the selection. The leader follows the discussion guide and calls on those wishing to speak. You will want to make eight positive contributions to each discussion. Points are made by initiating discussion, giving information, asking for information, raising questions, answering questions, giving a restatement of another's contribution, asking for clarification, giving examples, encouraging others, or relieving group tension. You need to address your questions and remarks to the group as a whole, not to the leader. The leader may call on any member of the group to offer a question or opinion, even if they have not raised their hand. The leader should not ask questions and offer opinions but rather concentrate on drawing out contributions from the rest of the group, making sure that each item is adequately considered before moving to a new question. The group should aim for a dynamic discussion with plenty of interaction among the participants to help accomplish the primary objective of the group which is to illuminate the selection.

4. Unsupported opinions (e.g. as "I didn't like it") do not gain points since they do not serve to illuminate the selection. You may also lose points for counter-productive behavior such as trying to dominate the discussion, being too quiet, or mocking another group member.

5. You should also mark your contributions with stars on the discussion sheet itself next to the items they represent. You should also make additional brief notes to document responses to items not originally noted on the guide. **If you miss a discussion period, your group will determine your required make-up work, subject to your instructor's approval.**

6. The discussion Guides are kept by you, once graded by the instructor and the discussion leader. The discussion guides for a unit are turned in with the unit exam. Once turned in, the grades on the guide are final. The instructor records points gained in this way: 8 (filled in discussion guide) + 8 (8 discussion points) = 16 (for a perfect score). Point/Grade ranges: 16-15 = A; 14-13 = B; 12-11 = C; 10-9 = D; under 9 = F.

FILM DISCUSSION PREPARATION GUIDE

Name _____ Date _____

Film Title _____

Culture(s) shown _____

Main subjects _____

1. How ethnographic or informed by anthropological questions is it? How? Be specific.

2. How much is the people's own view represented? How? Be specific.

3. Whose voice or point of view does the film present? How? Be specific.

4. What is the art/science or aesthetic production values/ethnographic values balance?

5. What is the influence of the film crew? How? Be specific.

6. Does the film create more or less sympathy toward the culture: empathy or antipathy?

7. Are shots or film scenes/sequences given a context? How? Be specific.

8. Does the film follow through on important acts? How? Be specific.

9. How visual and how wordy is the film? How effective are the visuals and the narration?

10. How much distortion of time and space, close-ups and long-shots do you see? Be specific.

11. What did you learn from the film? How does this film establish generalizations or state abstract concepts? Be specific, concrete, and detailed.

12. How did you feel during the viewing of the film and afterward? Why? Be specific.

13. How is the culture shown in the film similar to your own? Be specific.

14. How is the culture shown in the film different from your own? Be specific.

15. What is your personal reaction to the culture you viewed in the film? Why? Be specific.

TO THE STUDENT

1. You must come to class on the day of the discussion with your discussion preparation guide filled out. Your instructor has graded it prior to the beginning of the class. They will not count if turned in ungraded with your exam. Completed discussion guides are worth eight points. You will be seated in a circle or around a table in groups or as one large group. Names can be displayed until everyone is acquainted.

2. One of you will volunteer to serve as discussion leader for this specific material that earns the discussion leader 8 points. You cannot volunteer if your discussion guide is not completely filled in prior to class. The leader does not "play" teacher but acts as a moderator to budget the time allotted for the discussion and to move discussion along. You will collect these guides, mark the total discussion points each person earned and initial the score you marked. Return them to your group that day. You should not serve again as leader until all of you in the group have served as a discussion leader. Then you may serve again.

3. Once the discussion begins, **your instructor will remain silent and will sit away from your group**. You are entrusted with the responsibility of discussing the selection. The leader follows the discussion guide and calls on those wishing to speak. You will want to make eight positive contributions to each discussion.   Points are made by initiating discussion, giving information, asking for information, raising questions, answering questions, giving a restatement of another's contribution, asking for clarification, giving examples, encouraging others, or relieving group tension. You need to address your questions and remarks to the group as a whole, not to the leader. The leader may call on any member of the group to offer a question or opinion, even if they have not raised their hand.   The leader should not ask questions and offer opinions but rather concentrate on drawing out contributions from the rest of the group, making sure that each item is adequately considered before moving to a new question. The group should aim for a dynamic discussion with plenty of interaction among the participants to help accomplish the primary objective of the group which is to illuminate the selection.

4. Unsupported opinions (e.g. as "I didn't like it") do not gain points since they do not serve to illuminate the selection. You may also lose points for counter-productive behavior such as trying to dominate the discussion, being too quiet, or mocking another group member.

5. You should also mark your contributions with stars on the discussion sheet itself next to the items they represent. You should also make additional brief notes to document responses to items not originally noted on the guide. **If you miss a discussion period, your group will determine your required make-up work, subject to your instructor's approval.**

6. The discussion guides are kept by you, once graded by the instructor and the discussion leader. The discussion guides for a unit are turned in with the unit exam. Once turned in, the grades on the guide are final. The instructor records points gained in this way: 8 (filled in discussion guide) + 8 (8 discussion points) = 16 (for a perfect score). Point/Grade ranges: 16-15 = A; 14-13 = B; 12-11 = C; 10-9 = D; under 9 = F.

Ping-Pong Archaeology: A Non-Destructive Field and Lab Exercise

Janet Pollak

This is a one week (two class session) project that allows students to perform a controlled surface collection from a simulated site that you or other students can create. It is designed to be user-friendly for students and instructors alike, but it does require some planning time up front in order to be successful. Instructors do not need to have a working knowledge of surveying instruments for setting up a grid. Following the surface collection, students meet in the "lab" to study the collection and interpret the site. Since most students and even many archaeologists are perfectly capable of damaging any kind of actual site, ping-pong archaeology permits the instructor to construct a simulated site on any surface that will inhibit ball rolling. The instructor need not leave campus and the basic equipment is simple, inexpensive, and can be recycled each term. Finally, the exercise can be used for any size class and for four field introductory anthropology where archaeology is but one segment, or in a non-lab archaeology course.

Ping-pong archaeology grew out of the need to provide some sort of hands-on archaeological experience that would give undergraduates a sense of the "field" experience and an idea of the subsequent laboratory analysis and interpretation that occur under archaeological field conditions. The project was confined to two 75-minute class periods and was limited to campus because there was no time to travel to a "real" site. It has the advantage of teaching archaeological principles without damaging a real site as well. While most campuses contain numerous historic sites – and even prehistoric ones – I have steadfastly refused to collect, test, or excavate any of them solely for the purpose of teaching field procedures.

Ideally, ping-pong archaeology is best when conducted on a grass or soil surface. I obtain permission from the Athletic Department to use the soccer field on some occasions and the field hockey practice areas on others. You will need between 200 and 300 white ping pong balls (they come in packs of six, but can be recycled), waterproof colored markers, brown paper lunch bags, a roll or two of bubble wrap, a ball of string, a compass, graph paper, about five or six clip boards, some #3 pencils, metal or plastic pins (or you can cut up wire coat hangers), and some measuring tapes (in metric or US customary units). You should have five or six short tapes (6') and a longer one (50'). In addition to the open area outside with a non-roll surface upon which to place the balls, you will also need to use a room with some tables and chairs so the "artifacts" can be studied in the "lab." Since this is a one day only event, your department conference room would probably work. If you have an archaeologist on staff at your institution or if there are faculty in environmental science or geology, you will probably be able to borrow survey pins and measuring tapes. You will not need to employ actual surveying equipment, such as a transit or theodolite.

The first step in the exercise is to plan your simulated site. Try to identify an area of the campus, such as the cafeteria in the student union, library entrance, bookstore, chemistry lab, department secretary's office, or some area where you can sketch a map on graph paper, pace off distances, and enter key artifacts. Keep the identify of your site secret. Unpack the ping-pong balls, take out the waterproof colored markers and decide what colors and symbols to use for each of the artifacts or artifact categories at your site. For example, if your site is the snack bar in the student union, you could have green circles stand for salad bar items and red circles stand for hamburgers. Be creative, but draw only one symbol on each ball. You will need to provide an identification key for the students in the lab the day they work with the surface collection.

For the day in the field, do not proceed if it is raining as it is not worth it. You will need to take your sketch map and all the coded balls out to your site area ahead of time and place each one according to your master plan. Try to fill an area large enough to accommodate an entire class at once. That is, if you have chosen the department secretary's office as your simulated site and the actual office is only 10 feet by 8 feet, make sure your site area is 40 feet by 32 feet. It is very helpful to have some assistance with this task, such as a teaching assistant, an advisee, or former students. Once all of the coded balls have been placed, it is time to begin the exercise.

As the students come onto the field, the ping-pong balls should be clearly visible to all so they will know not to walk into the site. Their first task will be to set up a collection grid for the site and they will need to decide on the size of the quadrats (equal sized squares); alternatively, you can assign the size of the squares. They also must decide where the site datum point should be located and then orient the grid (North/South; East/West) with the compass. In this part of the project, setting up a grid with small squares will provide a better experience than deciding to make all squares 10 or 20 feet on a side or 10 meters or more on a side. If students are using just measuring

tapes, pins to push into the ground, and string to tie around each pin, they should be done in a few minutes. Of course, the grid they create will be just approximate and not very accurate. That is, some of the squares may not be correctly laid out. These initial tasks will keep only a few students busy. Those who are not engaged in the grid construction can be put to work filling out the collection bags. They can use black waterproof markers to set up the information that should appear on each bag and a part of this exercise should include having the students decide (with your guidance) what must be recorded.

Divide the class into as many as six teams of five or six students, if your class runs that large. Putting any more than about 40 students on this project at one time is extremely difficult. If you have a class of more than 40 students, it pays to divide them into groups no larger than 40 and conduct separate exercises with each group. Each cluster of five or six individuals is a collection team and the teams are then assigned specific squares or quadrats to collect. One person from each team will be the recorder or grapher and the others will be engaged in "mapping in" the ping-pong balls before any are picked up and bagged. Students will be able to write field catalog numbers in pencil on each of the balls as it is entered in the site map of the square. Be sure that students indicate the square designation and number each ball in the order it is collected from each square (example N5E10.1; N5E10.2, and throughout). This may seem a rather tedious procedure, but it gives students an appreciation for the need to pay attention to detail, to record data appropriately and systematically, and do what is diligently done on site. Plus, doing the numbering in the field as the balls are collected will permit the second or lab phase of the project to proceed immediately in the subsequent class. Pocket tape measures are used to ascertain the approximate locations of the "artifacts" in the squares. The use of string, spirit levels, and plum bobs to determine a more accurate location for each ping-pong ball is not really necessary for the exercise and will take up too much time in the first class. Once all the teams have completed mapping their squares and bagging the artifacts, the first phase of the project is done. One note of caution: on average I experience a 7% mortality rate for the ping-pong balls every time the exercise is conducted. Even though the grass is usually bright green and the balls are sparkling white, students still step on them from time to time. Of course, on the plus side, they do manage to map and pick up 100% of the "artifacts" placed on the field.

The second phase of this exercise takes place indoors. Before the class enters the room, be certain to cover all table surfaces with bubble wrap (first choice) or some other material that will not allow the ping-pong balls to roll off and bounce away. Make enough copies of your "key to the artifact symbols" so that each of the field collection teams can have at least two at their work stations. With all the square maps out, each team then empties the balls from each of the quadrat bags they collected. Because each of the balls already bears a field number with its square location, students then begin the task of identification via your key to the symbols. Since each of the teams has collected in a particular sector of the site, the final interpretation and identification of the site will probably not be immediately apparent to any one team. As the class hour progresses and each team begins to acquire a general understanding of the contents of their quadrats and the spatial orientation of the materials, you will have to gauge when to stop

the teams and conclude the project. Since the ping-pong balls are all identical except for the symbols drawn on them, students quickly learn to view them equally and dispassionately. No ping-pong ball is more interesting than any other.

The last phase of the exercise involves each of the teams, in turn, reporting their findings to the whole class. It helps if the classroom has a large chalkboard so students can post their conclusions. At this point, you may ask for overall interpretations of the site and request that each team come up with its best analysis. Finally, you can reveal the site's actual identity (department secretary's office, snack bar).

The same ping-pong balls can be used year after year, since the field catalog numbers are written in pencil. Just erase them. You can certainly recycle the symbols and devise new keys to match the next site you select.

The Illegal Antiquities Trade, Looting, and Archaeological Ethics

Harold D. Juli

As the only archeologist at a liberal arts college, one teaching challenge is to maintain interest among a student body who mostly come to the department for our cultural anthropology courses. Over the years, I have discovered that one of the appeals of our discipline, beyond the exotic and non-western, is its ability to present a unique perspective on current issues in society. When well executed, such an approach brings students a heightened awareness of topical issues seen through the lens of anthropology. I chose to develop a theme on illegal antiquities, looting, and archaeological ethics as a way to introduce a practical topic in my introductory archaeology course. This topic/theme is taught throughout the term, not as a discrete course unit, but periodically. It is designed to complement and enhance the regular coverage as the course unfolds. In this article, I will first discuss some of the reasons why I developed this theme and then describe how it has been constructed and implemented. The topic/theme is suitable for any size class, and the timing is flexible.

Why This Approach is Popular With Students

Issues of illegal antiquities and looting present an interesting challenge for instructors of archaeology because of their relevance to what is arguably archaeology's "hottest current topic:"

... The issues are interesting, complex, and loaded with ambiguity. In constructing the theme, I have been faced with the realization that the "standard archaeological point of view," namely that looting is reprehensible, destroys sites and that artifacts derived from looting should not be sold, while valid, is simply not a matter of universal agreement even among archaeologists, let alone museum professionals, antiquities dealers, or collectors.

... The issues relate to virtually every archaeological culture in world-wide perspective.

... The issues connect archaeology to real world concerns beyond research and the academy.

... The issues appeal to students because they connect archaeology to several related careers such as museum curatorial work and education, import/export business, art gallery entrepreneurship, customs agent careers, and the practice of law.

... The issues concern "ethics" in an archaeological context, and students today are very attuned to ethical issues since they are so prominent in our society.

Illegal Antiquities, Looting, and Ethics: Description and Implementation of the 7 Steps

Step 1. On the first day of class after completing the usual bookkeeping chores, I begin the theme by showing the first 15 minutes of *Raiders of the Lost Ark* (Steven Spielberg 1981). Students find the film clip exciting for several reasons: virtually all have seen the film, it is "cool" to watch a Hollywood film in class, and because they think they know what it is about. But, they have never considered its message from an archaeologist's perspective. During the film's well-known opening segment situated somewhere in South America in 1936, Dr. Indiana Jones and other characters introduce the viewer to a number of popular, but incorrect and negative stereotypes of archaeology as a discipline and archaeologists as professionals. These stereotypes set the stage for my treatment of several issues such as antiquities looting, site destruction, illegal export and purchase, and the role of museums. After viewing only the first 15 minutes in class, I distribute a handout titled **Raiders of the Lost Ark and Popular Stereotypes** of Archaeology. Figure 1 (in appendix) lists the relevant issues portrayed in this short segment. For example, "Indy" steals an ancient statue from a jungle temple and then meets his rival, the archaeologist Bellocq, who enlists an indigenous group to help him re-steal the statue from Indy. In the next scene, we see Dr. Jones teaching in a university classroom. When the class ends, his institution's museum curator offers to buy artifacts "no questions asked," after which Indy hands him artifacts without documentation, provenience, or associated cultural information. At the conclusion of this segment, there is a segue to the film's main focus, the lost ark of the covenant, now that Indy is established as an expert on ancient civilizations and the occult!

I have found this film clip to be an excellent introduction to many thematic issues and students love it. Figure 1 is discussed in detail, with the negative stereotypes described, corrected, or challenged by descriptions of what archaeologists really do and how they work and the fact that they don't steal or even own artifacts.

Step 2. The next time I revisit the antiquities theme, I distribute a short article for students to read for discussion in the next class period: "Getting Their Hands Dirty: Archaeologists and the Looting Trade" by John Dorfman (1988). This journalistic treatment presents an overview of the history and main controversies of the illegal antiquities trade, looting, and associated issues; it is short, interesting, and incisive. Students enjoy reading it and it makes them aware of the many conflicting issues and points of view. In the next class period, we discuss the Dorfman article along with a handout that was based on the article titled **Ethics and Archaeology: Two Points of View** (Figure 2 in appendix). The handout identifies 11 issues discussed in the article and presents them as opinions covering two points of view on each issue. Figure 2 lists these issues, including museum exhibition of looted artifacts, purchase of looted artifacts, and the roles of dealers and collectors in the illegal artifact trade.

In class, we review the points at issue, and I attempt to generate class discussion. This is the class where their eyes are really opened to the contradictions and complexities of each issue. For example, while most field archaeologists argue that looted artifacts without provenience have limited research value, epigraphers, while recognizing that looting destroys sites, nevertheless argue that looted artifacts may have substantial research value when they yield decipherable hieroglyphics. The case study in this example is Mayan and the discussion relates to glyphs on ceramic vessels originating in looted tombs. Given this contradiction, students begin to realize that the issues contain several conflicting perspectives.

Step 3. Several weeks later, I distribute another handout titled **Archaeological Ethics: Glossary and Concepts** (Figure 3 in appendix). I compiled the glossary and its 54 terms and definitions based on items from the Dorfman article, various publications, and *Archaeological Ethics* (Vitelli1996). The 23 readings in this book are integrated into the course and the theme. (This is a required text and chapters are assigned throughout the term. In this way, the theme is carried over in out-of-class reading so that at any point, students are reading or have just read a short article on the theme. This keeps it fresh in their minds and provides case study examples to supplement those I discuss in class.)

Step 4. When I return to the theme, I emphasize a different controversy, distributing a three page article "Stop the Charade: It's Time to Sell Artifacts" (1997) by Avner Raban, a 40 year veteran archaeologist specializing in biblical archaeology. This article throws the students a curve because although they have absorbed the perspective of most archaeologists – that looting and sale of artifacts is reprehensible – the Raban article offers a radical proposal by an archaeologist working in Israel where there is an abundance of excavated artifacts, especially coins and common ceramic vessels that are languishing in museums and storehouses. Raban argues that many of these artifacts, whether scientifically excavated or looted, have little monetary value because many represent poor examples of common items from various periods of antiquity. His proposal is to sell them under strict rules and government supervision and to turn them into a source of revenue to be used for pressing archaeological needs. Raban does not consider all artifacts "sacred," a proposal that differs from the standard archaeological point of view. He suggests that selling genuine artifacts will decrease the market for fakes because the average collector will be assured of

authenticity. Obviously, these suggestions are extremely controversial in the archaeological community. The article introduces a further source of ambiguity for students as they try to understand this complex, clouded set of issues and we discuss the ambiguities during the next class period.

Step 5. In a subsequent class (we are now 3/4 through the course), I show a 60 minute video titled *Plunder*, first aired in 1990 on the PBS series *Frontline*. This video addresses the issue of who should own and control the past. The first segment focuses on Maya site looting and includes rare footage of a TV crew that was allowed to accompany *huáqueros* (the term for looters in some areas of Mesoamerica) as they actually excavate tunnels and loot an ancient grave. This footage shows students a stark reality, especially when they realize that the actual thieves, usually poor peasants desperate for cash, reap very little financial gain for their efforts. The real money changes hands on the other end of the pipeline in New York, London, and Paris galleries.

This segment is followed by interviews with foreign government antiquities officials, curators, gallery owners, and auction house executives. In hearing the various points of view, students can understand why these issues are so contentious. It is also suggested that museums are sometimes complicitous in the illegal antiquities trade.

The video's major focus is a case study on the looting, illegal import, sale, arrest, and trial of a group of individuals involved in a prominent case during the 1980s concerning artifacts from what is known as the "Sipan treasure," an AD 500 Moche culture royal burial tomb in coastal Peru. The video ends with an unexpected verdict issued by a U.S. court in which the illegal importers of looted artifacts are acquitted and the looted artifacts returned to them. This verdict provides yet another jolt for students because they are expecting the opposite result. The court found the Peruvian antiquities laws to be vague, and their concept of "blanket ownership" was not upheld. As a result, students are exposed to another stark reality of the antiquities trade, that courts do not always support the laws of foreign governments regarding looted artifacts.

Step 6. The next class devoted to the theme features a student debate. The class is divided into half and students are asked to prepare opinions on the pro or con side of the antiquities/looting/ethics question. Once the students begin talking, the debate can be lively, even heated. Students usually enjoy the debate format because they can participate and at this point in the term, they are well prepared to argue a position.

Step 7. The final classroom activity is distribution and discussion of a two-page handout "Society for American Archaeology Principles of Archaeological Ethics," issued by the Society for American Archaeology and subsequently published in *American Antiquity* (1996). This completes the theme using a professional archaeological organization's statement on these issues. The statement contains eight principles of archaeological ethics covering issues such as stewardship, accountability, commercialization, public education and outreach, intellectual property, public reporting and publication, records and preservation, and training and resources. These principles are reviewed and form the basis for a class discussion. I conclude by talking about the issues developed throughout the term and their relationship to the eight principles of professional conduct.

References Cited

Dorfman, J.
1988. Getting Their Hands Dirty: Archaeologists and the Looting Trade. *Lingua Franca* May/June: 29-36.

PBS *Frontline*
1990. *Plunder*. W. Cran and J. Gilmore, producers. WGBH Boston.

Raban, A.
1997. Stop the Charade: It's Time to Sell Artifacts. *Biblical Archaeology Review* May/June: 42-45.

Society for American Archaeology
1996. Society for American Archaeology Principles of Archaeological Ethics. *American Antiquity 61 (3): 451-452.*

Spielberg, S.
1981. *Raiders of the Lost Ark.*

Vitelli, K. (ed)
1996. *Archaeological Ethics.* Walnut Creek CA: AltaMira Press.

Note: in Figure 3, only 5 terms are defined due to space limitations. The author is happy to supply definitions upon request.

Figure 1

Raiders of the Lost Ark and Popular Stereotypes of Archaeology

I put together this list after watching the first 15 minutes of *Raiders of the Lost Ark* (1981). The film is a very popular adventure fantasy based on archaeology and biblical themes. The main character, Indiana Jones, is a professor of archaeology at a U.S. institution. Along with two sequels, the film portrays archaeologists, archaeological research, and related museum issues in the following ways:

... Archaeologists work in remote and exotic places, e.g, jungles and deserts.

... Archaeologists hunt for ancient treasure and use any means necessary to acquire it, including looting and murder.

... Archaeologists carry weapons in their research, including pistols, knives, and bullwhips.

... Archaeologists hire indigenous people to help steal artifacts.

... Archaeologists compete with each other for looted treasure.

... Archaeologists teach in colleges and universities when not treasure hunting.

... Archaeologists are "sexy."

... Museum curators are interested only in artifacts and not the cultural information associated with finds.

... Archaeologists are experts on ancient civilization and the occult (defined as the study of mystic arts such as magic, alchemy, and astrology).

Figure 2
Ethics and Archeology: Two Points of View*

PRO	CON
Permit museum exhibition of all archaeological collections.	Do not permit museum exhibition of archaeological collections unless obtained legally.
Institutions or individuals should be permitted to purchase artifacts/art from antiquity.	Most artifacts available for purchase have almost certainly been looted.
Archaeologists should identify, authenticate, and/or study looted artifacts/art contributing to expansion of knowledge.	Archaeologists should not identify, authenticate, and/or study looted artifacts/art because it condones/encourages further looting/destruction.
Artifacts/art even without context have research value, e.g. linguistic, iconographic, and aesthetic.	Looted artifacts/art lack research value because context and provenience are missing.
Dealers, collectors, and museums encourage preservation, study, and display by acquiring artifacts/art already out of the ground.	Dealers and collectors encourage looting because they are willing to pay high prices for artifacts/art from antiquity.
Market forces are operating to bring artifacts/art to the galleries, museums, and collectors around the world; rare objects get high prices.	The illegal antiquities trade is violent, linked with drug traffic. Estimate: $120 million/year business and growing.
Vague laws in foreign countries or UN conventions should not keep us from pursuing our business and our passion.	Dealers, museum curators, and collectors are criminals for breaking the laws on importation of antiquities.
Many objects were imported legally (pre 1970 UNESCO convention).	Many objects were exported illegally from their countries of origin.
Artifacts/art are sometimes damaged in acquisition and shipping.	Looters destroy artifacts/art when attempting to reduce their size for easy shipping abroad.
Through display and publication, galleries and museums educate the public and further our knowledge of the past.	The educational value of looted objects is questionable and contributes to more looting.
The indigenous people's perspective is irrelevant since they cannot protect artifacts/art.	It is necessary to respect the indigenous point of view regarding their ancestors' remains.

* based on Dorfman (1988).

Figure 3
Archaeological Ethics: Glossary and Concepts*

Antiquarianism. An interest in old things. Today, archaeology and art history as modern disciplines have replaced antiquarianism.

Antiquities. Objects and art from the past, usually recovered through archaeological excavation or looting of sites, graves, or tombs. Often, antiquities acquired by one means or another hundreds of years ago, have been handed down in families through generations.

Antiquities Market/Trade. The world-wide trade in archaeological and art objects from the past. The market exists on many levels from individual to individual, dealer to gallery, gallery to museum. This market is both legal and illegal depending on how, when, and under what circumstances antiquities were acquired, donated, or sold.

Antiquities Laws. Specific legislation designed to protect archaeological sites from destruction and looting, as well as laws designed to control the illegal trade in antiquities.

Antiquity Dealers. Individuals who are in business to buy and sell artifacts and ancient art legally and often illegally.

Archaeological Pedigree
Archaeological Record
Archaeological Conservancy
Archaeological Site
Authentication
Avocational Archaeologists
Black Market
Certificate of Authenticity
Collectors/Collecting
Commercialization of Archaeology
Connoisseur/Connoisseurship
Conservation Ethic
Contextual Information
Cultural Patrimony
Epigraphy/Epigraphers
Ethics/Ethical
Forgery/Fakes
Glyphs
Grave Goods/Furnishings
Heritage Management
Huaqueros/Tombaroli
Huacas/Huacos
Iconography
Lithics
Looting/Pot Hunting

Mesolithic
Museum Collecting Expeditions
NAGPRA
Neolithic
Non-renewable Archaeological Record
Obsidian
Paleolithic
Preservation Law
Protohistoric
Provenience/Provinance
Reburial
Register of Professional Archaeologists (RPA)
Repatriation
Stela
Stewardship
Stratigraphic Excavation
Trafficking in Antiquities
Treasure Salvors
Trophy Art
Tumulus
UNESCO Convention for the Protection of Cultural Property in the Event of Armed Conflict, 1954
UNESCO Convention on Cultural Properties, 1970

37

"First Steps" in Hominid Evolution: A Lesson on Walking

Janet Pollak

Teaching multiple sections of Introduction to Anthropology to mostly non-majors who are fulfilling general education social science requirements not only presents opportunities for innovative pedagogy, it demands creativity. Moreover, since "critical thinking" and "intensive writing" (or writing as a mode of learning) are required at many colleges and universities, instructors have begun to experiment and reconfigure segments of courses and even entire courses. In the mid-1980s, I signed up for a week-long seminar in writing across the curriculum, audited the basic English composition course, and revised my Introduction to Anthropology course as a "writing" course. One of the faculty seminar's instructors then audited my class for a semester to assess the re-visioning. I developed fifteen writing and learning segments in the course that involved various types of writing and writing assessment. The most popular assignment focused on bipedalism in human evolution.

The exercise described here can be adapted to a variety of instructional formats, even those that do not incorporate much writing. You will need a full session (60-75 minutes) and, although class size is not a relevant constraint, it works better in rooms where students can get up and move around a bit. "First Steps" can also be easily used in a physical/ biological anthropology course as an introduction to bipedalism.

Because so many undergraduates continue to be stressed by nearly anything in the curriculum that falls under the general science umbrella, my unit on human evolution and the fossil record begins with an exercise that draws on the students' own knowledge and expertise of a motor activity that they have been acquainted with for nearly two decades: walking. I flip on an overhead transparency and distribute a copy to each student:

"Bipedalism: Human beings are proficient in the mode of loco-motion known as bipedalism or striding/walking on two legs. Imagine that you have been hired to write copy for an "owner's manual" of the human body. On this sheet of paper, provide detailed instruc-tions for standing from a seated position (without using the hands) and moving forward for about ten feet using only the legs." (See end of article for this statement; it can be copied on a transparency or photocopied for individual students.)

This "writing about walking" exercise is very deceptive because it appears to be much easier than it actually is. While it proceeds from students' prior knowledge and experience, it compels them to examine the process critically and focus on sequential steps in great detail. Expect that none of the students has ever dissected the act of walking before. There is one caution about using this particular exercise in every class, however. Sometimes a physically-challenged student is present so it may be a good idea to speak with that individual ahead of time and, perhaps, recast the exercise to address some other distinctly human motor skill that everyone in the room possesses, such as manipulating objects with opposable thumbs.

The bipedalism assignment is completed in class and students are allowed to move around and "practice" in order to review the discrete motions required to accomplish the tasks of standing and walking. Give them a few minutes to think about the exercise and make some preliminary notes. Then give them about twenty minutes to complete the assignment. While you do not have to suggest anything about "acting out" the motions, usually one or more students will begin testing various movements while others watch intently or squirm around in their seats to see what body parts move and in which order. In completing this assignment on paper, some students write lists while others write paragraphs. A small percentage of the group (generally less than 10% of a class) will make drawings.

After everyone is finished, collect the papers, shuffle them, and then ask for a volunteer. Clear the front of the classroom and place a side chair (without arms) in the center where all may observe. A volunteer comes forward and is asked to sit in the chair. Read the directions on the first paper (without revealing the author.) The volunteer is required to follow the directions to the letter, and the results are frequently hilarious. Students become instantly aware of which sets of directions are adequate or inadequate, based on what the volunteer is asked to do. Generally, at this first go-around, there are too few specific directions and not nearly enough precision for the volunteer to get to his/her feet, or, if they get the person standing, a number of key components for moving the legs appropriately are missing. While it is not necessary at this stage to read all the papers aloud, it is advisable to change volunteers after every three or four papers. Reading about a dozen or so of the first drafts should suffice. After each set of directions is read, ask students what they think is missing or what should be changed or eliminated.

Following this front-of-the-classroom segment, hand the papers back to the students for revision. This process should take no more than ten minutes or so and you may find that many more students are standing up and walking around to ensure they not only have the steps in sequence, but that they have included sufficient detail in their descriptions of each step. When the first drafts have been revised, divide the class up into groups of three or four (four should be the maximum) and have them peer-review their newly-configured directions. Students will have written their first drafts on the front of the sheet and their second drafts on the back. During the peer-critique phase, they are asked to note the suggestions they receive in the margins. If the exercise is to be evaluated, the papers are collected. (Instead of letter grades, I assign pluses, checks, or minuses.)

This assignment involves problem-solving skills as well as critical thinking and the need to identify a logical progression of movements in a behavior that most, if not all, students have never given much thought to. In all the semesters that I have assigned this exercise since 1986, less than five percent of a class comes up with a complete set of directions the first time through. For students, it provides a comfortable, yet substantive introduction to the "stones and bones" portion of the introductory course. It provides a very necessary preface to what students tell us is the most difficult area of anthropology with just enough humor and sense of accomplishment to tackle the complexities of hominid evolution.

Finally, the exercise could be expanded to illuminate the impact of culture on basic human motor skills. For instance, the type of footwear worn by young children will impact on the foot fall as they walk. Wearing an inflexible sole on a sandal that requires an individual to grip it with the toes may result in the entire foot hitting the ground at the same time, and not the heel-to-toe movement seen with other types of footwear or bare feet.

Footnote

1. For information on the other writing exercises I developed for my Introduction to Anthropology course, contact the author at: pollak_j@wpc.wilpaterson.edu.

Appendix

What follows are two examples of students' unedited first-draft directions for this exercise:

(1) # 1. Place your feet on the floor.
2. Lean forward.
3. Place the weight of your body on your feet.
4. Extend your legs at the knees.
5. Now you're standing.
6. Take your right foot and place it in front of your body.
7. Take your left foot and do the same same while your right foot is stationary.
8. Alternate back and forth between the right and left foot.
9. Now you are walking.

(2) # 1. Sit in a chair.
2. While sitting, stretch your legs straight out. (This is how you want your legs for step 3).
3. Stand up slowly maintaining your balance. Lock your knees. Your upper body should be straight up.
4. After standing in place with your knees locked and your body upright and balanced, take your left

foot slowly and lean forward a little, bending your knee and step forward about 6 inches. Remember to stay upright and maintain your balance.
5. Then take your right foot and place it about 6 inches in front of your left foot, maintaining your balance and leaning forward slightly to maintain your balance.
6. Continue this motion slowly until you are able to move faster.

BIPEDALISM: Human beings are proficient in the mode of locomotion known as bipedalism or striding/walking on two legs. Imagine that you have been hired to write copy for an "owner's manual" of the human body. On this sheet of paper, provide detailed instructions for standing from a seated position (without using the hands) and moving forward for about ten feet using only the legs.

The Trouble With the "Race" Concept: It's All in the Cards

Robert Graber

Because the populations of a species ordinarily are connected, at least indirectly, by some degree of gene flow, genes are constantly getting "scrambled" so that at any given time the species as a whole cannot be neatly subdivided into distinct subgroups. Astute zoologists recognized decades ago that this renders quite problematic the whole subspecies concept; biological anthropologists increasingly have recognized it as perhaps the fundamental reason that science could not arrive at a satisfactory enumeration of human "races." How the species breaks down will depend on the variable, or variables, looked at, so any particular set of racial categories is not so much a reflection of something real "out there" in the natural world, as it is the result of arbitrary choices by the racemaker. Statistically, the problem is that of discordant variation. But, as I learned long ago, this important concept is difficult to convey to students verbally. As a result, I invented a hands-on approach by designing two decks of cards and inviting students to try their hands at sorting them. This card game can be used in any introductory-level class that has one or more sessions devoted to the study of race, from four-field introductory anthropology to entire courses devoted to biological anthropology. I will describe the decks themselves, then explain how they are used in class to demonstrate the concept of discordant variation.

Figure 1 shows the "c" deck: four 3-by-5-inch note cards, each bearing a stick-person. Card "c1" bears the image of a short, solid, curly-haired individual; "c2" a tall, dotted, straight-haired individual; "c3" a short, solid, curly-haired individual; and "c4" a tall, dotted, strait-haired individual. (Actually, the stick people are not solid and dotted, but purple and orange, with black ink used only for faces and hair.) Figure 2 shows the "d" deck: card "d1" bears the image of a short, solid, straight-haired individual; "d-2" a tall, solid, curly-haired individual; "d-3" a short, dotted, curly-haired individual; and "d-4" a tall, dotted, straight-haired one. Note that the cards' labels are inconspicuous. Sixteen of these decks (8 of each kind) are sufficient for a class of up to about 50 students. You will need about a third as many decks as you have students, so if the class is really large, you will need many decks and a recruit or two to help pass them out; fortunately decks can be made quickly, and as is obvious from Figures 1 and 2, require no artistic ability. Feel free to photocopy and enlarge Figures 1 and 2 on heavy paper, cutting and pasting on 3 x 5" cards, and coloring orange and purple, or make you own variations.

After introducing the subject of biological variation among modern humans, I assert that with humans, as with animals generally, gene flow between populations (concepts covered earlier in the course) tends to make variation **discordant** rather than **concordant.** I write these terms on the chalkboard without attempting to define them in any detail. This brings up the next point in the lecture outline, "The Trouble with the Race Concept." Students invariably show heightened interest when they are told they will be involved in some "active learning." Teams of two to four will be given a deck of cards showing four individuals, all of the same sex; their assignment is to sort the four people into two races. I assure them that I will be coming around to check their races and that their grade for the term depends entirely on their success at this task. I pass out the decks, one to every two to four students, as seating dictates, to make for a pleasant social experience. The cards are purposely prearranged so that the "c" and "d" decks approximately alternate, but do not mix the decks.

After a few minutes, I wander around examining each group's result. The c-deck sorters are lavishly praised for having made such "good races," while d-deck sorters are questioned very briefly as to why they sorted as they did. "Here, trade decks with this group," I say encouragingly, "as I think you will have better success at making races;" and indeed they do. The other group, meanwhile, having received the "d" deck, gets cold water poured on its enthusiastic racemaking. Occasionally a group declines to sort the "d" deck, having recognized the arbitrariness of whatever they might propose; once, presumably acting on an unusually strong aversion to the very idea of racial classification, a group actually refused to even sort the "c" deck!

When everyone has had a chance to sort both decks (and the general hubbub has subsided), I restore order by asking the class in what variables the stick-people differ. Students quickly volunteer them: height, color, and hair form. "For both decks?" "Yes, for both decks." "What states are possible for each variable?" "Tall/short, orange/purple, and curly/straight." "For both decks?" "Yes, for both decks." "So, how do the decks differ?" Suddenly, silence. "In one deck," I point out, "you get the same cut no matter which variable you use, but in the other deck, **the cut you get depends on the variable you use.** Invariably I get raised eyebrows and nods. (The

instructor, on a pedagogical roll, wonders why the whole semester can't be like this.) Only then do I call attention to the little labels in the cards' corners. "Can you guess what the 'c' and 'd' stand for?" I ask, gesturing helpfully toward the chalkboard where the terms **concordant** and **discordant** remain, where I had written them several minutes before. It sinks in, students get the point, and the two terms and their importance to the "race" concept are now understood.

I immediately emphasize that I am not saying biological variation is completely discordant among humans, or any other species; only that it is sufficiently discordant to have confounded all attempts to divide the whole species up into scientifically satisfactory biological subgroups.

The next lecture point is entitled "A Better Approach," in which I talk about the insight that comes from looking at the distribution of single traits throughout the species; here we focus on clinal analysis of single traits. My favorite examples are skin color, nose form, and body build, all of which appear to represent adaptation through natural selection, to specific environmental features (directness of sun's rays, humidity, and temperature, respectively). I conclude by warning, however, that there is something seriously misleading about such examples and that we must not let them obscure the fact that humans expanded into diverse environments mainly by adapting culturally, not by adapting biologically. I point out that humans didn't inhabit the arctic by evolving thick fur any more than we ventured into space by evolving the ability to do without oxygen. I pick up the decks of cards at the door as students leave.

However you frame the sorting experience, it seems more effective and memorable than a strictly verbal approach to the concept of discordant variation. A former student I bumped into recently actually wanted assurance that I was still using "those cards"! Unusual teaching techniques, in my experience, generally take a while to work, then work for only a while; this one, by contrast, was an immediate and lasting success. When making up decks, use high quality materials because you will probably be using them for years to come.

Figure 1: The "c" deck

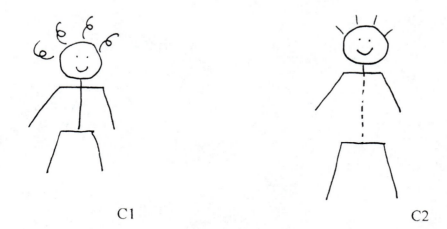

C1   C2

C3   C4

Figure 2: The "d" deck

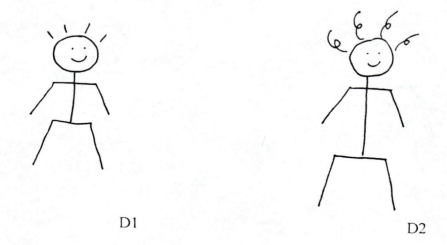

D1   D2

D3   D4

The Use of Biblical "Stories" as a Discussion Point for Evolution Versus Creationism

Clifton Amsbury

When I was teaching physical anthropology at a community college, invariably there was one person in the class who was powerfully oriented toward creationism. It was so consistent that I wondered if each was a "plant," put there to "correct" the evolutionism the student expected to hear from me. I discovered a way to handle that situation and wish to pass it on.

After the formal part of the first day's handling of enrollment sheets and other housekeeping chores, I picked up a small and obviously old copy of the Old Testament (also called a Hebrew Holy Book) that I had been given by a chaplain while in the U.S. Army during the second world war and started to read the first two chapters aloud to the class.

When finished, I called the class's attention to the fact that I had just read them **two** stories of the creation from the Bible. I also told them that the two stories were totally incompatible with each other. One story presented God as a King giving orders, reviewing the work at the end of each stage of creation and pronouncing it well done before ordering the next stage. The other story presents God as a Craftsperson doing the work himself. How can this be? Historians tell us that when the propagandists of David's new empire were preparing the origin myth of this kingdom of a united Palestine – or Israel – they needed the stories in it to appeal to diverse people, so almost all of the stories in the "historical books" of the Bible appear in at least two versions. The priestly version and the folk version cannot both be correct.

I then introduce the "science" story of creation, including the scientific method and experimentation. By doing this, I suggest there is a third story about creation, and not all three can be correct. I always told my classes that although they did not have to believe the third, i.e., the scientific story, they had to learn its premises.

Gender and Language: A Fieldwork Project

Peter Wogan

In this project, students write down compliments that they hear around campus, such as "I like your shoes" or "nice shot." To test hypotheses about the differences between men and women's speech patterns, the students then analyze the class's collective data, i.e., transcripts and standardized forms rating these compliments. Not only does this project make anthropology come alive through issues that concern real people, but through focused fieldwork, it raises important questions about gender, language, and anthropological methodology such as qualitative versus quantitative data, what people say versus what they do, and interviewing.

The project is well suited for classes such as Language and Culture or Gender and Culture, but it also works well in the linguistic anthropology unit of any introductory level class. The project is appropriate for both large and small classes and can be scheduled for use in one to five class sessions. I describe two versions of the project: the **Long Version** is a full-blown unit primarily designed for a small, discussion-based class, whereas the **Short Version** is aimed at a large class or one with only one or two sessions available for the topic.

Long Version

Class 1: Gender and Language. I begin by reviewing the central points in Janet Holmes's *Women, Men and Politeness* (1995), specifically Chapter 1 (a general overview of research on gender and language) and Chapter 2 (about interruptions). Holmes, like Deborah Tannen, makes the following hypothesis: males use speech more for status seeking and information whereas females (who interrupt less, for example) use speech more for social solidarity.

I then show the class a clip from the film *Good Will Hunting* to begin to explore Holmes's points about interruptions. Even though virtually every student has already seen the film, I review the characters and then ask students to pay attention to interruptions in a short scene in which Ben Affleck tells a story about an uncle who got arrested for drunken driving. After the clip, discussion focuses on the character Morgan, who interrupts so many times that Affleck tells him to "shut up." An alternative would be to play the audio version of a section of Deborah Tannen's *Talking from 9 to 5* (1994) (available as a "Book on Tape" in many public libraries). Ask the class if Morgan is being competitive by trying to steal the floor. Is he status seeking? Or are these interruptions actually a good-natured form of ritual teasing that builds solidarity among this male gang, much as females supposedly build solidarity by not interrupting. The students will inevitably come up with interesting interpretations, and you can conclude by noting the importance of context with its complex range of factors in determining the meaning of an interruption or any other speech event (Holmes would agree); this point will resurface again in the class research in terms of the importance of using both quantitative and qualitative data.

Whether you use the Tannen tape or not, at some point in the project it is worth discussing the authors who criticize research that neglects power dimensions, i.e., arguing that gender differences in language are not innocent misunderstandings due to distinct socialization patterns but, rather are reinforcements of male power. Although it is sometimes harder to get at this power question with only intra-student compliments (due to lack of sharp status differences), these discussions can give students good questions to think about while analyzing their own compliments, and the ostensibly conflicting interpretations lend themselves to good paper topics.

Introduce the fieldwork assignment by announcing that as a collective research group, the class will now test some of the hypotheses and in the process gain a first-hand sense of important anthropological issues. Essentially, the assignment requires students to record three or more compliments, create a written transcript for each compliment, analyze its meaning, and provide standardized ratings on various categories, such as the gender of the participants, degree of truthfulness, intended and received meaning of the compliment (from solidarity to envy and manipulations). Hand out and go over the compliment forms, copies of which appear in the appendix.

Class 2: Fieldwork Process. By the time of this class session, each student should have recorded at least one compliment and conducted one post-compliment interview and be ready to discuss various fieldwork issues, such as:

... Were there any special problems during the interviews and how were/are they best resolved?
... If you (the anthropologist) and the participants disagree on the compliment's meaning or truthfulness, who is right?
... Are you and/or the participants reluctant to

rate compliments as less than truthful or as based on envy or manipulation, and if so, what challenges does this present in filling out the forms and interviewing on such sensitive topics?
... Did the interview permission form's "science frame" increase or reduce interviewees' self-consciousness?

Go Over Paper Directions. In class, go over the most important parts of the assignment and its directions. This would include instructions to write a five double-spaced page paper that analyzes the meaning(s) of the class data on complement exchanges and answering the following questions:

... What patterns – especially in terms of gender, but also if relevant questions on status or age – do you find in the compliment data and what do these patterns reveal about American gender relations?
... How do these patterns compare with the findings in our readings?
... What is confirmed or disconfirmed, and why might this be the case?

Students should consider both statistical patterns in the class data and qualitative data that are the interpretations of their own and others' transcripts and discussions, citing both extensively. Instruct them not to cover every pattern or piece of data collected by the class. Instead, they should focus on specific patterns or issues that they think are particularly interesting and revealing and develop interesting, original points that show a careful reading and deep insight into the gender relations revealed by the data.

Class 3: Statistical Results and/or Rough Drafts. Once the full set of compliments is collected, it must be distributed to all by putting the class compliment forms on library reserve, photocopying the forms for each student, or having students send out their completed forms on a class email list.

There are several options for the next step which is what to do during the time between receiving the full set of compliments and the time students complete their papers. One option is to start a new unit. Another is to have a class devoted to reviewing each other's rough drafts of the papers. And another is to have the class as a group review two or three drafts of papers you have photocopied before class. Finally, and one that easily blends with the second option, is to devote a class session to an analysis of the statistical patterns in the class data.

Relative to statistical patterns, one issue that inevitably comes up is the difficulty of assigning ambiguous compliments to one and only meaning category. This points up the limitations of quantitative data. On the other hand, students will realize that qualitative data has its limitations as well: with only three or four compliments, it is very difficult to know whether you are seeing a gender pattern or just an idiosyncracy of personality. The solution of course is that both qualitative and quantitative data are needed. Toward this end, ask specific groups of students – either as homework for the day's class or as an activity in class – to do a very simple quantitative analysis of certain parts of the full set of forms. For example, one group analyzes gender and compliment percentages (what percentage of all compliments were female to female or male to male); another group analyzes gender and compliment meaning (e.g. what percentage of

"solidarity" compliments were male to male or female to male) and so on. Not only does this analysis allow time to finish the final paper, but it provides a chance for the class to see what types of insights you find interesting and surprising. Also, dividing up this quantitative work is simply a favor to the class as otherwise each student will have to do the full analysis separately for the paper.

Short Version

Some instructors might prefer the condensed version of the project that would involve only 1½ class sessions. Many teaching strategies from the Long Version are pertinent here as well.

Class 1. Introduce research on gender and language and hand out the compliment forms.

Class 2. Collect the student's completed forms and discuss some of the fieldwork issues raised. Alternatively, the entire class period could be devoted to a new unit. Within the next few days, you will need to do a simple quantitative analysis of the compliment forms looking at patterns such as the percentage of compliments that were male to female, truthfulness ratings for female to female vs male to male compliments.

Class 3. Briefly discuss the results of the quantitative analysis. Give a photocopy summary of the results to each student and ask them to analyze these patterns for the next exam. (For the exam, make up multiple choice or short answer questions that ask about the class statistical patterns.) You can also ask students to compare their own compliments with the class patterns and/or the patterns predicted in reading materials.

This short version has many of the advantages of the long version: it makes issues concrete, shows gender patterns (which are particularly striking with a large class), and bond the class by allowing them to see their collective statistical data, which is like a snapshot of the whole class.

Results and Conclusions

Whether the class findings confirm or disconfirm previous gender research is unimportant because the findings will be academically interesting and important. Some gender patterns have always been quite striking every time I do this project: the greatest percentage of compliments is always female to female and the lowest is always male to male; and male to male always shows the highest level of joking as well. Some of the most interesting papers I have seen have focused on issues of power, self esteem, envy, and truthfulness. Students have found this to be an interesting project because it impacts on their own lives.

The Compliment Forms that follow are collapsed for space saving. Lines between them indicate new pages. Additional teaching comments are noted in brackets.

Reference Cited

Holmes, J.
   1995. *Women, Men and Politeness.* New York: Longman.

Tannen, D.
   1994. *Talking From 9 to 5: How Women's and Men's Conversational Styles Affect Who Gets Heard, Who Gets Credit, and What Gets Done at Work.* New York: W. Morrow.

Notes

A tape of non-scripted, natural speech would be preferable in many ways to using a commercial film to show male/female speech, but this film works well not only because it is funny but also it is a familiar, at-hand example that suffices for these heuristic purposes.

There are a number of readings that demonstrate power dimensions in language, such as Nancy Henley and Cheris Kramarae's "Gender, Power, and Miscommunication" in Miscommunication and Problematic Talk, Nikolas Coupland et..al, eds (London Sage, 1991), or Mary Crawford's *Talking Difference*, (London Sage 1995), pp 97-198. Also, somewhere along the line, I recommend assigning a reading specifically about compliments: Tannen and Holmes have sections on compliments as does Robert Herbert "Sex-Based Differences in Compliment Behavior," *Language in Society* 19:201-224, 1990.

COMPLIMENT FORMS

YOUR NAME: COMPLIMENT #: 1   2   3   4   (Circle one)

[In order to have enough data to see patterns, the minimum number of total compliments recorded by ALL students is about 60; larger numbers are better for seeing patterns, but if each student is expected to read the entire data set, there is a trade off in terms of workload.]

SETTING (When, where happened):

RELATIONSHIP BACKGROUND (Relationship between speakers):

FULL TRANSCRIPT OF COMPLIMENT EXCHANGE (Use gender-marked pseudonyms for each speaker and note prosodic features):

                                                                                 _____

COMPLIMENT RATINGS FORM

YOUR NAME: COMPLIMENT #: 1   2   3   4   5 (Circle one)

GENDER: (Circle one): M-F (compliment given by male to female); F-M; F-F; M-M.

TRUTHFULNESS [Student makes this rating based on – but not limited to – interview with compliment giver some time after the compliment.]

   Rate the compliment on a scale of 1-5 for truthfulness. (Note: the lack of truthfulness in this context is not necessarily a bad thing; this might be a way of being "nice," comparable to asking "How are you?"). Circle one.

Least truly believed   Most truly believed

1   2   3   4   5

COMPLIMENT GIVER'S INTENDED MEANING (Circle one.)
[Student decides which letter to circle based on – but not limited to – the interview with the compliment giver.]

(a) solidarity (to be friendly, nice, supportive);
(b) possibly evaluative (praise that puts the compliment giver in the "superior" position, being the one to evaluate the other person; could be seen to be patronizing);
(c) envy or desire for that object/quality (wants it too);

(d) kidding, teasing (not for solidarity, but not malicious or critical vs. next category);
(e) critical, sarcastic, veiled criticism (kidding tone, but could contain criticism);
(f) manipulative (trying to get something, to manipulate);
(g) silence avoidance (way to initiate or keep conversation going – "ice breaker");
(h) embarrassing to recipient (made recipient embarrassed, uncomfortable);
(i) other (explain, under "Discussion").

COMPLIMENT RECEIVER'S INTERPRETATION OF COMPLIMENT MEANING (Circle one.)
(This designation is based on what the compliment receiver said, but if you disagree, note that in Discussion.) [Below, simply reproduce same lettered choices from "compliment giver's intended meaning."]

FORM OF COMPLIMENT RESPONSE

(a) deflection, then acceptance;
(b) persistent deflection, never accepts;
(c) rejection (ignored);
(d) acceptance (immediate acceptance, without deflection or qualification).

[Other categories could be added, such as object of compliment; possession; ability; appearance.]

_____

DISCUSSION/INTERPRETATION OF COMPLIMENT

YOUR NAME: COMPLIMENT #: 1 2 3 4

DISCUSSION. Discuss the reasons for your ratings (i.e., on truthfulness and compliment meaning), and add any other information about the interviews or the background context that helps to understand this compliment.

Linguistic Models in Anthropology 101
Give Me The Cup

Michael Sheridan

I think of introductory anthropology classes as intellectual buffet dinners. Our textbooks and lectures often fall into familiar domains of anthropological specialization, such as kinship, religion, and language. For many of the students in these courses, the unit on linguistic anthropology is their only exposure to the important issue of how language, culture, and society influence one another. Students often find ideas like the Sapir-Whorf hypothesis and linguistic insecurity stimulating notions, but it may be difficult for them to appreciate how language shapes their own consciousness. This exercise is designed to illustrate how the hidden meanings in the English language relate to social inequality. Other languages, of course, do the same thing, but it is easier to convince students of the ability of language to "do" such things through their own language.

In my lecture on linguistic anthropology, I lead up to this exercise by going over ethnolinguistics and sociolinguistics. I emphasize the evidence for female linguistic insecurity in English pronunciation, intonation, grammar, and vocabulary. I write a list of words on the chalkboard that has an implicit gender component (such as "manhole," "chairman," and "bachelor's degree") and ask the students for more suggestions. Then I summarize this material by saying that ideas about hierarchy and difference are built into our language use. I ask the students if words like those on the board shape the way they think. They usually do not agree or disagree strongly, but sometimes express their ambivalence with phrases like "I guess so" and "maybe a little."

At this point, I introduce the term "cultural model" to the class and write it on the board. I define cultural models as "implicit, non-conscious constructions of what is 'real' and 'natural,' shared by a group, and unconsciously embedded in language." I give them some examples of cultural models in vocabulary and grammar, such as:

... Arguments are war – he won, so he beat me, and I had to defend my position.
... Ideas are food – it's food for thought, and something to chew over, but I couldn't stomach the notion.
... Love is a disease – he got over her, but she's got it bad for him, so it broke her heart.
... Virtue is up – he's an upstanding citizen with ideals, but I would never sink so low, so he will have to come up to my standards.

Another cultural model involves the passive voice in Swahili. It is common for Swahili speakers in rural East Africa to use passive forms to avoid placing blame and to maintain an image of peace and harmony. This usage appears in both formal and informal contexts, from street conversations to legal documents. For example, one often hears that *kikombe kilivunjikwa* ("the cup was broken") but not that Mohammed *alivunja kikombe* ("Mohammed broke the cup").

After this introduction to cultural models, I announce that the class will conduct some experimental research on cultural models in American English. The exercise works best with 12-15 groups, so I break them into groups. I give each group 10 previously made up cards and explain that they are going to use common research methods in linguistic anthropology, ranking, and sorting. Each card contains a number and a phrase. Each phrase is a directive about a cup, used in a hypothetical two-person conversation. Ahead of time, you should make up as many identical packs of 10 cards as you are apt to need, one per group.

The list of phrases (and a number) are given below:

(1) Give me the cup.
(2) The cup.
(3) Could you please give me the cup?
(4) Would you give me the cup?
(5) Give me the cup, won't you?
(6) Can you give me the cup?
(7) I can't reach that cup.
(8) I want that cup.
(9) Can you get that cup for me?
10) I need that cup.

I tell the students that each group has to rank the cards according to the degree of politeness in the directive, from least polite to most polite. It usually takes 10 minutes for each group to reach consensus about the order of the cards. I ask each group to write down the order they have agreed on, and when every group has done so, I tell them to save the order and then to shuffle the cards. While they are shuffling, I take this time to remind them that many of the criteria of politeness are non-textual factors such as pitch, volume, and tone.

In the second part of the exercise, I tell the students to sort the cards into three piles:

... most likely to be said by a man;
... most likely to be said by a woman;
... could be said by either a man or a woman.

I ask the students to make a note of the contents of their three piles by their numbers.

Now is the time to compile the data. I make a chart on the chalkboard with ten columns and as many rows as there are groups of students. I write "least polite" above the upper left corner of the chart and "most polite" above its upper right corner. I ask the students to read me their ranked list of numbers, and I write these numbers across the board in a row for each group. The order of the groups' reports does not matter, so I move as quickly as possible to get all of the numbers on the chart. At this point, a typical chart looks like this:

least polite   most polite

2 8 10 6 1 5 7 4 9 3
8 10 2 1 9 7 6 3 5 4
2 10 8 9 7 1 6 5 4 3
2 8 20 6 5 1 7 4 3 9
10 2 8 1 9 6 7 5 3 4
8 2 7 1 10 6 4 5 9 3
8 2 10 9 7 1 5 6 4 3
2 10 8 8 1 7 6 5 3 4
6 2 10 8 5 4 1 7 9 3
2 8 10 1 7 9 5 3 4 6
8 2 1 7 9 10 6 5 3 4
8 2 1 10 7 6 5 4 3 9

The next step involves the sorting exercise by gender. I ask each group to tell me which numbers belong in the "male" and "female" categories, and as a student reads the numbers, I mark the chart by circling the female numbers and drawing triangles around the male numbers.

55

After I cover the chart with circles and triangles, I ask students to look for a pattern. Usually the triangles cluster on the left side of the chart and circles cluster on the right. I ask the class if men are really less polite than women, and if women sound masculine if they use directives such as "the cup." The exercise often leads to a lively class discussion of how gender hierarchies persist in American culture despite the efforts of feminist activists and advocates of "political correctness" in our speech.

Using Ads to Teach Anthropology

Spyros Spyrou

As a teacher of anthropology, I always struggle to make my teaching relevant to students' lives. I strongly believe that learning becomes meaningful when one sees its relevance to one's own life. In the absence of such key linkages between students' lives and experiences and what we teach them in the classroom, learning is often dry and uninteresting.

In many of my anthropology classes I use advertising to teach students about some of the discipline's basic concepts and to create the kind of engagement that will allow students to see anthropology as relevant to their lives. But why advertising?

First, advertising is a major aspect of our lives. We are constantly bombarded with it on TV and radio, on billboards, in magazines and newspapers, and even in junk mail. To ignore advertising is virtually impossible. We are surrounded by it and whether we wish to or not we are forced to deal with it, one way or another. But using advertising to teach anthropology is also convenient because students have easy access to ads. They can easily flip through magazines and find ads or even record TV commercials on videotape and bring them to class. Furthermore, the range of issues one could explore through advertising is huge – from basic issues related to culture, to issues of "race" and ethnicity, gender, class, and sexuality, to politics, ideology, and the family -- making it a very effective tool for addressing a variety of anthropological topics. And of course, advertising, especially visual advertising, can be very interesting and appealing to work with. It can allow students to work hands-on with ads and explore them in ways that bring otherwise abstract concepts and principles back home. In this way, it may encourage students to reflect on their own culture in a critical and productive way.

The possibilities in using advertising as a teaching (or more precisely learning) tool are many. I have used ads in a variety of anthropology courses including Introduction to Cultural Anthropology, Multiculturalism, and Race and Ethnicity. Because the scope of advertising in the contemporary world is broad, virtually any anthropological issue could be discussed in relation to it. Below I describe how I use advertising in an introduction to cultural anthropology course and outline some variations of it that I occasionally use. I usually schedule this exercise for two class periods, though a shorter time may be sufficient with smaller classes.

Personally, I prefer to use this particular exercise towards the end of the term though it could certainly be used earlier when the instructor wishes to introduce or exemplify a particular concept. My primary objective in using the exercise is to show students how anthropological concepts that are discussed in the course can be useful in understanding what goes on around us.

In one particular version of this exercise I focus on group stereotypes. During the class meeting before the planned day of the exercise I ask students to look through magazines they read or have access to, to find two or more examples of ads that portray a particular social group (e.g., men, women, children, Asians, Native Americans, or college students), and bring them to class.

To prepare students for the exercise I sometimes show them Jean Kilbourne's documentary film *Killing Us Softly* (1979) where she focuses on the use of gender in advertising and/or have them read a chapter from William O'Barr's book *Culture and the Ad: Exploring Otherness in the World of Advertising* (1994), both of which help students look at advertising critically and recognize its relation to culture.

During class, I pair up students and ask them to spend 10-15 minutes in discussing their ads with each other. To help guide their discussion, I give them the following list of questions:

... What is the primary message of the ad (e.g., that Levi jeans are good quality jeans)?
... What is the secondary message (i.e., the underlying cultural message) of the ad?
... How does it portray the particular group in question?
... Is it a positive or a negative portrayal? What kinds of stereotypes are portrayed, if any?
... Do you agree or disagree with the portrayal?
... Could there be more than one interpretation of this ad? What might they be?

Once students have had a chance to discuss their respective ads and to think through dialogue about them a bit more, I ask them to present their ads to the rest of the class at which time I encourage other students to comment on the ads. Students are very enthusiastic about the exercise and even

shy students who might have been relatively quiet in previous classes contribute. The discussion that surrounds each presentation provides us with an opportunity to talk about a variety of anthropological concepts and to raise a number of issues that students have been exposed to earlier in the course but now in a much more particular fashion. My role as a teacher is not to analyze the ads for them but to help them do so themselves by reminding them of relevant concepts that we have already covered in the course. Thus, in addition to stereotyping, we might talk about cultural values, norms and attitudes, symbols and symbolism, language and cultural metaphors, cultural variability, ideology, interpretation, "race," ethnicity, gender, class, and cultural change. Because students often differ in their interpretations of ads we often get into a discussion of multivocality and differences between intended and received messages. I also raise the question of cultural change and advertising: does advertising reflect cultural change and in what ways? At this point I enrich the discussion by showing students examples of ads coming from different time periods (e.g., about the portrayals of women in advertising through time) and how they reflect larger cultural changes in values and attitudes. Inadvertently, we discuss issues of power, hierarchy, and dominance between various groups in society.

The exercise never turns out the same way. Students and their interests differ each semester so that you always discuss the issues from different points of views and using different examples.

To complement this exercise or as an alternative to it, I have from time to time, used other variations of it. For instance, I have asked students to:

... collect, either individually or in groups, ads that deal with a particular category or theme (e.g., representation of African-Americans in advertising or representations of gender in advertising) and present them in poster form with captions;

... collect ads from foreign sources (e.g., French newspapers or Greek magazines), focusing on a particular theme (e.g., child-hood) and compare them with ads from the students' own cultures. (This could be either a writing assignment or an oral presentation.)

... collect ads that focus on a particular theme from different time periods and write a paper about the cultural changes that the ads reflect;

... collect ads that relate to a key concept or idea (e.g., "progress," evolution, war, or the body) and see how such concepts are metaphorically used in advertising.

Though in my experience print ads from magazines are the most accessible and convenient for students, it is possible to use the exercise with other media (e.g., TV commercials that students may record on videotape and bring to class, provided of course that they have access to the technology).

The beauty of this exercise is that it can take so many different forms and can be used in so many different ways. More importantly, from an educational standpoint the exercise actively implicates students into the learning process and helps them think about anthropological concepts in a concrete and interesting way. At the same time, it helps students reflect on their own cultures and think critically about the messages they are exposed to.

References Cited

Kilbourne, J.
1979. *Killing Us Softly*. Cambridge, MA: Cambridge Documentary Films.

O'Barr, W.
1994. *Culture and the Ad: Exploring Otherness in the World of Advertising*. Westview Press.

Teaching Cultural Anthropology Through Mass and Popular Culture: Seven Pedagogical Methods for the Classroom

Scott A. Lukas

In recent years cultural anthropologists have become more comfortable with the worlds of mass and popular culture, especially in ethnographic and epistemological senses. One of the overlooked values of the detraditionalization of contemporary cultural anthropology is the positive impact that studies of mass and popular culture can have on the anthropology classroom. Over the past five years of teaching introductory cultural anthropology courses, I have employed a strategic emphasis on contemporary culture in my classroom. Specifically, my students examine the connections between traditional theoretical and methodological facets of anthropology and the worlds of popular culture. What I have found to be most fascinating is using popular culture as an apparatus of pedagogical technique itself. What follows is a description of a number of these approaches. They can all be modified for the specifics of your class in terms of size, level, or content.

(1) Class Ethnographies

I have assigned class ethnographies in my introductory anthropology classes for a number of years. The introductory ethnography, generally a paper of ten to fifteen pages in length, is no doubt a common assignment for many anthropology students, but here the assignment has a specific regional twist. The students read two professionally written ethnographies during the term. Each highlights different cultural areas; one is written from a third-person-detached perspective, the other is illustrative of reflexive first-person ethnography. Typically the students feel overwhelmed when it is their turn to write a partial ethnography. I stress that their works are of an obviously smaller scale and that they should view the two professional ethnographies as works of insight, not models. I stress that ethnography is both scientific and personal, both analysis and observation. Because I currently teach in a city based in a tourist and service economy, I ask my students to tailor their ethnographies to reflect either work or leisure experiences in the community. The ethnographies that have been produced are quite outstanding. I am always pleasantly surprised at how the students integrate traditional anthropological concepts with their contemporary field sites. Some of the more interesting topics have included the dynamics of being a ski lift operator, working in a fast food restaurant, and being a casino blackjack dealer. Class ethnographies may also be assigned according to a specific emphasis in individual anthropology classrooms. An example would be assigning the class ethnography on the topic of religious belief and practice for an anthropology of religion course.

(2) Material Culture Presentations

I developed material culture presentations following an early interest in archaeology. I incorporate the material culture presentation in my cultural anthropology courses because I feel it effectively stresses the significance of culture and material culture in anthropology and because it emphasizes critical thinking related to everyday objects. Prior to the assignment the class focuses on the significance of material culture in anthropology. For the assignment my students are asked to find one object of material culture. There is no stipulation about the object, other than that it must be brought into the classroom and that it may not be a picture. I believe that by having students bring in a three-dimensional object, the class presentations take on a more engaged, less class report, style. The students give a five to ten minute presentation on the object. First, they speak on a descriptive level highlighting the physical, tactile, and other sensory aspects of the object. Next, they consider the production of the object. This is a very interesting area as some consumer items are often of ambiguous origins; other times they reflect the unfortunate sides of the production of mass culture objects. The final portion of the presentation emphasizes connections between the object and systems of culture. Students may tie the object to a cultural institution or to a particular aspect of everyday life. This technique continues to be one of the most successful pedagogical methods I have employed. The list of objects considered by students has included Beanie Babies, processed food packages, an Eisenhower political button, and a cell phone.

(3) Anthropology and Nontraditional Film

I use film to emphasize key course themes in all of my classes. Because I believe that we anthropologists are afraid to venture outside the boundaries of our discipline, and in particular in the use of films and videos, for a number of years I have been integrating "nontraditional" films in cultural anthropology classrooms. I say "nontraditional" in that I choose examples not on the list of traditional ethnographic films (*The Ax Fight, Trobriand Cricket*) and because the films are those that many of my students have never before seen. Using such films can lead to exciting classroom experiences. A first viewing means that a majority of the class will watch and then reflect on the film in unique and personal

senses. Using a film never intended for an anthropological audience allows a deeper understanding of traditional anthropological concepts and themes. I have screened Werner Herzog's *Strosek*, a film about three misplaced Germans who travel to rural Wisconsin, to emphasize cultural contact zones and culture and human values. Errol Morris' *Vernon, Florida*, a documentary about a small rural United States community, is shown so that students will consider the theories of psychological anthropology, including typical personality, as well as the students' common reactions to the film and how these reactions relate to cultural relativism. Errol Morris' *Gates of Heaven*, a film about the politics of California pet cemeteries, is shown so that students will consider the anthropology of religion in a less traditional sense. There are any number of intriguing and nontraditional films that can be effectively integrated in the cultural anthropology classroom. These have worked well for me.

(4) Instant Camera Project

A technique that I have used in my visual anthropology class is the instant camera project. The intent of the assignment is to stress the relationship between cultural content and representational method in anthropology. In visual anthropology, we analyze films as they relate to these two areas. Recently I began to incorporate more media in class considerations of visual culture. In addition to working with the visuality of the World Wide Web, I ask students to reflect on visual culture as it is manifested in everyday optical devices, the tools of what is sometimes called "camera culture." The assignment involves the use of instant cameras. I originally asked the students to purchase Polaroid Pop Shots cameras because I wanted to have consistency in the size and number of photographs as well as the level of photographic control available to the photographer. Since its original inception, I have allowed students to use other cameras because of the expense of disposable cameras. The students are asked to mount their photos on paper and, if they so choose, provide captions. The captions may include personal statements, statements of informants or quotations from texts. Regardless of the formal aspects of the assignment, students are instructed to use the cameras to document a cultural theme or a biography. In the past, students have chosen to reflect on local political issues such as "The Cultural Picture of Water" and "Pictures of Tourism and the Environment." The second option again yielded interesting results, with some students choosing to picture and narrate their own lives; others focused on persons they deemed important in their lives. When there is a balance of the two options, I ask them to present their storyboards in class. The opportunity for all of us to reflect on visual representation in the areas of biography and other cultural themes is invaluable.

(5) Critical Collages

The critical collage is an assignment I have incorporated in visual anthropology and most recently in my introductory cultural anthropology classes. This project utilizes the availability of images of popular culture. I tell the students to focus on either autobiography or a cultural theme. The actual assignment takes place outside of the classroom. It requires them to produce a critical collage, i.e., a collection of cut-up images and pictures on a letter sized piece of paper. I specify the size of paper out of convenience to the students, but I have received much larger collages as well. I ask that they avoid the web on this assignment. One can imagine that an autobiography collage could be easily completed through a few keyword searches and downloading of web images, but I feel that this would not emphasize the components of the project. Instead, students are instructed to use images from popular magazines and newspapers. Typically these images end up being parts of advertisements and product ads. The point of the collage is to critically think about our personal existence in a mass-produced consumer world, and to think about our personal and political options for changing it. One student produced a collage that was a set of three images of the planet earth. Each was of a different scale and size. The largest image had glossy images of conspicuous consumption, the smallest had images that were smaller and more difficult to see. These included pictures of the homeless and global starvation. As the student explained to the class, she used the three contrasting scales to focus on personal commitment and capitalism. It is easy to be a part of the world of consumerism, she offered, but by looking more closely at the (smallest) world, we can see that the luxuries of some people are the poverties of many other people. In addition to the critical insights on mass culture that such collages provide, I also think that the assignment emphasizes the nature of the embeddedness of popular culture in all of our lives. Finally, some collages use advertisement pictures in the method of ditournement whereby the original messages of the ads are altered by the student's collage.

(6) Magazines and Body Image

I teach introductory cultural anthropology courses from a holistic and integrative perspective. I like to give students overviews of anthropological theories and methods and incorporate anthropological topics throughout the term. One of the most important integrations of theory and topic is my segment on feminist anthropology and the anthropology of gender.

Students study the significance of feminist anthropology in the development of professional anthropology. In order to have them understand the significance of praxis as well, I ask them to do a short group exercise. The exercise is one that is familiar to many gender studies classrooms, but I think it is as important to cultural anthropology students. Each of the student groups is given a set of popular magazines; if possible, have at least one magazine for each person in the group. The magazines are varied by content and targeted audience. The groups are also given a supply of sticky flags. They are asked to spend ten minutes working through the magazines. As individuals, they work to place sticky flags on the pages of appropriate examples. An appropriate example is any visual composition that highlights a major theme or theory we considered in our readings and class discussions on feminist anthropology. Then the students present their flagged pages to their colleagues who discuss the themes and theories related to the image compositions. The small group work is then summarized and shared with the entire class. I really enjoy this exercise because of the ways in which it emphasizes the concepts we explore in the anthropology of gender in the classroom. A set of two images -- an exoticized woman on an island and a professional man in an office -- can illustrate a concept like the male to culture/female to nature divide more effectively than I could lecture on the issue. I also think that the exercise can assist students to better consider the significance of gender in their everyday private and public lives.

(7) Theories and the News Pages

Anthropology students need not only learn the major theories and concepts of anthropology, but they need to be competent in understanding how the theories and concepts relate to the real world. I call this goal "making the theories speak," and I believe that it both reinforces the theory/concept while developing critical thinking skills and social science methods in students. I focus the assignment on theories, but the idea may be modified for any concept in cultural anthropology courses. First, students must understand fourteen major anthropological theories. In the past I have used handouts and readings to introduce the major theories (from unilineal cultural evolutionism to anthropology as cultural critique), followed by discussion groups and even theory skits where groups present a drama based on a theory and the other groups attempt to interpret the theory being presented. Following the introduction I ask students to "go out and find the theories," a sort of epistemological scavenger hunt. Each student is given three or more letter sized sheets of paper. On the top of each page is the name of a major theory (depending on the size of class I often have to assign more or less pages and sometimes assign the same theory to multiple students). Each student then takes the pages and is asked to fill in the space by the next class period. I suggest that they find one or more news stories which would explain or illustrate the theory on the page. This assignment could be modified to use pictures, but I think that it is important to connect each of the theories to lived cultural contexts of the sort offered in newspaper or web stories. Some interesting results have included a story on a community's water management problems (cultural ecology), a newspaper editorial on automobile names (cognitive anthropology), an article on the use of cultural savagery in popular culture (unilineal cultural evolution), and an article on good and evil (structuralism). By involving students in letting the theories speak for themselves, I can more effectively teach the theories and also have the students critically think about current events in the news.

I have incorporated these techniques in my cultural anthropology courses because they allow me and the students to study anthropology through mass and popular culture. Ultimately, they develop critical thinking skills in students as they stress the need to carefully consider popular culture. Most importantly they allow students to learn cultural anthropology in ways that stress reflexive thought and work.

Acting Out Anthropological Concepts

Juliana Flinn

Over several years of teaching introductory cultural anthropology, I became increasingly discouraged at how well students might spit back a definition word-for-word yet be unable to recognize an example of the concept, explain it in their own words, or apply it. They were memorizing, not learning, and they rarely went beyond definitions. I was also frustrated with student passivity; they expected me to spoon feed them definitions for terms rather than actively attempt to make sense of a concept, how it is used in anthropology, and its relevance for analysis. Finally, too often I noted in discussions that the same few people spoke up; most were too shy or uninterested and had no voice. Thus over the years, I've developed (and swiped!) exercises, activities, and simulations in which students have to engage with the material and in which it is practically impossible for anyone to just sit and vegetate. Some of the simplest, which I describe in this article, involve students acting out some very basic, common concepts covered in introductory cultural anthropology texts. The technique can be adapted to almost any class, and I mention briefly how I have applied it in an undergraduate theory class.

I teach at an urban, primarily commuter school. Many students fit courses as best they can around work and family responsibilities. Many who take introductory cultural anthropology do so simply because it fulfills a requirement, and although we have some very bright students, many – especially at the introductory level – are poorly prepared for college, a few honestly resent the expectation that they should even have to read a book, much less several books, for a class

rather than just listen to a teacher talk and take some tests. Luckily my classes are relatively small, ranging from about twelve students to fifty. In the introductory class, I usually use a textbook along with readers and/or ethnographies. This is the context in which I have developed my bag of tricks, but the technique I describe here should be suitable elsewhere.

In order to encourage students to read, think about what they are reading, and work with the material, I have them act out basic concepts from their reading. This takes place before discussion or lecture on the topic, but the reading is assigned in advance. The concept of **consensus** is one example. I used to describe the process and how it differs from voting, and I used to give a hypothetical example of the class coming to a consensus decision about where we all should eat. Instead, I now give them an issue that truly matters to them and tell them that I will abide by their consensus decision if they can reach it within the time limit I set. I tell them that they have five minutes to decide which chapter to omit from the final exam and that everyone has to agree (or at least no one can object). Students take four exams during the term and then a comprehensive final exam; I don't care about omitting some material on the final, especially since it would already have been covered on an earlier test. Students are clearly motivated to take the exercise seriously. With smaller classes, I let the class as a whole deliberate. I don't designate a particular process or leaders; I simply give them the time limit and tell them that all have to agree – or else all the material is fair game for the final. When I recently had about fifty students, I divided the class into four groups and had each select a representative. The representatives were to consult with their groups and meet as a "council" to reach the decision. The representatives could go back and forth between their groups and the council, but they still had a time limit; I gave them ten minutes instead of five. I give five, two, and one minute warnings.

After the decision (they have never yet failed to reach a consensus within the time limit), instead of lecturing about consensus, I can ask questions that elicit a number of key points. I can ask them the difference between consensus and voting. I can ask them to consider circumstances under which it is more likely and less likely to work. I can ask them about some of the mechanics of the process. By this time, the students have come to know each other in the class, and they tend to turn to certain people for leadership. Some students sit and don't really participate in the decision. Some initially disagree with others but give way eventually. Some argue more forcefully than others. Students can discuss this process based on what they just experienced, and I encourage them to discuss how it would work in societies they have been reading about. Anything that does not emerge in discussion that I would previously have simply lectured about I can easily add.

Another obvious place in the introductory class for acting out is with concepts about **distribution of goods and services.** Again, students should have read about them before coming to class. I divide the class into five groups and give each of them one of these concepts: generalized reciprocity, balanced reciprocity, negative reciprocity, redistribution, and market exchange. My instructions are to design a specific example of their assigned concept in order to act it out in front of the class. They are not to label the example, but merely act it out. I tell them that each person in the group has to have a part to play (though not

everyone has to talk). As they prepare, I visit each group – and usually once is enough – to ensure that they have come up with an appropriate example. I steer them in a new direction when necessary. Rarely is a group clearly wrong, but at times the example could be confusing. For instance, I discourage using Christmas presents as an example since it has elements of more than one concept. I discourage using money in examples except for market exchange. They are free to use examples from our own society or any other.

Then I take the groups in the order in which I like to teach the concepts. The group presents its skit in front of the class. (Some examples are minimal and take less than a minute. Sometimes students are more creative and present more elaborate cases.) The students sit down, and then I ask the class questions to elicit more thoughts on the concept. What was demonstrated? How or why could they recognize it? How did it differ from another? What are other examples? Under what circumstances would they expect to find it? Did it do anything else besides distribute goods? Whom would they expect to engage in such transactions? Through such questions, I usually manage to elicit most of what I would otherwise have lectured on, and I simply add anything else. Then I proceed to the next group and repeat the process.

Another obvious place I have found for this "trick" is with **postmarital residence patterns.** Before I can say anything very interesting about them, students need to know what they are. Again, without first explaining them, I divide the class into groups. For a small class, I assign two groups; for larger classes, three or more. If just two groups, I assign one matrilocal and patrilocal patterns and the other avunculocal (because it always takes longer). With three groups, I assign one to each; with four, I give two of them avunculocal residence to ponder. (I don't have them act out the others, but it is certainly feasible.) I tell each group to assume that they are all living together under their assigned rule of residence and that they range over three generations. They are to figure out how they could be related to each other. One person in the group should draw a diagram on a piece of paper, a group that has to have at least three generations and include everyone in the group; another student should write it on the chalkboard. I go around to each group to be sure they have come up with something appropriate. If there is a problem, I simply point out where it is. I have to pay particular attention to avunculocal residence, but so far the students have always eventually figured out an appropriate example.

When I first started this last example, I was amazed at how often I heard comments such as "You mean I'm living with my sister!" or "Both my brothers are together with me?" or "I'm living with who?!" These comments have convinced me that students acquire at least a slightly more sophisticated understanding than they would have if they had simply memorized a definition.

Again, I take each in turn and ask questions. Who is being kept together? Why might keeping those people together make some sense? Under what circumstances would you expect to find this? What could be some consequences for women? Why do we bother studying these concepts?

Other examples from my introductory class are more specific to my own background and experience, but other instructors should draw on their backgrounds as well. With linguistics, for example, I have an exercise to help students learn a bit about **morphemes**.

My field language has numerical and possessive classifier morphemes not expressed in English. I have made a selection of terms such that the morphemes are readily identifiable and students can make educated guesses at their meanings. It allows them to actively engage in a linguistic exercise. In another part of the course I bring in one or more people to **play music,** and I teach and call a traditional American dance. I then ask students to compare it with a Micronesian dance they have watched on a video and to consider how each may be related to the culture it is a part of. Other instructors can pull from their own backgrounds to create similar exercises that encourage active learning and analyzing on the part of the students.

These examples are all very basic and simple, but the general idea can be more widely applied and made more sophisticated. For example, after seeing problems with student understanding of theory, I adopted a variation of this technique in our undergraduate theory course that is required of majors. Very briefly, each time after discussing a theory, I ask students to apply the theory to specific data. Often I bring in data from my own fieldwork, but sometimes I bring published but very descriptive ethnographic material. For structuralism, for example, I bring in some myths and fairy tales. I divide the class into small groups of about four students each and have them attempt to apply what they have learned. Unlike the activities in the introductory class, however, students attempt the activity only after a discussion of the material.

In sum, I constantly look for ways in which students, working with one another, can act out, simulate, or apply what they should be reading and hearing about. In addition to the active as opposed to passive learning which is theoretically taking place, this technique helps ensure that the quiet and the uninterested become more involved and have a voice. Although I have no quantitative data to support this statement, my impression is that a higher percentage of my students participate in class discussions – especially after one of these exercises – than was the case before I started using this technique. Students get to know one another, and I have even noticed study groups forming in recent years, a rare but valued event at a commuter campus.

Introductory Fieldwork: The Meaning of the Gift

David Sutton

In teaching introductory anthropology I tend to put less stress on what anthropologists have "discovered" and more on what we do: anthropology as an approach to seeing the world. Thus I was eager to find a way to incorporate a short project fairly early in the term that would give students the chance to get out and do an ethnographic interview, and to have the experience of moving from data to conceptualization of that data. I decided to bring home the in-class section on gifts and exchange with a project that explored the "meaning of the gift." I find that nearly all students are fascinated by the idea of analyzing gift-giving (broadly defined), as it is something that they are universally involved in, and many of them have strong ideas concerning "generosity," "altruism" or "basic selfishness" as elementary human traits. This project gives students a chance to relate their own practices directly to the "exotic" materials we are working through in class.

I have found that this assignment works equally well in small or large classes, and equally well in a class of anthropology majors or a class of students taking anthropology to fill a general education requirement. The first time I used this assignment, it was in a class of 170 students, most of whom were majoring in subjects like forestry, business or nursing – a tough crowd. While a large class obviously makes grading a consideration, I believe that this assignment can be graded by graduate assistants (see below). Even when I did my own grading of the 170, it was possible to accomplish this in less time than I had imagined. Another option would be to grade the assignment on a credit/no-credit basis, and then to test the ideas on an exam.

The Setup

I usually spend about a week going over ideas about gifts, commodities, and exchange. I introduce some basic anthropological concepts, though without trotting out Mauss et al. The basic ideas are that in most societies gifts are explicitly about creating obligations, i.e., social ties, rather than free expressions of sentiment, and that they have the potential to create hierarchy, or at least can index the status of the giver and the receiver. I also suggest that most economic activities – the usual producing, distributing and consuming – are embedded in, and part of the process of creating and maintaining social relationships rather than simply an attempt to get the maximum amount of "stuff" to the maximum number of people, sometimes called the Walmart approach to economics. I also talk about the way that objects and persons can blur in contexts where the same individual is producing most of what the individual distributes. I have used a number of different readings which seem to "work." At an introductory level, I use Richard Robbins' (1997) summary of different approaches to gifts and exchange, as well as Lee Cronk's "Reciprocity and the Power of Giving" (1997). When I teach higher level courses, I use Lewis Hyde's "Some Food We Could Not Eat," (1979), as well as James Carrier's "The Ideology of the Perfect Gift in American Society" (1990) which introduces important ideas about why Americans divide "gifts" from "market transactions," as well as why gift-giving is particularly problematic in U.S. society. The author suggests this is because gifts do create obligations, which goes against our commitment to individualism, and also because it is difficult to express sentiment through the giving of mass-produced commodities. Students are particularly impressed by his explanation of why we wrap Christmas presents (to put our personal touch onto impersonal commodities), while in many other cultures this is not necessary. They also seem to like the fieldwork stories of failed reciprocity that I believe we all have in our experiences. I tend to use this opportunity to mix in a number of stories of my fieldwork on a Greek island, such as when people yelled at me for bringing them a gift of local pastries and told me to "never do that again" (because I had tried to repay their gift too soon, and with local products rather than waiting to bring them something from the U.S. on a return visit).

Finally, at all levels I use Richard Lee's "Eating Christmas in the Kalahari" (written in 1969; reprinted in 1997). At the beginning of the section on gifts, I introduce the notion of different "types" of exchange: potlatching, or competitive gift-giving; Kula, or the gift that accrues history with each act of giving, the "Indian Gift" that demands a return (Hyde 1979; Cronk 1997), the "American gift of sentiment," and the gift that is specifically meant to create long-term social obligations. Of course, I stress that these gifts do not represent different societies, that they exist potentially in all societies, though some may stress one type of giving over another as an "ideal." I also try to get across the notion that "generosity" and "self-interest" also exist in all societies, though they may be channeled in different ways. In U.S. society, the tendency is to try and restrict generosity to the private sphere of family and friend relations, and restrict self-interest to the public sphere of market relations, though in fact each motivation can spill over into the other sphere.

The Assignment

The appendix includes the assignment Hand-out, which can be photocopied and used, or changed to suit your specific purposes. I usually give the students about 10 days to complete the assignment. This means that it doesn't have to take away from class time or assigned readings if you don't want it to. It can be done "on the side." But it could also become a larger unit: after students do the interviews, they discuss in small groups during class time the results of their interviews and what kind of categories they might use to make sense of the gifts they describe. Either way, I stress to students that the list of questions is not meant to be a survey, but rather meant to stimulate conversation in the interview, and that not all questions need be asked. Most students seem to understand this, and I've found that the tendency is to apply the questions more mechanically in the self-reporting part of the assignment, but not in the actual interview. If language and culture is part of your course, it also gives you a chance to ask students to think about these issues of non-linguistic communication or gender difference in presentation and acceptance of gifts.

The Results

I am always intrigued by what students come up with in this assignment, and students repeatedly report that it got them thinking about a part of their culture to which they had never paid much attention. Some of the most interesting papers, not surprisingly, are about gifts that "failed," thus placing into relief cultural assumptions about gift-giving that normally go unstated and thus unanalyzed. For example, one student wrote about a disastrous gift she gave to someone she had worked for on a contract basis. The gift was interpreted as a "bribe," since it was given from a position of less power to a position of greater power (her "boss"), and effectively ended their relationship. But students also have written fascinating papers concerning "Kula-like" gifts. Many female students reported on gifts passed on to them from grandmothers when they had come of age, which were, like Kula goods, usually useless, but which carried family history in them. Some of these exchanges, indeed, included the grandmother passing on family secrets to the grandchild. And like the Kula (and some of the other gift types we talk about) there was an expectation that the gift was not "property," but would be passed on to the grandchild's grandchild in the future. One or two bright students even made the link to matrilineal kinship patterns. Another "Kula-like" gift that a number of students write about is the "gag gift" -- a peacock-feathered hat or a deflated basketball, which is wrapped up elaborately each Christmas and passed to a different member of the (usually extended) family. Students seem to recognize that this gift is Kula-like in that its main purpose is to create a history, or a series of stories of past owners of the gift.

Other students provided interesting analyses of gifts of money – both in family contexts and in those ambiguous contexts (gift or commodity transaction?) of tipping restaurant servers, trash collectors, or giving food or money to the homeless or to street performers. Students write perceptively about how even money can be given the aura of a gift through its presentation, or through earmarking it for a specific purpose, i.e., to pay for tuition, to stop the student's phone from being disconnected, rather than simply dissipating into multiple purchases and being forgotten. Gender issues also often come out of these papers, as males and females in the class analyze the divergent gendered expectations of, say, Valentine's gifts, or male/female expectations of gift-giving in relation to first dates.

The main pitfall I have discovered is that some students tend to interpret whatever they get as an "American gift," i.e., a gift of sentiment not meant to obligate the receiver. Usually I spend time talking in class afterwards about how it is hardest to analyze the "American gift" as an example of our own culture because we retain our culture's assumptions that this is the true meaning of the gift, i.e., gift as pure generosity rather than obligatory and creating social ties. Indeed, I have considered insisting that at least one of the gifts analyzed in the paper must not be an "American gift."

Grading for this paper is fairly straightforward, and can be done without a huge time commitment. It can also be done with graduate student help if criteria are made clear. I tend to use 85 as a baseline grade if the student writes a clear, well-organized essay, does a reasonable job on both the "self" and "other" interview, and spends a page or so attempting to analyze the gift using the readings. From there I grade up or down according to whether the student spends time on the details of the exchange, or shows originality in selection of a gift to talk about or in its interpretation.

Class discussion after the project is particularly useful because it not only brings out some of the interesting interpretations discussed above, but it also gives a chance to review ideas about gifts and exchange without making it a "review session."

Summary and Benefits

This is a simple project which can be done with little labor investment on the part of the instructor, it makes the familiar strange and the strange familiar, and students seem to get a kick out of it. Most importantly, it introduces students to two important aspects of doing anthropology: the ethnographic interview and moving from data to interpretation. I like to use this early in the term so I can give the students a more extended interview/observation project later in the term with the knowledge that they have the basic tools with which to carry it out. I hope that you accept this project as my gift, and that I've convinced you that it's an offer you can't refuse!

References Cited

Carrier, J.
1990. Gifts in a World of Commodities: The Ideology of the Perfect Gift in American Society. *Social Analysis* 29:19-37.

Cronk, L.
1997. Reciprocity and the Power of Giving. In *Conformity and Conflict: Readings in Cultural Anthropology*. J. Spradley & D. McCurdy eds, 157-163. New York: Addison, Wesley, Longman.

Hyde, L.
1979. *The Gift: Imagination and the Erotic Life of Property*. New York: Random House.

Lee, R.
1997. Eating Christmas in the Kalahari. In *Conformity and Conflict: Readings in Cultural Anthropology*. J. Spradley & D. McCurdy eds, 26-33. New York: Addison, Wesley, Longman.

Robbins, R.
1997. *Cultural Anthropology: A Problem-Based Approach*. 2nd edition. Itasca, IL: F.E. Peacock Publishers, pp 146-153.

Note:

To illustrate the idea of creating long-term obligations, I always show the first scene of *The Godfather, Part 1* (which always seems to wake up the jocks slumbering in the back row) in which Don Corleone reprimands the undertaker, Bonasera, for asking him for a favor in exchange for money, rather than offering friendship and respect. The scene ends with the clincher line "Someday, and that day may never come, I will call on you for a service. Until then, accept this as a gift on the day of my daughter's wedding."

"The Gift" Assignment

(1) First, think of a recent exchange that you were involved in that was in some way special, notable, or memorable. Take some time to think of an event that you might be able to analyze. Possibilities could include holiday gift giving, birthdays, Valentines day, or even treating for a meal, tipping a waiter, or giving money to a street performer. You should write down the following information about this exchange in as much detail as possible:

... what was the relationship between yourself and the person exchanged with?
... what was the occasion for the exchange?
... how was the object presented? What are the rules governing presentation and receipt of the object? What was said and what was communicated through body language?
... was price a consideration in the exchange, and how so? What was the exchange meant to communicate? Was there anything else about the exchange itself that might make it memorable?
... was this exchange given in response to a previous exchange? Is there an expected reciprocation? What might be the timing of the reciprocation? Are there any non-tangible reciprocations expected as a result of the exchange?
... did the exchange cause any intensification, strain, or other sort of change in the relationship?

(2) Once you have done this for yourself, find a friend/roommate/relative who is willing to sit down with you for at least a half an hour and discuss a gift exchange in which he or she was involved. Ask for a description in as much detail as possible. When the description is finished, ask the questions above to stimulate further discussion. You should jot down notes during the conversation, so that immediately afterward you can write down what you have been told, perhaps including verbatim quotes that you think are interesting or revealing.

(3) **The Paper**. The paper should be four to five typed manuscript pages in length. It should integrate a presentation of your materials with a discussion of anthropological ideas about gifts and exchanges taken from the readings. It might be useful to comment on what kind of gift best describes what you found: for example, was the gift a "Potlatch," a "Kula" exchange, an "Indian Gift," a "Don Corleone Gift" or an "American Gift?" Justify your conclusion referring once again to the readings.

Ethnography, Humanity, and Imagination Seeing a Culture and Society Through the Eyes of an Individual

Phillip Carl Salzman

I have always felt that the great gifts of social and cultural anthropology are illuminating the intricate wholeness and complexity of each society and culture, showing their systematicness, and celebrating the great arc of cultural and social diversity through history and around the world, while appreciating the richness and accomplishment across this diversity. The medium of this illumination and celebration is the ethnographic record produced by anthropologists. It is not without some just pride that we offer to newcomers to anthropology, such as the students in introductory level courses, samples of this ethnographic record in the form of ethnographies, selections from ethnographies, or secondary summaries of ethnographic studies.

If strengths often are associated with corresponding weaknesses, we may want to reflect on shortcomings or limitations that arise from our prized ethnographic record and the modes of analysis and representation that underlie it. Even for those of us who assign full ethnographies to our introductory students, these accounts of societies and cultures tend to be highly abstract, reporting patterns, general tendencies, and principles. Particulars and specifics tend to be adduced, usually briefly, to illustrate the patterns, tendencies, and principles. Not to put too fine a point on it, ethnographies, by and large, tend to be bloodless.

What is often absent in our ethnographies is individual, unique human beings. We seem often to be presenting human life without the people. (Excepted, of course, are the biographical or autobiographical accounts done for ethnographic ends, but these make up less than one percent of ethnographies.) Perhaps, given our main interests and the constraints of research and publishing, there is no way to avoid this. Of course, we know the people behind our ethnography because we lived, spoke, laughed, and cried with them. But our introductory students do not have the benefit of our experience. Therefore, in introducing anthropology, I searched for a relatively easy and efficient way to emphasize to students that we were talking about human beings and not just abstract social and cultural systems. Furthermore, I wanted to get the students to appreciate the point of view of an individual living in his or her society and through his or her culture.

So I assigned a paper in which each student would construct a fictional individual (a Samoan, or Ju/Hoansian, or Bedu) with certain age, gender, and status characteristics, and describe – based on the assigned ethnography, with full citations – that person's life and experience, including observations of others. I call this exercise a "sociobiography," because it is meant as a portrait of a (fictive) individual as a social being and carrier of a culture, and at the same time being a portrait of the society and culture through the eyes of a (fictive) individual. A sheet of student guidelines is given at the end of this article.

What results from student's efforts? What follows are two brief excerpts from good student papers that will illustrate the kind of material that students produce for this assignment.

Excerpt 1 from a Middle East course:

Nuha and I talk about many things. We are thoughtful girls by nature and spend many of our free hours discussing our lives and those of the other women and men in our neighborhood. The woman we like to talk about most is Jameela who is a hurya *or free woman* (Maher 1978:111). *We like to hide and watch her flirt with the men who employ her to dance for the menfolk at weddings. The women cry, "Shame!" when we tell them (it would be very bad for our reputations if we were caught) but they want to know everything about her: how she dressed, what colors she painted her eyes and lips and how she laughs and her eyes sparkle when the men say stupid things. She is very beautiful and mysterious and I often fantasize about her life although I will never tell anyone this private secret, not even Nuha, for fear of the shame and dishonor I would face. When I have these thoughts I remember what my brother used to call me when he was angry:* abel shitan *or rope of the devil. Through our sexuality, which is uncontrollable, we weave a web of evil around men to trap and ensnare them* (Rosen 1978:568). *Even my brother, with whom I share some confidences, does not trust me and watches to make sure I do not endanger our family honor by meeting boys secretly, for example* (Dwyer 1978:20). *Although he admits that I possess the virtues of common sense, wisdom, social responsibility, modesty, uprightness and ingeniousness, he still thinks that if I were left alone with a boy my naivete would not protect me from the clutches of this more cunning young man* (Dwyer 1978:95).

Dwyer, D.
   1978. *Images and Self-Images.* New York: Columbia University Press.

Maher, V.
   1978. Women and Social Change in Morocco, in *Women in the Muslim World*, L. Beck and N. Keddie, eds. Cambridge MA: Harvard University Press, pp 100-123.

Rosen, L.
   1978. The Negotiation of Reality: Male-Female Relations in Sefrou, Morocco, in *Women in the Muslim World*, L. Beck and N. Keddie, eds. Cambridge MA: Harvard University Press, pp 416-431.

Excerpt 2 from the same Middle East course:

The marriage is not easily arranged [by Abu Malik of the al-Aqta, who wants to pacify the aggressive Al-Slailikh]. *Although large in number, Al-Slailikh's grazing land is in poor condition and their tiny oases* [sic] *do not permit the growth of more than a few date trees. Mahmud* [leader of theAl-Slailikh] *views the marriage as a potential means to gain access to al-Aqta's large oasis, and after receiving an enormous brideprice for Zeina (10 camels, 50 goats), he approves the idea* (Note 2: it is not uncommon for brideprices to go unpaid for some time. Immediate payment of a large brideprice indicates the importance held for the marriage by the suitor. Peters 1978:321.) *Abu Malik's next difficulty is Zeina's male first cousin who, bearing first right to marry her, must consent to her being given away. It costs Abu Malik two camels and 20 goats to reach an agreement with the cousin.* (Note 3: Discussion of parallel-cousin marriage in Peters 1970:386.)

Abu Malik's marriage to Zeina does indeed ease tensions between the two clans, as Mahmud and Abu Malik begin to realize their respective predicaments: namely, al-Aqta's problem of too much property and too little manpower, and al-Slailikh's difficulties in meeting the needs of so a large a group with so few resources. The friendship which develops between Abu Malik and Mahmud, his new father-in law (Note 4: Favorable relationships may develop between husband and father-in-law. Peters 1965:386), *proves beneficial to both clans and they begin to cooperate in areas where conflict had prevailed, such as the oasis areas which is developed to allow the al-Slailikh members to grow grains and cereals. It's conceivable that in the future the larger clan will envelope or graft the al-Aqta, forcing a further revision of the tribal geneology* [sic] (Note 5: Evans-Pritchard 1949; Peters 1970).

Evans-Pritchard, E.E.
1949. *The Sanusi of Cyrenaica*. Oxford: Clarendon Press.

Peters, E.
1965. Aspects of Family Life Among the Bedouin of Cyrenaica. In *Comparative Family Structures*, M. Nimkoff, ed. Boston: Houghton Mifflin.

Peters, E.
1970. The Proliferation of Segments in the Lineage of the Bedouin of Cyrenaica. In *Peoples and Cultures of the Middle East*. L. Sweet, ed. NY: Natural History Press.

Peters, E.
1978. The Status of Women in Four Middle Eastern Countries. In *Women in the Muslim World*, L. Beck and N, Keddie eds. Cambridge MA: Harvard University Press.

Conclusions

I have given this assignment repeatedly over the years in the introductory level world cultures course and in intermediate level area courses. Most students seem to get involved enthusiastically in the assignments. Comments, even the anonymous ones on course evaluations, are almost always positive. For my part, I find the quality of student work on this assignment is generally high.

The assignment is a small step toward helping students to understand that our research subjects are individual human beings and in many ways like them. It is thus a modest effort in humanistic anthropology to provide balance with the scientific concerns of other parts of the course. While it would be ideal, but impractical, to take all of our students into the field to meet people and even to bring our informants to class to speak to students directly, our students' imaginations, disciplined by ethnographic reports, can be their, and our, best allies.

Sociobiographical Essay

The assignment is based on Mead's *Coming of Age In Samoa*. The assignment is to write an account of ordinary life and characteristic events **from the point of view of a particular (fictional) Samoan individual** with specific age, gender, occupational, and social characteristics. We can call this kind of exercise a **sociobiography**. The objective of the sociobiography is to provide a sense of the specific human reality of social life and cultural conception as manifested in the life and experience of a particular individual. This account should thus reflect the individual's cognitive (thinking) processes, affective (emotional) structure, and social relationships. The essay should show what it is like from day to day to live in a Samoan village (according to Mead) and how the institutions and customs guide and impinge, assist and inhibit a particular individual in a given position. By means of this account of an individual's lifetime, the reader should learn about (at least several of) the main social structures (organized sets of roles and relationships), cultural frameworks (ideas and concepts), and customary activities and practices of the society in which the individual lives.

A successful sociobiography will (1) present effectively (either in the first or third person) the point of view of a **particular** individual, (2) illustrate through the protagonist's activities and/or observations the nature and workings of the **main social institutions and cultural patterns** in the society, and (3) document carefully with **multiple page citations** the source of **each item** of information used. Material supplementary to the basic ethnographic text, such as information and perspectives presented in lectures, films, and other readings, are not required or necessary, but are not prohibited and may be used if cited and if they serve to deepen and enrich the account.

The essay will have a **maximum length** of 1500 words (5 double-spaced pages), not including notes and bibliography. The essay is due on _____.

Student Experiential Learning on Social Control, Class, and Gender

Carolyn Epple

In the introductory four-field anthropology course, my students conduct mini-field projects. The projects occur at the end of the term to encourage student synthesis of course concepts and (a bit deviously on my part) to heighten student participation during those restless last few weeks of term. Students chose from one of three projects: (1) political structures/ social control, (2) economic systems/social class, or (3) gender. Overall, the projects help students realize the ideas and practices they accept as "natural" or "given" are instead cultural constructions. Prior to the assignments, class readings provide background on the nature of systemic oppression and social stratification, indicators of racism and sexism in language, and the significance of belief systems in organizing daily life. The assignments also dovetail with basic introductory anthropology texts and provide opportunities for cross-cultural comparison. The projects are suitable for any introductory-level class that is concerned with any of these topics.

Theory Overview

The assignments derive from my own hodge podge of discourse theory (a la Foucault) and gender performance. I break down the systems of hierarchy and cultural practices into six components: beliefs, traits, expectations, social systems, institutionalization, and consequences. An immediately accessible example (if grossly simplified) is woman's status. The Judeo-Christian origin story (belief) teaches that woman is responsible for humankind's fall and that she is derived from man. We learn to mark gender as significant (trait) and impose all sorts of expectations on to gender. Such beliefs and expectations, in turn, are reinforced and enacted in families, medicine, education, the judicial system, and religion (social systems). With institutionalization, such as in an elementary classroom treatment of girls versus boys or laws governing women's but not men's reproduction, different consequences emerge: women continue to receive lower pay and they occupy fewer leadership positions. Because the consequences align with the initial beliefs, we accept the consequences as "proof" of the original belief/premise, and thus reify the belief as a "valid" explanation.

By walking students through how our beliefs inform our expectations and cultural practices, they begin to realize that there is nothing "natural" about a woman's lower status. Nor is there anything natural about differential arrest rates by ethnicity or different privileges granted to upper versus lower socioeconomic classes. Instead, they get a glimpse into how cultural beliefs and values are our own arbitrary creations, how we function as a culture, in part, because we multiply and reinforce the "realness" of those beliefs, and how, when we rely unthinkingly on cultural beliefs to explain social phenomena, we cannot see the cultural processes that maintain stratification.

The assignments ideally build on each other. The political/social control topic introduces social rules and underlying values. The economics topic emphasizes how values and beliefs single out certain traits and inform expectations. The third topic, gender, examines how, via our enculturated statuses and roles, we reinforce these beliefs/values, mark difference, and perpetuate stratification for ourselves and others.

78

The Assignments

For each assignment, students are given a list of activities and observations to record. I also include definitions from the text and questions to consider. Students engage in the projects on their own, and turn in copies of their notes at the beginning of their respective weeks. I review the notes to have a sense of items to highlight in class and provide comments to assist them in completing the final paper. Generally, we work in class on interpretations of their observations.

(1) Political Organization and Social Control. Students who conduct this project select a specific location, such as the dorm, home, the workplace or the classroom and write down the site's formal and informal rules. Students note how they know certain rules and regulations: possible sources include posted signs and learning the regulations/rules from others. After they have a good feel of their site's rules, they spend one day carefully abiding by the rules and observe how they are treated by others, comments they receive, and how they feel about themselves. On a subsequent day, the student breaks one of the site's rules and makes the same observations. For obvious reasons, I instruct the students to select a rule that has no legal ramifications. One student who was a hospital volunteer, for instance, observed the hierarchy at a health clinic as manifest in the kinds of uniforms, who spoke to whom, and who was allowed in certain areas. She attempted on several occasions to make eye contact with and to speak to physicians, but without success. She also observed that physicians would make eye contact with each other, and to a lesser degree with nurses.

I also instruct students to observe and record the following: how do these rules and meanings vary with gender, class, ethnicity, age, physical ability, or sexuality? How do these rules give society a way to control certain people but not others? How do these rules become internalized? How do shared rules help create a certain social stability?

During class time, we list the observations on the chalkboard, collectively tease out the meanings underlying the rules, and hypothesize what beliefs give the rule this meaning. For instance, holding the door open for the next person may indicate courtesy and thoughtfulness. The underlying belief may derive from "do unto others as you would have them do unto you." Some of the more frequently mentioned beliefs are the work ethic, a hierarchical arrangement of society, a heavy emphasis on cleanliness, and fear of contamination. Since each of these relies on Judeo-Christian tenets (e.g., Protestantism and capitalism, the Great Chain of Being, and purity and godliness, respectively), students begin to see how deeply religion intertwines with daily activities. With this, students begin to see the first piece of the exercise: beliefs often tell us what to look for and how to interpret what we find.

Students may need a bit of extra encouragement to understand how ethnicity and gender impact the rules. I often use David Cole's (2000) work on racial profiling to illustrate how different expectations (and the ensuing systemic stratifications) result in different kinds and degrees of social control. We also list in class the different responses and personal feelings students encountered on the day they abided by the rules versus the day they broke the rules. The comparison illustrates such key concepts as informal versus formal rules, law versus social sanction, internalization of cultural values, and the dynamics of social control.

(2) Economics. The students who conduct the economic field project examine how markers of class, such as attire, affect shopping experiences both at an exclusive store and a discount store. For the first part, students go to both stores wearing their "bumming around the house" clothes (one student went in her pajama bottoms). They cannot put on make up, take a shower, fix their hair, walk in with an air of authority, and express interest in making a purchase. If they decide to buy something (optional), they are to use only small change. To connote higher class at both kinds of stores, during the second part of the project, students wear their best outfits, style their hair, walk in with an air of authority, and express interest in making a purchase. If they decide to buy something (optional), they are to use new bills. Students should conduct their experiment on similar kinds of days (i.e., weekdays, weekends, or holidays) and at approximately the same time of day.

At both kinds of stores, they observe and note facilities layout, such as: size of parking lot, kinds of cars, availability of shade, distance from the building, lighting, security cameras, noise and lighting, carpeting, and bathrooms. They also observe and record characteristics of the store staff and of other shoppers, such as attire, ethnicity, and age range. When attempting a purchase (in both kinds of stores and in both kinds of attire), they note the following interactional variables: time until someone offers assistance; presence and number of other shoppers (to control for delays); friendliness of store staff; reactions from other shoppers, such as side glances, efforts to ignore/engage; response to form of money used (small change versus new bills); and presumptions of class, such as offers to open a charge account or to be put on a mailing list.

To discuss this in class, I organize the data into the six columns mentioned above: beliefs, traits, expectations, social systems, institutionalization, and consequences. The class begins by listing the traits that were significant, such as kind of attire, hair style, age, and ethnicity, followed by expectations for each trait. Students quickly see that the traits and expectations are not the same for the different kinds of stores. The discount store places less emphasis on different attire than do more exclusive shops. We then return to the first column, beliefs, and for each trait and expectation, list its respective underlying ideology.

I present two very short and clear excerpts from Weber's *Protestantism and the Spirit of Capitalism* to illustrate the association between virtue and hard work, as evidenced by wealth. Accompanying readings on differential pay by ethnicity and gender illustrate how beliefs target specific traits, imbue these traits with expectations, and lead to different outcomes. Using students' examples and the readings, we examine how social systems (family, religion, education, medicine, and the judicial system) institutionalize the expectations (enculturation, church doctrine, treatment in schools, differential access to health care and disparities in kinds of care given, and laws, respectively) and thus perpetuate stratification, and to varying degrees, shared cultural values.

This project can generate potent insights on ethnicity and "race." Regardless of how they were dressed in the more exclusive stores, all African American students were followed by security or watchful sales staff, while European American students were followed in the exclusive stores only if they were male and wearing casual attire. Several African American students were also followed

80

in the discount stores. Students see clearly how "whiteness" entails numerous hidden privileges. Because the students almost invariably received better treatment when better dressed, students become their own "living proof" that social categories and stigmatization are human-made and not "natural."

The experiences help students develop several critical insights. For one, students observe how persons of a lower status (be it class, gender, ethnicity, or ability) should appreciate and emulate those in higher status; However, those in a higher status (i.e., wealthy patrons at exclusive stores) are not obliged to appreciate individuals in a lower status (i.e., individuals perceived to be of lower class). Second, by seeing how class is so arbitrarily determined, students begin to grasp that other social categories may also be arbitrary and constructed. For instance, many of the European American students noted that it was not fair to be treated as somehow "bad" simply on the basis of attire, particularly when these same sales people had treated them well when the students were dressed up. In response, African American students pointed out that European Americans' experience with attire, was, by comparison, a minor annoyance, although analogous to what African Americans experience every day. In these discussions, students also begin to realize that there is no "real" basis for treating people differently and that the usual categories of class and ethnicity are not conceptually substantive but rest on bias and assumption. This awareness provides the basis for the third and final field project in which students learn how a concept may not be conceptually real but is nonetheless socially perpetuated.

(3) Gender. The gender assignment is again a comparison between accepted and unaccepted roles. Students choosing this project begin by wearing their typical attire, undertaking usual activities, and recording where they notice gender and why, and how much gender plays a part in their actions. On another occasion, students engage in dress, behaviors, and/or practices associated with the opposite gender in which they do not already engage. Attire is often the easiest for students to do, and given its symbolic meanings, cross-dressing can yield great material for discussion and interpretation.

During the fall term, I suggest that students use Hallowe'en Day as an opportunity to don other-gender attire, but they must be in costume all day, including class and work. The experience will vary for men and women, and only once has a male student undertaken this project, and he was extremely wary. Instead of cross-dressing, he sat in a local bookstore in a noticeable area and read gay magazines very openly; subsequently, at about the same time of day and in similar attire, he went to the same store and read sports magazines. Of the women, one student cross-dressed an entire day, but at a different campus. An older student, who was already slated to be an usher at her brother's wedding documented everything from the fitting of the tuxedo to dancing at the reception. Another woman student, who wore jeans and baggy shirts regularly, went hunting with her boyfriend and his friends, and later, without her boyfriend, shopped extensively at the local bait shop.

During their gender nonconformity experience, students noted responses of others, where they felt the most and least comfortable and why; personal difficulty in undertaking the assignment and why; how often/where they noticed their gender and why; how/if they were more aware of gender than when engaging in typical gender behaviors; and the significance of gender in interactions. Students also observed and recorded how these experiences may have been impacted by class, ethnicity, closeness of kin or friends, and religion.

During the class discussion, we again used the same six components, beliefs through consequences, to summarize and present students' experiences. Among the more significant insights students gain is that the two genders are often rigidly opposed. Indeed two African American women stated they had never realized the distrust and suspicion African American men endure. Another illustrated how we signal our gender identities vis a vis the opposite gender: when she was dressed as a man at a football game, she struggled not to engage in "feminine" behaviors or otherwise reveal she was a woman, particularly when the men around her were "being rowdy."

In describing and listing the traits that were significant, students begin to realize the widespread effects of gender in cultural practices, ranging from speaking styles, to clothing, to kinds of jokes, to perceived authority. Readings reinforce these observations and present larger systemic issues as well, such as the gender pay gap, childcare, and violence. Overall, students begin to see two key (and largely inseparable) pieces in the construction of social categories. First, they better understand how we internalize our social norms, such as the student who wanted to somehow signal she was not a man at all when surrounded by loud men. Second, the project illustrates how we reinforce the "realness" of social categories for each other, as when one woman described how she was severely chastised by an older man for chewing tobacco at a local bar. In such clear, lived examples students can see how we depend on each other's responses to affirm and perpetuate what is meant by "appropriate" gender, how in a binary system we mutually reaffirm the difference between the two, and how we use our internal gender statuses to correct those who stray.

Class discussion focuses on why we have a binary gender system, how we are excluded if we do not comply with these expectations, why it is OK for a lower status (woman) to emulate a higher status (man) but not vice versa, and how we reinforce others' gendered behaviors. The exercise also permits discussion on cultural beliefs about gender, the numerous ways gender encodes our behaviors, and how difficult it is to step outside our enculturation.

Finally, a word of caution is in order. While many of these experiences can produce great insights for the student, the exercises may be particularly risky for people who are already stigmatized and marked in our society. It is imperative to remind students not to put themselves at risk and to carefully think through the possible ramifications of their actions. For instance, when an African American student wore her brother's clothes and for once, walked through a "bad" part of the neighborhood, a passing car slowed down to assess what gang she was in. She quickly removed her cap and explained it was an experiment. She was able to proceed unharmed, although very unnerved.

Writing Assignments

The students synthesize their experiences in a 6 to 8 page paper. They provide a brief summary of their project, and then analyze their observations using the framework described earlier. Students map out how beliefs cause us to identify certain traits and imbue these with expectations, and how sociocultural systems and practices reinforce the validity of those traits. The assignment also entails a comparison with other cultures, taken from the textbook, and self-reflection on what their experience tells them about the meaning and workings of culture and discrimination.

Reference Cited

Cole, D.
1999. "No Equal Justice: Race and Class in the American Criminal Justice System." In *The Social Construction of Difference and Inequality: Race, Class, Gender, and Sexuality.*" T. Ore, ed, pp 319-337. Mountain View CA: Mayfield Publishing Company.

Family Altars in Introductory Anthropology: Making Kinship Relevant

Jeffrey H. Cohen

We have all likely experienced from 30 to perhaps 400 blank stares and audible groans when, in the course of our introductory classes in anthropology, we utter the word "kinship." For reasons that I still do not fully understand, students seem to fear kinship. Certainly part of the problem comes from the charts that challenge students to pay attention, and although reading a matrilineage or following a Crow system probably does not rank with the excruciating pain that comes with conjugating Latin verbs or reciting algebraic theorems, nevertheless, our students seem to be under the assumption that kinship and the charts that come with it border on the unintelligible.

We are not helped in our jobs to present kinship and the role of the family in culture and society when most of the anthropology texts we use make a series of distinctions between the "west and the rest." Natives "do" kinship; industrial nations do not. For non-western peoples, the family is presented as the most crucial of structures in the maintenance of cultural traditions and social cohesion. In western systems, the family is in crisis and the role of kinship in society is limited by our society's industrially based mobility.

Raymond Scupin describes the family as holding "diminishing importance" in the fourth edition of his introductory text book (2000:267). Conrad Kottak makes a similar point and argues that kinship systems and the family in North America have changed in fundamental ways (2000:194-195). Both authors are correct in their arguments and each documents how the organization of the American family has changed and how kinship works "differently" in our culture/country. Furthermore, each outlines how the American family has transformed over the last decades including the decline of nuclear families and the rise of same-sex marriages.

Nevertheless, text-based discussions of American kinship make it hard to effectively communicate the family's continued strength and importance in socio-cultural life. In addition, I believe we add a further layer of confusion when we present native systems in a monolithic fashion (the so and so **are** matrilineal and live in extended family units) while documenting the crises and changing structures of American families. Perhaps this is one way we contribute to "othering" native people – they do not change, we do.

For the majority of students, a fairly typical ("old fashioned") nuclear family is likely the norm. In addition, same-sex marriages or single parent families are more than likely as alien to them as the polyandry that textbooks describe among the Paharis.

As teachers, we are left with two challenges. First, we need to better explain why kinship is important, not just for native peoples in non-western settings, but for the average North American. Second, as we make kinship matter, we also have an opportunity to ignite interest in, and a valuation of anthropology. There are at least two ways in which we can make this happen, and neither demands an extensive amount of preparation, training, or time. Either of them can be used in any size class and in any introductory level course. One approach is to ask students to put together a family tree or family genealogy. This is an effective way to show students why descent matters and remains an integral (if behind the scenes) part of their lives. I often ask for a few volunteers and we work through their genealogies in class on the chalkboard. A bonus is that we can share just how messy studying culture and society is, how the real and ideal often do not mesh, and how cultural models are regularly reinvented to make sense of a world that does not fit with our expectations.

A second activity that I began this year is the construction of "family altars." Asking students to make family altars is a great opportunity to get them to think about kinship and family from more than a descent perspective. I ask the students to design their altars with two anthropological models in mind. First, they are asked to take a fairly traditional functionalist approach to their families and talk about who on/in their altar is important to their socialization, safety, and growth. Second, they are asked to think like symbolic anthropologists. I want the students to look beyond or below the surface of the relationships, people, and things in their altars and interpret how meaning is constructed. I want them to decipher the cultural symbols in their altars and make their "values, beliefs, and worldviews meaningful and intelligible" (Scupin 2000:130). I do not want to see a display of family members who are loved by a student. Rather, I want the students to tell me why the people, places, and things in the altars are personally and culturally meaningful. Thus, students are able to practice a bit of anthropology upon themselves, defining the functional and symbolic significance of their families. (See instructions as given to students as a handout at end.)

In the class meetings leading up to the assignment, we tour a series of web sites and look at a series of real altars from various cultural/religious groups: Buddhist, Shinto, Catholic. Students are encouraged to make **their** altars as "real" as possible, using family photos when possible. Finally, I encourage them to share this work with their families, something that makes the assignment even more special for those students who take it seriously.

The essays that are collected with the altars are often more important to the evaluation of a student's ability than the altar itself. Is the student able to effectively link a functional definition of social practice with members of her or his family? Can the student interpret the cultural information in a symbolic way? The altars become a basis for in-class discussions, and they are effective props for students who fear talking in public. Finally, the evaluation of the altars and essays can be used to better prepare students for exams. Misperceptions and questions are often more clearly evident from the evaluation than asking for questions in the classroom setting. For example, one student just did not understand what socialization meant. I was able to use this young man's essay as a way to set up a meeting where we could discuss his errors and better prepare him for the rest of the course.

The response from students to this project is very positive. There are altars and essays about broken homes and abusive relationships, but the majority are sensitive portraits of parents, grandparents, siblings, and friends. There are also moments of clarity. One student left a section of her altar blank in order to communicate that she is young and has yet to experience a great deal of her life. A second represented each member of her family with a special symbol that is associated with that person (a high school swimming champ is a wave, for example). A third decorated his altar with the foods that are central to celebrations that bring his widely spread family together. Not only are these effective examples of how kinship and the family continue to function in America, they are effective examples of active learning and critical thinking.

It takes very little time or effort to do this kind of a project and the payoff is excellent. I believe that if I were to call some of these students who went through the project in 20 years and ask what they remembered from this particular class, it would be this assignment. I also know for a fact that many of the altars are going home to families and will be shared around the table.

Building an Altar

For this assignment, you should have completed reading the appropriate chapters in your text on the structure and functions of the family. Most authors tell us that the family changes in industrial societies and the nuclear family becomes particularly important. Beyond that, the family is an important unit in terms of:

... the emotional support it gives its members;
... the social and economic training and networking it affords;
... the cultural knowledge it teaches.

In this assignment, you will make an altar that celebrates the importance of your family (and family here can be real or fictive). Make a drawing on paper (no larger than 11 x 17) that depicts the people, places, and things in your family that you want to celebrate. This can include images of family members past and present, important places in your family's history (and in your own history), and items that may hold an important place of family lore (a religious item like a family bible, or some kind of food that is unique to your family; it might even be something that seems rather silly such as a basketball you used when you were young and played with a grandparent who has now passed away). Arrange these items following the drawing below:

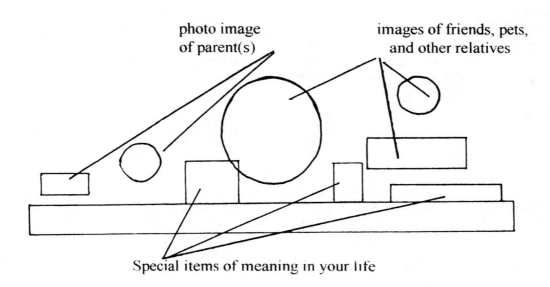

photo image of parent(s)

images of friends, pets, and other relatives

Special items of meaning in your life

Finding pictures of "real" altars may help you arrange your materials.

Once you have completed your altar, write a brief, 2-3 pp description of what your altar represents. Your description should be written in as anthropological a way as possible. Don't write about how much you love a parent or grandparent; rather write why the people, places, and things on your altar are important and from a kin-based, cultural, and social perspective.

Dynamic Ethnography, Methods, and Next-Door Anthropology

Lorenzo Covarrubias

Learning to do ethnography, and teaching it, can be one of the joys of the anthropological experience. The roads can be many, but the stated goals are the same: to give students some exposure in our preferred method of conducting field research the anthropological way.

Usually, as was the case during my undergraduate (and graduate) methods courses, this meant for each student to try a variety of research tools -- interviewing, observation, kinship charts, note taking – as part of a series of class assignments. Once completed, it was hoped that students would have a detailed glimpse of the methods of ethnographic research. However, an issue that can derive from this approach is that students may see each class assignment in which a different method is used, as an end in itself, a kind of self-contained deliverable, rather than as part of the holistic approach that we instructors purport to follow.

Dynamic Ethnography

One way that I have found to address this concern is to present methods courses as project-oriented in which each student will add something to the complexity of an existing community to be examined. To do this, I often provide a subtitle in the class syllabus to make it less abstract in the eyes of the student participants. Thus Anthropology X became "Isla Vista: The Changing Face of a California Town." And Anthropology Y became "Castroville, CA: History, Society, and Culture of a Rural Town."

By focusing and organizing the courses this way, I have been able to transform introductory ethnographic methods courses into full-fledged field-oriented research projects in which each student becomes an integral part of a group endeavor. During the first week of instruction, we go over the course syllabus as if it were a kind of research design where I expand on why I have selected that particular community and what I mean by the course subtitle. This means that previous to the beginning of term, I must do preliminary research on the community selected to identify potential themes that could be addressed through ethnographic methods. In other words, I have to make sure that this approach won't backfire, becoming a hodge-podge of student interests that may or may not be doable.

The description that follows basically concerns a field methods course in cultural anthropology. In its most intense form that needs close mentoring and guidance, 15 students is probably the maximum number. However, with some work on the part of the instructor to make assignments small and doable, it could be modified to suit the field work part of any level course, from introductory anthropology through area courses.

Setting the Stage

The first idea I sell is that by enrolling and staying in the course, students have become instant **student researchers**, that we have a **group project** ahead of us, and that it will be completed with the **individual contributions** of each. When I refer to them as student researchers, I emphasize that they have stopped being simply students. They have added responsibilities, they are now researchers not only grade seekers. When I introduce the concept of a group project, I reiterate that we are all in this together. It is then that I describe the course goals at length and how it will be through the application of some or all of the research tools to be learned and applied – interviewing, questionnaires, participation, observation, note taking, keeping a field diary, bibliographic research – that the research project will take form. At this time, the subtitle becomes handy and as I expand on it, they understand the importance of a precise title that also serves to guide their research.

If I use any "tricks" in these courses, it is when I refer to their own mini research as an "individual contribution." When I was a graduate student, the words "group project" gave me the shivers. In such group projects, each student had individual excuses that we handily transformed into reasons for failure to do certain work. I had to work, someone else lived too far, another had language problems, and still another didn't have a car. The causes were as varied as the individuals, but the real cause was that we were in fear of the unknown, the group project. I address the issue by clearly stating that the needs at hand will be addressed solely through the individual contributions of each student, plus the assistance and guidance that I provide. The sense of relief that I notice in their faces when they hear that their individual contributions will not be violated is astounding. It is at this point that I am tempted to let them in on my own little secret, that due to the nature of the project in which each student can exchange field-based information with each other, near the end of the term they will have become such a tight-knit group that they will never know they had been tricked!

The Field Settings

During the course of teaching using this field technique, I have used two field settings, each with its own peculiarities. Although neither is likely to be adopted by another instructor, a brief discussion of these settings will help anyone picking a nearby site as a field setting.

Isla Vista. Adjacent to the University of California, Santa Barbara (UCSB), exists the community of Isla Vista. I.V., as it is known locally, has a reputation as a party heaven, and is often referred to as a college town. This densely populated area of about a square mile has around 25,000 inhabitants, the vast majority of them being students. However, a little known fact is that about a quarter of its population is made up of Latino families, the majority being from Mexico and some from Central America.

A research course in which the objective is to understand key or salient elements of a community next to a university, is what I refer to as "next-door anthropology." In the case of Isla Vista, the objective included a need for students to realize that this little town acted as a reflection of larger happenings in the state of California. Thus the subtitle selected for the course was "Isla Vista: The Changing Face of a California Town." A methods course was then instantly transformed into a class setting in which, through ethnographic learning, particular issues would be addressed.

This approach allowed the student researchers to develop their own projects. I often tell them that the trick of a successful project is to turn personal interests into academic endeavors, that any topic if well presented is doable, and that through the ethnographic way, the student – not the instructor – will know more about the topic that was selected. In fact, I tell them that by the end of the course, I will be the one asking questions and wanting to know more. Students had to come up with their own topics to research and the only rules that had to be strictly followed was that the title of their project had to include the words "Isla Vista" and that the information had to be gathered through the use or combination of the research techniques introduced in class.

Castroville. The rural town of Castroville (Monterey County) is near to California State University, Monterey Bay (CSUMB). It is located about five miles away and is known proudly and locally as the "Artichoke Center of the World." There are about 5,000 inhabitants, mostly engaged in agriculture or in agriculturally-dependent activities. At least 80% of the population is of Mexican origin with many of the original settlers of Portugese and Italian descent.

In contrast to urban Isla Vista, rural Castroville posed different challenges. First, I was not aware of its existence until I arrived in the area to teach; secondly, most students at the local university had never set foot in it, with some only driving through as they were going somewhere else. Third, one could not just walk there.

I used these limitations to advantage. Since students chose their own projects from within the subtitle "Castroville CA: The History, Society, and Culture of a Rural Town," they were essentially doing part of a community study. They were intrigued when I told them that no one at the university would be able to challenge their field-based findings.

Again, the rules were the same as stated above: the title of their work had to include Castroville, and their study had to be carried out through the research techniques introduced in class and through our readings.

Results

The work that results from this project has been excellent, not least of which is the team-like atmosphere that ensued. In the case of Isla Vista, the projects included topics such as "Growing Up a *Mexicana* Female in I.V.," "The Housing Conditions of Latino Families in I.V.," The *Pepenadores* (Urban Recycles) of I.V.," and "Being a Latina Mother in I.V." to name a few.

The Castroville project is equally successful. The topics included an analysis of a revitalization project, an examination of a family-owned Mexican food outlet, and a description of bilingual programs in local schools. Other topics included studies of family interactions, migrant workers, issues of alcoholism, and gay life in this rural community.

This type of dynamic ethnography had a true empowering effect on students. There is something uniquely powerful about works informed through ethnographic approaches. Students **know** it is their work and they present it as such. And, by the end of each project, the rigors of their field-based studies united them far beyond expectations.

Getting Into the Act:
Using Classroom Role-Playing as a Type
of Participant Observation

Mary Riley

One of the hallmarks of anthropology is that we study cultures by "getting inside the heads" of people in order to better understand the way they see things, what they believe about the world and their place in it. While it is fun to teach how radically different other societies can be concerning the way they treat marriage, kin relations, birth, death, sex, gender roles, and cosmology, sometimes teaching our students abut exotic customs only serves to reinforce the notion that the "other" culture is even more strange, odd, offensive, or morally repugnant than before they began to study the "other" culture in some depth. I have seen many students' faces blanch when I begin to explain how cross-cousin marriage worked in lowland South American societies, with the usual response being "Don't their children turn out mentally retarded?" or something equally negative.

One of the more difficult things to convey in the classroom is that "other people" are not all identical, cookie-cutter copies of one another, or of one proto-typical Native Person, all living and going about their business with no sense of self-consciousness or collective group consciousness. People living within a specific culture may try to live according to specific cultural rules, but this action of attempting to live according to a certain societal ideal is processual, ongoing, and is not a passive enterprise. Decisions must be proactively made by the individual person or family in order to ensure that behavior is in line with societal rules. Or, alternatively, in order for someone to show disagreement with

something or a wish to flout societal rules, the verbal expressions or physical behaviors must be chosen and properly executed in order to communicate this sentiment to others in society.

It took a good part of the 20th century in anthropology to finally figure out that so-called "traditional" or "primitive" peoples are in fact, conscious beings who manipulate their environment, circumstances, social rules and networks just as much as we do in North American society.

Many students in my classes tend to become bewildered about two major realizations about "people in our society" and "people in other societies," namely that people in "other" societies do not live passively, timidly observing every taboo, rule, and superstition that they are supposed to believe in, and that people within our own society may be more traditional, superstitious, and desire to conform socially than we tend to expect.

One way that I get beyond this stumbling block is to come up with class exercises designed to make the student put him or herself in the place and role of a person in another culture and according to a broadly written cultural scenario I have written in advance, have them solve a problem that involves them in a social event. This event requires negotiating and working together with others in that culture. While writing cultural scenarios and coming up with characterizations takes time, and each class will have different scenes and characters, the "on the ground" aspects makes the students step into the role of being, for a short period of time, a participant/insider in that culture, even one step beyond the participant-observation role of the anthropologist.

The Setting

I teach at a four year institution that focuses on the visual and performing arts and is located in the center of a large city with many students commuting between school, work, and home. There is a high number of older and non-traditional students working toward their bachelor's degrees; additionally, many of my students are "into" role playing and acting because of the focus of the college. The exercise that follows was developed for my urban anthropology class with a maximum enrollment of 25. Nonetheless, this exercise could be adapted for use in larger classes, introductory level cultural anthropology classes, or other upper division classes in anthropology. The exercise could be equally successful with students who have had no role playing experience.

The Exercise

The exercise itself is simple, but it does require planning and write-up before the lecture itself. In a nutshell, I write a cultural scenario that I then use in class to illustrate a particular point of a lecture or concept we are currently working with. Within the cultural scenario (or script), there are character profiles and/or group profiles (such as a family or a company) who are faced with a specific problem or dilemma that needs to be explored, discussed, or resolved. There are two keys to writing this kind of exercise for class lectures. The first is that the cultural script or scenario is written to illustrate where the character (or family or company) is "coming from," the nature of the problem or dilemma, the cultural knowledge or resources available to the character to help make an informed decision, and hints at the available choices for the character to make. The second key is that the characters (or group characters) must negotiate with one another to come to a decision or resolution that pleases all or most people in each party.

This written description of the scenario makes the exercise sound harder than it actually is. What follows is a specific exercise that I wrote for one of my lectures in urban anthropology that focused on the experience of ordinary people deciding to migrate to a city and adapt to urban life. It can be used as a model for picking themes to investigate and scenarios to write for your own classes. Obviously, adjustments will have to be made for class size; for example, if the exercise best accommodates 25 and the class size is 50, then two different exercises could allow each student to participate in one, being part of the "audience" in the other.

The Migration/Employment Exercise

For this exercise in migration and urbanization, I write five broad-ended scenarios, complete with family and company profiles, for a class of 25. Then I break the class into groups of 5 each and give each group one of the character profiles (which may be a family of five or a company of five). In my case, I assigned two families and three companies. The students in each group decide among themselves who will play what role (i.e., in the family profile, the choices would be parent, child above age of 18, child in grade school; in the company profile, the choices could be employer CEO, human resources representative). I deliberately keep some of the scenarios "open-ended" so that for example in the case of companies, the company officials can decide what benefits they want to offer future employees or how they are going to negotiate with prospective job candidates in interviews. In both profiles, I write out what resources each side has in terms of their human capital, what they need financially from a job in order to make the household break even, what other strategies they need to think about as individuals, families, and companies in order to think through negotiations with two or three companies when deciding where to work.

See Appendix for sample profiles to use in writing your own scenarios and profiles.

What resulted the first time I used this exercise was that the class got so into it that I had to stop every now and then just to keep the peace. The students were clearly having fun with the wheeling and dealing aspect of the exercise. In job interviews, for example, employers that promised paid health insurance (medical, dental, visual), 401 (k) plans, three week vacations, and on-site child care were met by guffaws and groans of disbelief by others in the class, who responded "that would never happen in the real world." It took a good deal of negotiations back and forth between the first family and each of the three employers, and after they made their decision, the next family negotiated with the three employers.

Results

Unintended results included an increase in class discussion and student participation in general after the exercises. Students commented on how the exercises allowed them to get to know each other in ways different from what they normally experienced. Also, the level of "pragmatic" discussion increased as well: discussing real-life decision making and events in other cultures, without having to fall back on stereotypical outcomes.

The students understood that a number of factors influenced each particular situation, and those factors have to be discussed as well before any assertion could be made as to what someone would or would not do in a given cultural situation.

Other Versions of the Technique

Role playing and writing scenarios must by their very nature be tied fairly closely to specific course materials, and beyond a discussion of the technique and a model of what I do in one course, specific design and use is teacher and course specific. However, I have also used this technique in creating other cultural scripts: for example, in negotiations for arranging an Indian marriage using dowry. In this exercise, I purposely made the families of the couple different, i.e, asymmetrical so the two families would not be equal in terms of human capital, and made the cultural rules of post-marital residence patrilocal to take the woman out of her own natal residence. Other cultural scenarios could be written for:

... a mock session between government officials, indigenous representatives, and multi-national development companies seeking to set up operations on indigenous lands;
... a woman shopping for a family of five on $50 a week and deciding what she will buy with her children in tow whining that they want candy and the latest Pokemon cards.

The possibilities are endless.

Caveats and Conclusions

Make sure your scenario and character profiles are written so they do not encourage stereotyping or predict stereotypical behavior. One way to do this is to make the script "demand" that the student think actively about how to come to a decision regardless of the cultural knowledge and resources available. This way a student does not have a character who will make a totally irrational decision based on "the culture made me do that." While the student should be drawing on culturally relevant information to help come to a decision, the character the student plays still must make a lone decision based on a number of available choices, as an individual. In this way, students learn that people in other cultures act in accordance with their cultural rules but are also trying to work together with the wishes of other members of the society, and in particular those of family and friends.

This exercise accomplishes three goals: it makes students get involved in role playing cultural scenarios that are based on real life situations, it is fun so even shyer students get involved, and students see that despite the cultural rules of knowledge that cultures have to guide and set limits on situations, decisions are **actively** made by individuals or corporately. They see that people in other cultures have to play with the same ambiguities and uncertainties when they make decisions just as we do in our culture. It makes the "other" closer to "us."

Appendix Materials

What follows are two character profiles I wrote for the migration and urbanization cultural scenario described above. I wrote two family profiles and three company profiles for this exercise, but space prohibits more than a single example of each. In this exercise, the class of 25 is split into 5 groups of 5 people each. Each group is given one of the five different character profiles which everyone in that group will read and discuss. The group will decide which decision to make concerning their life situation (if the group is a family) or their corporate situation (if the group is a company). Each character profile is different from the others given out, so what the other groups decide to do as opposed to what a single group decides to do reflects the uniqueness of each group's circumstances.

Family Profile #1

Your group consists of a family headed by a single mother with two nearly-grown children (college age) and one younger child (grade school age). Mom is considering moving the family from the outer suburbs of Chicago where they now live to a neighborhood in Chicago with affordable housing and easy access to public transportation. At her current place of work in the outer suburbs, Mom makes about $12.00 an hour at a job in the service industry (totaling about $25,000 a year). After working full time for twelve years, this is the most she has been able to make since her career history was interrupted by intermittent periods of being a full-time, stay at home mother when her two older children were younger. Mom does own the house they all live in with the mortgage paid and of course no rent.

She has sent her children to good public schools for their education, which has been one tangible benefit of living in the outer suburbs despite her relatively low income. Her two oldest children currently attend community college on a full-time basis and receive substantial financial aid because of their mother's low annual income and the fact that two children are enrolled in college at the same time. The youngest child is currently attending a public grade school located about 1.5 miles away from home.

As a family group, consider what the best decision would be in terms of moving to Chicago or staying in the outer suburbs, given the following factors:

... the household would need an annual income of at least $35,000 a year in the city in order to pay for the cost of renting a large apartment/small townhouse for the four people;
... tuition for continuing the college education of the two older children will be more expensive in Chicago (unless they go to the University of Illinois at Chicago) but Chicago offers tremendous   opportunities for both children to decide to work, go to school or do both at the same time;
... the quality of the grade and high schools is said to be much poorer within the city limits of Chicago, but magnet schools do exist, and first-tier suburbs (Evanston, Berwyn, Oak Park) are also known for their better schools.

In short, should the family decide to:

... have Mom seek a job at Company 1, with both older children going to school and working part time?
... have Mom seek a job at Company 2, with both older children going to school and working part time?
... have Mom seek a job at Company 3, with at least one of the older children working full time. and foregoing school until the other child has graduated from college?

What salary can Mom hope to ask for when negotiating for a job at each Company?

In addition, where should the family live? In the city (which neighborhood)? In one of the first-tier suburbs? How will family members get to work and school, public transportation or by car? Or should the family stay put where they are in the suburbs until the youngest graduates from high school and gets into an "Ivy League" college?

Company #1 Profile

Your company makes widgets for the gizmo industry and is located on the southwest side of Chicago, close to an El and a number of bus lines. You have about 200 employees, 30 of which are managerial/professional, 50 are clerical, and the other 120 are either factory workers or unskilled laborers (such as janitorial). Your company offers "competitive" salaries that are no better or worse than what other companies offer to its employees, and the fringe benefits employees can take advantage of are considerable (health insurance, continuing education/ partial tuition reimbursement, vacation/sick days). Management has to keep an eye out for the bottom line, however, and the overall salary and benefits offered to new employees is continually reviewed.

Under the current salary guidelines, unskilled workers are paid a starting salary of about $7.50 an hour (about $15,600 annually), with health insurance benefits (but no opportunity for continuing education/tuition reimbursement). Skilled (office, clerical) workers receive a starting salary of $11.00 an hour (about $23,000 annually) with health insurance benefits and some opportunity for continuing education and tuition reimbursement. Managerial and professional employees, depending on their department, are paid anywhere from $33,000 to $85,000 annually, have health insurance benefits, the most continuing education/tuition reimbursement opportunities, and also have additional fringe benefits (company cars and cell phones). An employee's ability to rise from an hourly position to a salaried/managerial position depends on experience on the job and educational credentials (college diploma or certification).

With your Board of Directors, decide what salaries and benefits you are willing to offer prospective employees from the families that come to talk with you. Interview each family and find out who is interested in what jobs that are currently open at your company.

Creating Cultures:
Taking the Pain Out of Writing in Introductory Courses

Suzanne LaFont

Introduction

Today's teaching environments offer new challenges that must be met with creative solutions. For many educators the emphasis in writing across the curriculum has come at a time when class size is increasing and the level of student skills is uncertain. To meet these new challenges, I developed a writing assignment that takes the pain out of writing (and grading writing) in introductory courses. The assignment, which I call *Creating Cultures*, first requires students to create their own cultures, designing a history and environment, as well as political, economic, social, and belief systems. The culture is then introduced to a new technology, and students describe how that new technology prompts change and alters the different aspects of their created culture. This article provides the "how to" details and highlights the advantages of the *Creating Cultures* writing assignment.

The two major objectives of the *Creating Cultures* writing assignment are to encourage students to think critically about the complexity of social change and to clearly demonstrate their knowledge of anthropological terms and concepts. While formulating the assignment, I tried to design a project that would meet these objectives while at the same time taking into consideration the constraints that instructors face in terms of time and other aspects of being mere humans.

The most important feature of this assignment is that it is fun! Students seem to enjoy being creative and even the most challenged students can do well because they are allowed to demonstrate knowledge in an informal manner. Students also benefit from the clear grading guidelines that are laid out in the instructions, and feel empowered by being able to decide their own level of grading feedback. (See appendix for these materials.)

Creating Cultures has also been designed to benefit instructors because it addresses three interrelated issues that converge to make grading writing assignments problematic: fairness and consistency in grading, time constraints, and reading burn-out.

Fairness and Consistency in Grading. Many instructors feel insecure about grading writing assignments fairly. *Creating Cultures* has a clearly defined and easily followed grading scale: proper usage of 10 anthropology terms is worth 10 points each, equaling 100 points. Students are increasingly grade conscious, so providing them with a concise grading scale takes the guess work out of how their papers will be assessed. They can clearly and immediately see where and why points were deducted and how the final score was calculated. This reduces grade discontentment considerably.

Reduces Grading Time. To address the time crunch issue, I formulated an on-demand feedback option for students. Students can opt for three different grading levels: "no return," "return," and "return with comments." "No return" papers are simply not returned to the students (you may be surprised at how many students choose this option). "Return" papers are returned with minimal comments. "Return with comments" papers are given the full editorial treatment.

This gives instructors the information they need to spend time on the papers of students who will benefit from their comments and editorial efforts. Importantly, it minimizes the time spent on papers written by students who are not interested in comments and feedback, thus eliminating the guilt we feel when letting grammatical and spelling errors slip by uncensored.

Reduces Reading Burn-Out.
Reading burn-out is another common problem with grading papers in introductory courses. Maintaining enthusiasm and consistency throughout grading marathons may be almost impossible. How many papers on the *Fierce People* or the *Forest People* can we read without losing our minds? And more importantly, are the same standards applied to the first paper as are applied to the 100th paper? Do we start off with high standards and gradually lower them throughout the grading "event" or do our senses become dulled as we go along, encouraging us to overlook mistakes?

By allowing students to create their own cultures, *Creating Cultures* produces unique and highly individualized papers. These papers are often fascinating to read because they include references to our students' lives and values, and demonstrate their creativity. They foster an appreciation and a deeper understanding of our students, and we sometimes learn how they feel about us. In addition, the *Creating Cultures* project basically eliminates plagiarism. The construction of this assignment is so specific that any attempt to copy from another source is easily detected. And finally, it fulfills some writing requirements.

Directions for the Writing Assignment *Creating Cultures*

The most efficient way for you to understand the *Creating Cultures* assignment is to read the description and directions as if you were a student. The assignment that I distribute to students follows as an appendix. Written instructions are the best way to cut down on misunderstandings concerning the assignment. I also take the time to discuss the assignment in class. Please feel free to use these directions or modify them in any way that best suits your teaching needs.

Variations on the Creating a Culture Theme

To make sure I receive original papers every term, I continually change the theme. What follows are suggestions for variations:

... change in division of labor;
... increase in sexual dimorphism;
... introduction of a new religion;
... introduction of a new political system;
... introduction of a new subsistence strategy;
... a drastic environmental change;
... genetic engineering;
... a new evolutionary feature;
... indigenous peoples reclaiming land;
... writing in the first person as the leader of an "endangered" people.

Most Common Problems

Some students have creative blocks or seem shy about creating a culture. I suggest they imagine a culture they would love or hate to live in, or a culture they would like to visit. If they really seem stuck, I make generalized suggestions.

Warn your students against futuristic cultures. While the future is a legitimate topic for social change, I have found that many students become so involved in the details of their space-age cultures that they often lose sight of the assignment and turn in (often excellent) science fiction stores that do not fulfill the assignment.

Students often want to write about real cultures (usually their own) rather than create a culture. I stand firm and insist that their culture must be imaginary. It can, of course, resemble a living culture.

Conclusions

Creating Cultures transformed a negative teaching obligation into a positive experience for me and for my students. Rather than dread the grading of one hundred introductory level essays, I look forward to reading them. I find I can match their cultures with their personalities, and am able to appreciate what they have learned about social change and anthropology. Many students have actually thanked me, saying they enjoyed working on the assignment. Even students who seem uninterested often rally enthusiasm for the project.

Notes:

A less formal version of this project was first suggested to me by Professor Betsy Hegeman from John Jay College of Criminal Justice. I would like to acknowledge and thank her for her contribution.

The references to *The Fierce People* and *The Forest People* are of course to the classic ethnographies by Napoleon Chagnon and Colin Turnbull, respectively.

Creating a Culture: Directions for Your Essay

The Content of Your Paper

One of the requirements of this course is a five page essay. For this assignment, you will create your own culture, designing a history and environment, as well as political, economic, social, and belief systems. Your culture will experience dramatic change due to the introduction of a new technology. Your essay should detail how this change will affect your culture.

One half of the essay should describe your culture before the "event," and the remaining half should discuss how the new technology altered the political, economic, social, and belief systems of your culture.

The essay is abut social change. The aim of the project is to enable you to combine creative thinking while demonstrating your knowledge of anthropological concepts. Your culture may live on Cloud 9 or in the sewer pipes under the city. It must, however, "make sense." By making sense, I mean for example that your culture cannot have great cities and subsist by hunting and gathering (unless you provide some mechanism that allows for that possibility).

Grading Criteria

You must incorporate at least 10 of the anthropological terms that we have learned this term into your essay. See last page for a list of acceptable terms. Be sure to clearly demonstrate that you know what the term means. Also, be sure to underline your terms.

Correct example: the pastoralists on Creatania engage in unicorn herding as a way of life. One aspect of their social system is patrilineal descent which means that only males inherit unicorns from their parents. Unicorns are important to marriage arrangements because they are used for bridewealth. The groom and his family present them as gifts to the bride and her family before or during marriage.

Incorrect example: the pastoralists on Creatania practice patrilineal descent and bridewealth. (Although this sentence uses the underlined terms correctly, it is unacceptable because it does not demonstrate knowledge of the terms.)

You will receive 10 points for proper usage of 10 terms. Five points will be subtracted from your score for each term that you use incorrectly. Your paper will also be evaluated for how well it fulfills the assignment, e.g., full credit will not be given to papers that are too short, too long, lack social change, or that do not make "sense."

Grading Feedback

You have the option of turning in a first draft for suggestions for improvements at least one week **prior** to the final due date. Grades on papers turned in on the due date are final grades. No papers will be accepted after the last day of class. Because the papers are due on the last day of class, I will not return them to you unless requested to do so. If you wish to have your paper returned to you, you must write "please return" on the top of the paper. If you want me to correct your grammar, structure, and English in general, you must write "please return with comments" on the top of the paper. I will bring these papers with me to the final exam. All other papers will be stored in my office and may be abandoned or picked up at a later date.

The Format

Your essay **must** conform to the following specifications:
... it must be typed and spell checked (some grammatical errors will be forgiven but there will be no mercy for spelling error's;
... you should use a 12 point font (this document is in 12 point font);
... left/right, top/bottom margins should not exceed 1 inch;
... it must be double spaced throughout;
... it must not exceed five pages;
... the pages must be stapled together; no loose pages, no folders; no plastic covers.

Anthropological Terms to Use in Your Paper

You must use at least 10 of the following terms while describing your culture. The list is in no particular order:

patrilocality	sexual selection	hunter-gatherers	demography
lactation	bipedalism	social stratification	estrus
population pressure	origin myths	subsistence strategy	creationism
sexual dimorphism	epidemiology	theory	evolution
ethologist	egalitarian	conflict resolution	neolithic
megalithic	taxonomy	natural selection	paleolithic
misognyn	population density	hominid	prehistory
human universal	foraging	innovation	endogamy
matrilineal	cosmology	polygyny	patriarchy
supernatural	monotheism	polygamy	patrilineal
fallow	assimilation	neolocality	gender
pastoralists	anthropomorphism	bridewealth	matriarchial
secularization	horticulture	reciprocity	biodiversity
meritocracy	rite of passage	achieved status	caste
ethnobotany	socialization	material culture	creole
ethnography	non-material culture	holism/holistically	ritual
cultural relativity	participant observation	diffusion	dowry
genealogy	cultural contact	feminization of poverty	ideology
bilateral descent	ethnocentrism	human rights	acculturation

aboriginal   serial monogamy   market economy   deforestation
artifacts   ascribed status   conspicuous consumption   fossils
carrying capacity   applied anthropology   cross-cultural comparison

Fieldwork and the Observer's Gaze: Teaching the Ups and Downs of Ethnographic Observation

Daniel M. Goldstein

Although formal instruction in field research methods has become a fairly standard component of an anthropological education both at the graduate and undergraduate levels, this training typically emphasizes the techniques of method over the experiential aspects of doing fieldwork. This is largely the result of pragmatics; while it is fairly easy to teach our students the nuts and bolts of ethnographic research methods (e.g., how to be a patient observer, how to identify and interview an informant, or how to perform network analysis), and to encourage reflection on the inherent difficulties of doing fieldwork abroad (e.g., coping with health problems, getting official permission, and dealing with culture shock), it is much more difficult to provide students with a firsthand glimpse of the fieldwork experience itself. Even more difficult to teach (possibly owing to the scant attention devoted to the issue even by professional fieldworkers) are the politics of doing ethnographic field research; the ways in which who we are and the methods we use shape the kinds of interactions we have with those whom we study, and the kinds of findings our research produces. Short of sending students abroad for an extended period (highly impractical in a typical anthropology course, not to mention the prohibitive cost of an entire class studying overseas), how can we create for them an opportunity in which they can begin to experience some of the realities of the fieldwork process for themselves?

The teaching technique described in this article is an attempt to convey to students the complex range of issues that come into play in the process of doing anthropological field research, beyond the scope of basic methods training. It asks them to perform one simple activity – observe the behavior of people riding in an elevator and record the results – and to reflect on their findings. The goals of the exercise are twofold. First, the activity is designed to give students an initial foray into fieldwork by sending them off campus, out into the field, to conduct their own research observations. In the process, they learn something about human behavior in a designated locale. The second and perhaps more subtle goal is to expose them to the politics of doing research by allowing them to experience firsthand the kinds of tensions and suspicions that studying others can arouse. Though it can be used in classes devoted to anthropological methods, I have used this activity most often in my introduction to cultural anthropology course with very positive results. It is a quick and easy way to provide students with a taste of what ethnographic fieldwork actually "feels like," and to encourage reflection on such themes as objectivity, interpretation, and the impact of the observer on the observed in the fieldwork encounter.

It should be noted that this activity need not be conducted in an elevator in order to be successful. All that is required is a public space in which surveillance and a heightened awareness of strangers are likely to be encountered. For people teaching on campuses in towns where there are no buildings tall enough to have elevators, doing observations in a convenience store (with advance permission), for example, would be a good substitute for the elevator.

The Activity: Observing Elevator Behavior

Identifying a Fieldsite. The first step in conducting this exercise is to ask each student in the class to identify a "fieldsite," which here means a particular elevator in which their observations will take place. I suggest to them that they think of a tall, busy building in the city but not on campus that is likely to have an elevator, and go there. They need to take a notebook and a pen/pencil to record their observations. Students may coordinate their fieldwork with friends in the class, but may not do the actual observations together, i.e., only one anthropologist per elevator at a time. In the past, students have conducted observations in the elevators in hospitals, office buildings, government towers, residential apartments, and shopping malls.

Students are told to spend at least 10 minutes riding the elevator up and down, observing the behavior of the other riders (many end up riding for longer periods, as the activity catches their interest). If they have the time and inclination, they can make repeat visits (perhaps at different times of the day) to supplement the initial 10-minute ride. I advise them not to speak to the other riders (unless spoken to first); they should confine their activity to visual observation. They are also encouraged to spend a few minutes outside the elevator, observing how people wait for the elevator and how they go about boarding or exiting it.

Observation and Data Collection. Recording fieldnotes and reflections is an important component of this exercise, as it is in all field research. I advise students to draw a line down the middle of the first page of their notebooks, heading the left-hand column "Observations" and the right-hand column "Reflections." In the Observations column, they should record everything they observe or notice during the elevator rides. What are people wearing? How do they conduct themselves? What kinds of interactions can be witnessed between riders? Where do people stand as they enter? How do they exit? In the Reflections column, students are to record their own thoughts, feelings, ideas about or interpretations of the observations they are making. Students can add to this column after the observation period has ended, as further ideas occur to them on reflection.

Importantly, in instructing them on how to conduct their observations, I urge students to be aware of the impact their own presence might be having on the behavior of the people being observed. I suggest that if people are ignoring them, they should position themselves near the front of the elevator so as to better observe what people are doing, perhaps turning to face the people as they observe them. Students are encouraged to reflect on people's reactions when they notice that someone is watching them and taking notes. They are also told to note their own emotional reactions during the observation, and to describe them in the Reflections column.

Write-Up of Findings. After completing their observations, students are asked to write a description and analysis (four to six pages, typed, double-spaced) exploring what they learned from this experience. Students are asked to recount some of the observations they made and to interpret what these say abut elevator behavior. In addition, students should reflect on the process of doing ethnographic observation, specifically noting the reactions of elevator riders to being observed. I ask students to consider what, if anything, surprised them about the behavior they witnessed. How did they feel while doing the observation? What kind of responses do they think their observation produced in the people they were observing? To what can they attribute people's reactions to them?

Debriefing the Observation Experience. On the day that their papers are due, I group students into triads to compare their experiences. Each group is asked to identify three to five things that everyone in the group observed, and one or two words that described how they each felt while doing the observation. We then go around the room eliciting group reactions, which I jot down on the chalkboard. This is an important component of the activity, for by noting similar observations across the class, students begin to perceive patterns of behavior emerging from their individual observations. Students also come to realize that their own reactions to the process (discussed below) are remarkably similar to those of their classmates, and that these indicate certain facets of the ethnographic enterprise that I try to draw out in discussion.

Findings and Conclusions

One of the most surprising aspects of this activity is the rich variety of information and insights that such an apparently simple exercise can produce. In addition to providing insight into the behavior of elevator passengers, the activity also gives students a glimpse of the many problematic dimensions of doing anthropological fieldwork. At the same time, it affords them the opportunity to reflect on their own role in the observation, and on how sometimes the observer can have a profound impact on the phenomenon that he or she is attempting to observe. Students can

be encouraged to think about the questions this raises for anthropologists trying to perform objective studies of the behaviors of others (cf. Scheper-Hughes 1993).

In a brief period of study, students are able to record a wealth of observations regarding the behavior of people in elevators. Many of these reflect the discomfort that people seem to feel when placed in close quarters with strangers, an insight that students gain when they begin to analyze the data that they have collected. Students also note that the context in which the elevator is located (a hospital versus an office building, for example) may have some impact on the kinds of behaviors observed. Some common observations gleaned from student reports are summarized in the appendix as Table 1.

Most students note the effect that their observing has on the subjects of their observation, who often seem to express suspicion or anxiety when they realize they are being studied. Students report feelings of uncertainty and ambivalence, ranging from the mild ("intrusive," "awkward") to the extreme ("criminal," "inhuman,"). Other descriptors appear in Table 2 of the appendix. Despite these feelings of trepidation, some students also report growing feelings of confidence as the activity proceeds: though most begin by feeling nervous and uncomfortable, some of them gradually gain a sense of their own ability to do this kind of work, a trajectory to which most experienced fieldworkers can relate. Some students even report a feeling of power, as they come to perceive their capacity to make others uncomfortable by their very presence, or from their perception of behavioral patterns of which the other elevator passengers are oblivious. During the debriefing, I try to draw connections for them between their own feelings and those of "real" ethnographers doing field work; their reading of Anderson (1990) further reinforces this comparison.

Parallels in Ethnography

One of the most remarkable aspects of this exercise is the way in which it exhibits multiple parallels with anthropological fieldwork as it is typically practiced in non-Western contexts. At the most mundane level, for example, students report field-related health problems from riding the elevator that are familiar to many an anthropologist, notably nausea and other physical discomforts from going up and down in the lift. Their self-described emotions are also familiar to experienced anthropological fieldworkers: feelings of skepticism, doubt, boredom, anxiety, or frustration with the pace of the work; fear for their personal safety; and the gradual acquisition of a sense of oneself as an anthropologist. Students encounter ethical dilemmas, as they question their own right to violate the personal space of others in the interest of "science." Many students report encountering suspicion or even outright hostility from the people they are observing. Elevator riders may turn their backs on the would-be anthropologists, quiz them in an unfriendly tone on why they are staring at them, or in some other way indicate their displeasure at being studied. Occasionally a student will have a run-in with a security guard or some other "official" person, who questions their activities and denies them permission to conduct their research and makes them leave the premises.

I take care to point out that the suspicions that their observation activities evoke in the elevator passengers have strong parallels in the responses received by anthropologists doing participant-observation in a variety of settings. Perhaps the key to this is recognizing that the subjects of our studies may often harbor doubts about the legitimacy of our activities as anthropologists, and are fearful about the ends to which the information that we collect about them may be put. This is particularly true when the anthropologist does an inadequate job of explaining the purpose and goals of the study to her or his subjects (a point that Anderson [1990] makes very clearly). Additionally, the fact that students are writing down their observations in a notebook may be particularly alarming, as the ends to which their written information may be put are open to misconstrual. I point out that writing about others gives the author a certain power over his or her subjects that they may resent out of fear of being misrepresented in print (Goldstein n.d.). Parallels with Miner's classic (1956) Nacirema piece can be effectively made here by drawing connections to the power of the author to misinterpret and hence mistakenly portray the subjects of his or her study.

References Cited

Anderson, B.G.
    1990. *First Fieldwork: The Misadventures of an Anthropologist.* Prospect Heights IL: Waveland Press.

Goldstein, D.M.
    n.d. On Ethnographic and Other Forms of Representation: Encountering Suspicion in the Field. Unpublished ms.

Miner, H.
    1956. Body Ritual Among the Nacirema. *American Anthropologist* 58:503-7.

Scheper-Hughes, N.
   1993. *Death Without Weeping: the Violence of Everyday Life in Brazil.* Berkeley: University of California Press.

Table 1

Elevator Observations: Patterns Noted in Observation Exercises

People move far away from each other.
People avoid eye contact with one another.
People stand near buttons and move when someone enters.
Children acknowledge other riders more frequently than adults.
Status differences are apparent in dress.
People give the observer strange looks.
There is a "struggle for personal space."
People seem to need to focus their eyes on something.
People ignore the observer, though they are aware that they are being observed.
There are gender differences in elevator behavior.

Table 2

Elevator Reflections: Terms Used to Describe Self Feelings While Doing Exercise

Out of place	Awkward
On a Mission	Authoritative
Uncertain of own motives	Amused
Gratification	Confused
Surprised	Intrusive
Confident	Foolish
Guilty	Uncomfortable
Powerful	Removed
Inhuman	Embarrassed
Foreign	Criminal
Worried about getting enough data	Giddy

Reading Textiles for Cultural Messages

Robin O'Brian

In my introductory anthropology courses, I use an exercise where I show the class different textiles and items of indigenous hand-loomed clothing gathered during my fieldwork among Maya women in rural Mexico to demonstrate numerous points about sociocultural anthropology. While my own textile collection is from Central America, such an exercise would work well with textiles or other craft items from other cultural areas. All the instructor needs are things to show that have specific messages within specific cultures. The exercise could work equally well in appropriate area courses. Since this is an "instructor show" exercise, there is no limit to class size.

I begin by placing all of the items on a table and asking the students to come down to the front of the room to look at the items and to try to figure out what the items are and how they might be used. Depending on the size of the class, students can be encouraged to try items on. They can work separately or in pairs or groups. After about 20 minutes, I ask students to present their findings to the class, again by pairs or groups or as individuals. This initial portion of the exercise allows students to apply what they have learned so far about anthropology to tangible items. They also learn how their own views of another culture shape what they hypothesize because we then discuss how the items are actually used. Students will, for example, attribute various ritual or other traditional meanings to items that were in fact made for the tourist market; this allows students to think about how their own ideas about the "other" color their perceptions of cultural artifacts such as textiles and clothing. In addition, it also introduces discussion about craft production, the role of tourism, petty commodity production, "authenticity," and "quality."

I then ask students to tell me how the items of clothing might be used to signal various aspects of the culture. Students already know different concepts, e.g., social organization, technology, gender systems, and cosmology, and they are familiar with ethnographic examples drawn from my fieldwork. What I want them to tell me are:

Social organization: different communities signal membership by wearing different styles of clothing. Women persist in wearing traditional dress. Small children, especially girls, begin wearing traditional items early as they are incorporated into their communities.

Gender system: as noted above, women continue to wear traditional dress more frequently and completely than men; women are traditional weavers among the Maya and their industry and skill are demonstrated in the wearing of traditional dress and properly dressing their families. Increasingly as well, women are becoming breadwinners in their families as they produce for the tourist market.

Cosmology: the colors and designs of traditional items have supernatural meanings that the wearer thus underscores through her or his dress. Women's blouses in particular are heavily brocaded around the neck – the woman is the center of her blouse, as her community is in the center of the world.

Technology: because traditional items are woven on the backstrap loom, some students can note how technology, in this case the loom, produces a concrete item that can communicate the above meanings. When I want to underscore the role of technology, I supplement the textiles with photographs of weavers (from books) in various cultures that use backstrap or other simple looms and have the students explain to me how this technology can constrain design, in this case the limitations introduced by the way the loom is strung. Designs are always geometric; circular items (e.g., flowers) are embroidered on the finished piece. This last part of the exercise also allows me to present both male and female weavers from a variety of cultures in Africa, Asia, Europe, and other parts of the Americas where such weaving has been practiced. This allows the students to see similarities as well as differences in different cultures.

Ideally, the above is what I want students to tell me about this particular set of textiles. If they do not, I incorporate the materials into the discussion. If you make a note of what you want students to be able to say about the textiles or crafts, it is not difficult to fill in what they do not tell you.

Coming of Age in Statistics

Robert Bates Graber

One of anthropology's most important and controversial books is Margaret Mead's 1928 volume *Coming of Age in Samoa*. Against the widely held opinion that adolescence is inevitably a difficult time of life for biological reasons, Mead argued that it is cultural rather than biological factors that determine its difficulty. Her study of young girls in Samoa persuaded her that traditional Samoan culture, especially because it allowed the relatively free development of sexuality, made adolescence quite easy. Recent claims that her study was deeply flawed have been vigorously refuted and the debate goes on. In any case, a widely unnoticed fact is that Mead presented data that are excellent for introducing anthropology students of any level to bivariate analysis. One virtue is that her data provide an occasion to link statistical analysis to general theorizing; another is that the sample size of 25 is small enough to allow meaningful manipulation in a classroom exercise; and yet another is that adolescent sexual experience is a subject guaranteed to arouse student interest. Although this exercise is written for an in-class exercise, it could be assigned as homework with highlights reviewed in class. It could be used when the subject of "methods" comes up in either an introductory four/five field or cultural anthropology course or as a piece of a methods course where qualitative and quantitative methods is the topic.

About a third of the girls Mead studied lived, dormitory-style, in the missionary-pastor's house; most, however, did not. Ask students what effect this might have had on the development of sexuality. The obvious hypothesis would be that living with the pastor might have inhibited sexual experience relative to those living "outside," especially if Mead's characterization of the traditional culture was accurate.

The last two pages of this article are handouts for students doing the exercise; one is data taken from Mead's book and the second is a set of blank tables for students to fill in. Have students tear off and separate the pages for convenience. Ask them to sort all 25 girls into the blank tables by writing each name in the appropriate cell. Note that the cells are labeled a, b, c, and d followed by parentheses. Students should count the names in each cell and record each cell's total (called its *frequency*) in the parentheses. They should do this for both blank tables.

Ask students what these results mean. The upper table reveals that 16 girls ($a + c$) lived on the "outside," while 9 ($b + d$) resided in the pastor's house. Of the 16 outsiders, 10 were believed by Mead to have had homosexual experience, while of the 9 insiders, 7 were believed to have had homosexual experience. Note that 7/9 is a bit higher than 10/16, suggesting – but not proving – that living in the pastor's house was more likely to promote than to inhibit this kind of sexual experience. Moving to the lower table, students can count and see that 10 of the 16 outsiders were believed by Mead to have had heterosexual experience, while only 2 of the 9 insiders were believed to have had heterosexual experience. Because 2/9 is considerably lower than 10/16, there seems to be evidence that living in the pastor's house did inhibit this kind of sexual experience. Here the discrepancy between the fractions is somewhat greater than for the first table, so we would tend to think that the data provide better evidence for the inhibition of heterosexual experience than for the promotion of homosexual experience.

Scientifically, we would like to be able to compare the tables more simply and precisely than this. A statistic useful for this purpose is known as *gamma*. Gamma, which can be applied to tables of any size, when applied to two-by-two tables is sometimes referred to, for historical reasons, as "Yule's *Q*;" it is calculated as follows:

$$\text{Gamma} = (ad - bc) / (ad + bc)$$

where *ad* denotes the product of *a* and *d*, and *bc* denotes the product of *b* and *c*. Gamma ranges from negative one to positive one. Our tables have been arranged so that a negative gamma will suggest an inhibiting effect on sexual experience, a positive gamma will suggest a promoting effect. Have students compute gamma for each table, recording the result in the space provided on their tables. (The calculation is quite easy even without a calculator, except for converting the final fraction into decimal form.) Once completed, ask students to summarize the results.

Before attaching too much importance to these results, we should consider whether the observed cell frequencies are more "lop-sided" than would be expected by chance. Have students consider cell *d* of the upper table. Ask if the observed frequency of 7 is really suspiciously high. After all, 17/25 of all the girls are said to have had homosexual experience; of the 9 residing in the pastor's house, we would expect 17/25 of these 9 to have had such experience even if where they resided made no difference. Multiplying 17/25 by 9 gives a "random expected frequency," then of 6.12 for this cell – only .88 less than the observed frequency of 7. The *chi-square* statistic is based on such differences for all the cells in a table, and it allows an exact answer to the question of whether the observed frequencies are the sort of thing we would expect by chance alone. In fact, for two-by-two tables, a chi-square value greater than 2.71 can be shown to result by chance less than ten percent of the time; greater than 3.84, less than five percent of the time; and greater than 6.63 less than one percent of the time. Social scientists conventionally rely especially on the five-percent value – the ".05 level" – so a chi-square value of less than 3.84 leaves us a bit reluctant to conclude that anything is necessarily "going on;" the observed results do not differ much, that is, from what would be expected by chance.

Without going into details, we can find chi-square for a two-by-two table this way:

$$\text{Chi-square} = (ad - bc)^2 \, n / (a + b)(c + d)(a + c)(b + d)$$

where *n* denotes the sample size (25 in our tables) and the other letters have the same meaning as before. You may not want your students to tackle this computation without calculators, but have them fill in the chi-square values for each table, recording the result in the space provided. This can be done individually as homework or in class as a unit. Again, ask them what interpretation there is for this finding.

113

Social-scientific use of statistics was young in 1928; perhaps your students will be surprised to know that with gamma and chi-square, we already have gone well beyond the analysis carried out by Mead herself in her controversial classic.

TABLE 1*

Table Showing Homosexual Experience, Heterosexual Experience and Residence or Non-Residence in Pastor's Household.

No	Name	Homosexual Experience	Heterosexual Experience	Residence in Pastor's Household
1	Luna	yes	yes	no
2	Masina	yes	yes	no
3	Losa	yes	no	yes
4	Sona	yes	no	yes
5	Loto	yes	no	yes
6	Pala	yes	no	no
7	Aso	no	no	no
8	Tolo	no	no	no
9	Lotu	yes	yes	no
10	Tulipa	yes	no	yes
14	Lita	yes	no	no
16	Namu	yes	yes	no
17	Ana	yes	no	yes
18	Lua	no	no	no
19	Tolu	yes	yes	no
21	Mala	no	no	no
22	Fala	yes	yes	no
23	Lola	yes	yes	no
23a	Tulipa	yes	yes	no
24	Leta	yes	yes	yes
25	Ela	yes	yes	yes
27	Mina	no	no	yes
28	Moana	no	yes	no
29	Luina	no	no	yes
30	Sala	no	yes	no

* **Notes**: This Table is adapted from Appendix V, Table 1, in Mead's book. For our purposes, it only gives data on names, homosexual experience, heterosexual experience, and residence in pastor's house.

All data are from Margaret Mead *Coming of Age in Samoa*, 1928. New York: Morrow.

I want to thank Tara Johnson for her assistance in this project.

Residence in Pastor's House?

	No	Yes
Homosexual Experience? No	a ( )	b ( )
Yes	c ( )	d ( )

Gamma = _____, Chi-square = _____

Residence in Pastor's House?

	No	Yes
Heterosexual Experience? No	a ( )	b ( )
Yes	c ( )	d ( )

Gamma = _____, Chi-square = _____

Culture as "The Rules of the Game:" Simulating Fieldwork While Playing Cards

Susan Birns

Background and Acknowledgment

One summer, my daughter Sylvia returned from summer camp having learned an extremely entertaining card game which she proceeded to play with me. Later, when I was preparing to guest lecture in her middle school social studies class, we decided to use this game as a teaching tool because the analogy to culture and anthropological field work was too good to pass up. It was very effective and I subsequently adopted its use in my introductory anthropology classes. The most fundamental premise of the game is that you are not allowed to discuss the rules; this made publishing them in this volume somewhat problematic. In order to remain true to my key informant, my daughter, the game that follows is an altered and greatly simplified version of the original.

The Rationale

A fundamental challenge in teaching introductory cultural anthropology to nonmajors is engaging them in both the subject matter and the class environment. This exercise helps achieve both of these goals while teaching important anthropological content. The primary focus is on culture as "the rules of the game." Students experience important components of conducting fieldwork in an unfamiliar setting. Discussion introduces them to the subjects of ethnocentrism, enculturation, participant observation, and culture shock. Though developed for courses in cultural anthropology and for classes of no more than 30 students, the strategy could be adapted to four-field introductory anthropology and for larger classes as long as the class is subdivided into units of no more than 30 for card playing purposes. Additionally, it would serve as an excellent introduction to an entire fieldwork course.

This exercise is most effective when used early in the term. In addition to the fact that field work is typically covered at the beginning of an introductory anthropology course, this game can play an important role in establishing the classroom atmosphere because it provides an informal context in which students relate to each other, as well as to their instructor. They see their instructor in what they believe to be a noninstructional context (dealer in a card game). Throughout the game, they laugh, relax, and develop a nascent sense of group identity as they ally themselves with each other, as novices, in opposition to their instructor, the apparently capricious "pro."

This exercise requires students to play a card game with a "pro." Only the pro knows the rules, but this knowledge is not conveyed via direct instruction. Students learn rules by making educated guesses that, when correct, allow play to continue and by inadvertently breaking the rules and receiving feedback and penalties from the pro. Some rules are familiar from the outset; many are completely unpredictable. The goal is to involve students in the learning process, not to teach them the game. This is a very important point to keep in mind.

This exercise works best with a pro to student ratio of no more than 1 to 30. The only materials required are two decks of regular playing cards and a room with moveable desks. Since the pro must be consistent in punishing most rule-breaking behavior, one to two hours must be invested in learning the game prior to using it in class the first time. Conducting the exercise in class takes approximately one half hour (15-20 minutes to play the game and 10-15 minutes to deconstruct the experience).

This article will teach you a card game called MCLA Rummy, known only to members of "The Secret Order of Anthropology Professors" (hereafter referred to as SOAP). (For anyone interested in origins of acronyms, MCLA stands for Massachusetts College of Liberal Arts.) Reading past this paragraph is tantamount to initiation into SOAP and implies commitment to abide by its provisos. The rules of MCLA Rummy are privileged; you must agree to discuss them **exclusively** with other SOAP members, no one else! When your students ask you to discuss game rules, which they undoubtedly will, you must refuse. Instead, if time allows, take the opportunity to discuss the basic principles of secret societies with them. **Should you decline membership in SOAP, please glue the remaining pages of this article together immediately!**

The Setting

In an effort to engage student curiosity and get them talking before class begins the day of the exercise, I rearrange the classroom furniture prior to student arrival by placing 5-7 desks in a tight circle in the center of the room and pushing the surrounding chairs out towards the perimeter. Students often express anxiety as they enter because their classroom environment has been disturbed and they don't know what to expect next. The field work

simulation has begun and we haven't even started the exercise yet! I also perch on the corner of my desk, smiling, and shuffling the double deck of cards as they arrive for class. In response to questions about "What's going on?" all they receive is a smile -- no explanation.

When it is time for class to start, I announce that we are, in fact, playing cards in class today and I recruit between four and six volunteers. I ask if there are any "card sharks" in the room, people who have had experience playing a variety of card games. If so, I ask them to become volunteers. Experienced card players help get the game moving because even familiar rules, like "following suit" do not present themselves as logical strategies to novice card players. I also suggest that first round volunteers be people who are willing to laugh at themselves and easily tolerate other people laughing at them. I ask the volunteers to sit in the chairs and the rest of the class to stand huddled around the players so that all spectators can see the cards as they are played. I, too, take a seat and play begins. After several minutes of play, I rotate no more than one or two of the spectators in as players. After another five minutes, I substitute another player or two.

Note: in an effort to maintain linguistic flow without succumbing to the sexism of English grammar, I will refer to players as male and the dealer/pro as female throughout the exercise.

The Rules of the Game

(1)   The object of the game is to be the first person to get rid of all his cards.

(2)   Use two decks of well-shuffled, regular playing cards.

(3)   There is no formal instruction in the rules of this game. The dealer/pro only punishes incorrect behavior by administering a penalty which is always one card per offense.

(4)   Cards are always distributed by the pro face down.

(5)   Cards are always dealt from the top of the deck.

(6)   Each player, in turn, tries to match the top card on the discard pile by following suit (playing any heart on top of a heart, spade on top of a spade) or by matching the number/picture (jack on jack, six on six).

(7)   There is a 10-second time limit on play. If the correct person does not play within 10 seconds, they are orally chastised, "10 seconds" and receive a penalty card.

(8)   A player who goes out of turn or provides an incorrect response is told, "wrong move" and receives a penalty card.

(9)   When a player is unable to play a card from his hand, he must take one, and only one, card from the top of the deck. Even if the card drawn is "playable," he is not allowed to play it this turn.

(10) It is quite possible that you will "exhaust" the deck more than once during a hand. When this occurs, make a mental note of the direction of play and whose turn comes next. Then remove the top card from the discard pile and leave it face up on the playing surface as the discard pile. Shuffle the other cards and return them face down as the playing deck.

(11) The cardinal rule is that no one is ever allowed to talk during the game except the dealer/ pro. If spectators talk, hush them. If a player talks, give him a penalty card and say, "talking." If the player sputters an objection, or otherwise verbalizes, give him another penalty card and repeat the name of the offense, "talking." Do this whenever any player speaks at any point during the game -- this is mandatory.

(12) No one (including the pro) is ever allowed to discuss the rules of this game! Included in this prohibition is one player indicating to another that it is his turn to play. If a player "elbows," "kicks," shakes his head, or even stares at another player, the pro administers a penalty and says "telling rules."

(13) In this context, it is important for the pro not to inadvertently "teach" rules by looking in the direction of expected play.

(14) The dealer/pro has the option of penalizing players (one card per person per offense) for "unnecessary laughter" whenever she feels like it. You may apply the penalty every time anyone giggles, or you may apply it intermittently. It's up to you, but do it sometimes. If several people laugh simultaneously, penalize each of them. The important point is that while you administer punishments, you must articulate the offense. In this case, as you place a card in front of the perpetrator, you announce, "unnecessary laughter."

(15) The dealer announces the name of the game. "We are about to play MCLA Rummy."

(16) Dealing in either direction (it's most effective if you vary the direction of the deal from round to round), the pro deals each player (including herself) three cards (one at a time). The deck is placed centrally and the top card is turned over so that it lies face up next to the deck, thus creating a discard pile. If the card is one that ordinarily requires special action (it is an ace, 3, 4, 8, or face card) -- ignore the special action (at the beginning of a hand only). The pro then announces the direction of play. "MCLA Rummy begins to the dealer's...(right or left)." The only correct response is for the identified person to pick up his cards. If anyone else touches his cards prior to the designated person, the dealer responds, "touching the cards" and deals him a penalty card. Allow ten seconds to pass and if the appropriate player has not picked up his cards, give him a penalty card and announce the offense, "MCLA Rummy begins to the dealer's...". The penalized player figures out it is his turn to act and picks up his cards. Everyone else can then pick up their cards. Apply the penalty to anyone who fails to pick up his cards within 10 seconds while announcing, "ten seconds" to each offender.

(17) The identified first player must place a card from his hand onto the discard pile. He must match either the suit or the number of the top card on the pile. If he is unable to make a match, he must draw one card from the top of the deck, but is not allowed to play it even if it is a match. Play then moves in the direction that the pro announced at the start of the hand.

(18) Whenever a face card is played, the card must be verbally identified by the person playing it. As he places the card on the desk, he must say "queen of hearts" (for example). Failure to do so results in a penalty and the admonition, "failure to say queen of hearts." The player must repeat "queen of hearts." Failure to do so, results in an additional penalty and verbal reproach every 10 seconds until he names the card. When students verbally identify non-face cards (4 of hearts or 10 of spades), they receive a penalty for "talking."

(19) Whenever a red "4" (heart or diamond) is played, all other players must draw one card or receive a penalty for "failure to pick a card."

(20) Whenever an "8" is played, the direction of play reverses. If the person otherwise next in line to play plays, he receives a penalty and the admonition, "wrong move."

(21) Whenever a "3" is played, the next player's turn is skipped.

(22) Whenever an ace is played, the player must say, "please pass the salt." If not, the dealer admonishes, "failure to say please pass the salt" and administers a penalty.

(23) Immediately before playing his second-to-last card, a player must knock once on the playing surface to give warning that he is down to his last card. Failure to do so results in a penalty and the admonition from the dealer/pro "failure to knock."

(24) When a player plays his last card he must announce, "MCLA Rummy." He has won the first hand. If he fails to make this announcement, he receives a penalty, and the hand continues.

Interpretation

Play the game for 15-20 minutes. By then, most students will have learned some of the rules. However, remember SOAP's primary principle: no discussing rules except with SOAP members. If students press you to confirm their hypotheses, turn it into a teaching moment and explain the operation of secret societies and your membership in SOAP. Refusing to discuss rules with students is truly important. Like other cultures, campus culture changes through diffusion. The more widespread knowledge of the game becomes on any given campus, the less useful it will be as a teaching tool. Its success is completely dependent upon the element of surprise. In addition, this version of the game has been simplified from its original form. This is advantageous for training trainers, but makes the game less interesting to actually play for any length of time.

Reconvene your class to deconstruct the exercise. Inform students that the only rule you will ever discuss with them is that you are prohibited from discussing the rules with them. Ask why they think you conducted this exercise with them at this point in the term, when you are on the brink of discussing field work. Be sure they have incorporated the following points into their analysis:

... Culture is the tool that helps us know how to behave appropriately in varying situations and helps us interpret the meaning of other people's behavior as well.
... The process of enculturation is akin to learning the rules of a new game. In some instances we learn via direct instruction, but much of the important stuff we learn by doing.
... We acquire important information by behaving appropriately, but often learn even more by making mistakes.
... If we're smart, we do not learn exclusively from our own behavior, but by carefully observing the behavior of other people.

Understanding all of the above is essential in conducting successful ethnographic field work. That's why we call our research methodology "participant observation." In addition, a field worker must learn to be comfortable feeling somewhat uncomfortable -- being the "odd person out." This comfort is not always easily achieved and culture shock may be the consequence.

Ask students to identify their feelings as they played. Some will insist that the game has no rules; you are capricious and invented them as you played. You point out that just because they cannot detect a pattern, does not mean there is no pattern. Others will express frustration with some of the rules. You wouldn't allow them to talk; you didn't tell them the rules prior to playing the game; and most outrageously you still refuse to discuss rules with them. You identify their attitude as ethnocentric. Culture novitiates are not in a position to judge the operating principles of another way of life, certainly not according to the standards that are familiar and comfortable to them. Their initial task is to learn the new rules and understand them in the context in which they occur.

Students may note that you tricked them. The game is identified as a form of rummy, yet it does not follow most of rummy's rules. You do not meld cards on the table, nor do you collect runs in your hand.

You explain that it is common for anthropologists in the field to be duped by false expectations. When told they are going to have the opportunity to participate in a "funeral" they may expect a particular set of behaviors that bears no relationship to what they will actually encounter.

Ask students to identify ways in which the game does not accurately simulate the situation in the field. Be sure they understand that in the field, everyone else will know "the rules of the game," while the field worker's job is to decipher them. Here, the majority is ignorant of the rules. Students have lots of company in the learning process; they are all in the same boat. True field work is typically a lonelier enterprise in this regard. Other components of the simulation not necessarily found in the field include: there is no language barrier; the environment is altered, but familiar; the duration of the simulation is extremely brief.

Most students love this exercise. They enjoy the exposure to concepts they are exploring in their readings, while feeling like they've been given a gift - an opportunity to play cards in class instead of having to "work"! In addition to preparing them for the mini-field work project that follows (I require them to attend services in a religious sect significantly different from the one in which they were raised), it makes our classroom a more relaxed context in which future learning can occur.

Editor's Note: use the author's suggestion to practice by yourself before trying this out on a class by dealing out hands to 3-4 "invisible" people, face up so you can read and play the cards, giving oral admonitions and penalty cards as appropriate. This does not simulate the entire experience, but will give you practice seeing what can happen and visualizing the rest. Or, use three or four colleagues as players and induct them into the secret society of SOAP. This will look good on all of your Vitas. And be warned! This strategy is diabolical.

Reading Between the Lines: Representing Diversity, Conflict, and the Broader World in International News Stories

Susan Buck Sutton

Engaging students in close reading of a single article clipped from the international news section of the newspaper is an effective active learning exercise for my introductory course in cultural anthropology. This is an exercise that focuses attention on the dynamics of contemporary events outside the U.S. at the same time that it serves as cultural critique of certain ways such events are understood within the U.S. (See Nanda 1997.) Even the shortest article of this type has provoked animated discussion on issues of perspective, representation, causality, globalization, and the students' own relationship to the broader world. Students leave the classroom feeling empowered to read, critique, and interpret international news stories, something many have previously avoided as threatening, irrelevant, or confusing. They come to see how certain styles of reporting present the broader world as a chaotic and fearsome place. And they make direct connections between the headlines they regularly encounter (even if only as background noise while turning to the comics or sports pages) and the themes we have been discussing in the course. So do I. Although I developed this exercise for cultural anthropology, it would work easily in a four-field introductory class and with appropriate selection, area courses. Although best in small to medium sized classes, it could be adapted and used in large classes as well, with students writing critiques or answers to questions.

Preparation

This exercise rests on structured classroom discussion of a newspaper article that the instructor has chosen. You can assign students to read the article and even write short papers as preparation for the discussion, or you can ask them to respond on the spot as you hand out copies of the article.

When I first began this exercise, I thought that success rested on choosing just the right article. Over time, I have come to see that the article can be selected almost at random, and indeed that part of the excitement generated by this exercise is that students recognize that all reporting, indeed all writing, is susceptible to this kind of critical analysis. I recommend selecting a fresh and timely article each time, giving relevancy and immediacy. It also gives it a dynamic quality as both you and the students mutually engage in the construction of knowledge, both exploring the article for the first time (King 1994:15).

The only selection requirements I set are that the item must come from the news section of the paper, that it be the kind of article found in most American newspapers on a daily basis rather than a lengthy analytic piece, and that it concerns some event outside the country. News stories that concern ethnic conflict are particularly productive.

The second step is to compose a set of appropriate questions to stimulate and structure the discussion. Since focused questions are the key to active learning, critical thinking, and construction of knowledge in the classroom (Bonwell and Sutherland 1996; Brookfield and Preskill 1999; King 1994), I pose questions that enable students to recognize the discursive structure of the article, analyze its message, and make connections with course material. I construct the following kinds of questions:

(1) Content and clarity:

... What is the incident described in the article; what does the article tell us about the incident?

... What are we told, if anything, about the larger situation surrounding this incident; about the nation(s) involved; their history; their internal dynamics?

... Is the article clear or confusing about the situation; if confusing, why; what kinds of information would help us understand the situation better?

(2) The author's perspective and emphases:

... Does the author state his or her assessment of this situation directly?

... What does the author's selection of what and what not to tell us reveal about the author's perspective?

... Are there any specific words or phrases that create a strong image; if these words or phrases were omitted, would the tone of the article change; are these words or phrases ones you recognize as common to reports on situations like this; what impact does it have that you have heard such words and phrases before?

(3) The groups and individuals involved:

... What specific groups or individuals are identified in the article; what are we told about each?

... Might there be other groups involved in this situation who are not identified?

... Who gets to speak in the article; whose views are reported verbatim; whose are paraphrased; whose are not presented at all?

... How might members of each of these groups feel about the article?

(4) The author's assumptions with respect to culture, causality, and global connections:

... Does the article suggest or imply any basic causes for this incident; what sorts of causes does it consider; what sorts of causes does it not consider?

... If we are not told much about why this is happening, what does this lead the reader to think about the situation?

... What does the article see as motivating the people involved in the incident; what does this lead us to think of them?

... What implicit assumptions concerning culture and ethnicity undergird the article; what kinds of social units are identified; how much variation is noted within them; is culture seen as something flexible; are social boundaries seen as fluid?

... Does the article make any connections (political, economic, other) between the U.S. and the nation(s) being discussed; what connections might there be?

(5) The overall impression given by the article:

... What overall impression of the situation emerges from the article; what does this lead the reader to think of this situation in specific, and the world outside the U.S. in general; is this broader world portrayed in a way that makes it seem comprehensible and familiar, or in a way that makes it seem very different from the U.S.?

The third step is for you to acquire enough background on the situation being reported in the article that you can help the class move beyond it toward the end of the discussion. If the news item concerns a part of the world with which you are already familiar, you are ahead of the game. If it does not, you can make the fact that you were able to learn enough about the situation to clarify the article in just an hour or so in the library or on the net serve as an example to students of how they might go about developing a broader view of the world by themselves.

The Discussion

If the class is small enough, I have found it productive to break it into small groups first, each taking question or a series of questions, and then to reassemble the class as a whole to see if we can reach a higher level of analysis by letting our answers build upon each other. (See Brookfield and Preskill 1999.) In the small groups, students develop detailed familiarity with the article and some mastery over part of its narrative structure and strategies. In the class-wide discussion, we work toward putting all this together and understanding the larger issues that frame such reports. I view my role as providing the linkages that keep the discussion moving forward and the kind of contextualization necessary for students to make connections between the article and what we have been discussing in class.

Although the particular article selected gives each discussion its own momentum, the following issues surface with some frequency:

... the conditions of international news reporting (how considerations of profit, deadlines, and editorial policies structure such articles, the information they contain, and the perspectives they employ [Lacy and Simon 1993; Seib 1997; Verschueren 1985]);

... the nature of writing and representation (including general discussion on the deconstruction of texts, the nature of objectivity, and the idea that bias rests in selection and omission as much in overt statements of opinion);

... the world as a chaotic place (that many of these articles portray the groups under consideration as entirely uniform and self-contained by overlooking internal variation and social mixing, while allowing single individuals to speak for the group as a whole);

... the world as a generic place (that many of these stories adopt a verbal shorthand, replacing cultural and historical specificity with stock phrases that do not lead us to think in any new way about the events they describe);

... an essentialist view of diversity (that many of these articles portray the groups under consideration as entirely uniform and self-contained by overlooking internal variation and social mixing, while allowing single individuals to speak for the group as a whole);

... connections to the U.S. (that with a little thought, we can identify ways in which this situation might connect to our personal lives and to the position of the U.S. in the global arena, connections that underscore the relevance of understanding international news and undercut the tendency of many articles to describe the world as a disconnected place in which each region moves largely under its own momentum);

126

... why most Americans do not read the international news section of the paper (that the reason many Americans do not regularly read such articles may lie as much in the articles as in the non-readers, a point that most students find quite empowering).

After you have worked through such issues, students are primed to want to know more about the situation. It is at this point that the background research you have done can most usefully be brought forward. Bringing in your expertise too early can put an end to student examination of the article. By this point in he exercise, however, students have reached an understanding of what is missing and are often eager to fill in the gaps. After telling them what I have learned about the situation and how I learned it, I find it fruitful to conclude the exercise by connecting it to the rest of the course. Explicitly identifying what anthropology offers for thinking through such situations gives students the final piece they need to read not only between the lines, but on a different page altogether.

References Cited

Bonwell, C.C. and T. E. Sutherland
1996. The Active Learning Continuum: Choosing Activities to Engage Students in the Classroom. In *Using Active Learning in College Classes: a Range of Options for Faculty*. T.E. Sutherland and C. C. Bonwell, eds. San Francisco CA: Jossey-Bass, pp 3-16.

Brookfield, S.D. and S. Preskill
1999. *Discussion as a Way of Teaching: Tools and Techniques for Democratic Classrooms*. San Francisco CA: Jossey-Bass.

King, A.
1994. Inquiry as a Tool in Critical Thinking. In *Changing College Classrooms: New Teaching and Learning Strategies for an Increasingly Complex World*. D.F. Halpern, ed. San Francisco CA: Jossey-Bass.

Lacy, S. and T.F. Simon
1993. *The Economics and Regulation of United States Newspapers*. Norwood NJ: Ablex.

Nanda, S.
1997. Close Encounters of the Third Kind: Selected Themes, Resources, and Strategies in Teaching Cultural Anthropology." In *The Teaching of Anthropology: Problems, Issues, and Decisions*. C.P. Kottak, J.J. White, R .H. Furlow, and P.C. Rice, eds. Mountain View CA: Mayfield Publishing Company, pp 113-126.

Seib, P.M.
1997. *Headline Diplomacy: How News Coverage Affects Foreign Policy*. Westport CT: Praeger.

Verschueren, J.
1985. *International News Reporting: Megapragmatic Metaphors and the U-2*. Amsterdam: John Benjamins.

The Cultural Dialog Project (CDP): Approaching Ethnographic Texts Through Playwriting and Performance

Mark Pedelty

Victor Turner pioneered the use of theatrical techniques in the anthropology classroom, intending to "put students more fully inside" the cultures they study (1986:146). However, such techniques are still not widely used and tend to be restricted to the graduate level. Nevertheless, those anthropologists who have experimented with performance techniques for anthropology undergraduates – such as Patricia Rice's "Ethno-Improvisation" technique (1985) – have discovered that students respond well to such exercises.

Many undergraduates are not yet enculturated into the academic world of text-and-talk and have a hard time learning through reading, lecture, and discussion alone. Outside the classroom, they live a multi-mediated and multi-sensory existence, yet inside it the world is often reduced to verbal discourse. This exercise, the Cultural Dialog Project (CDP), attempts to involve other sensory dimensions in order to provide a fuller sense of the ethnographic experience as a lived phenomenon, while bringing the text back to life. The CDP encourages students to imagine ethnography as an oral, aural, and even kinesthetic encounter. Perhaps more importantly, it gets them to do the reading.

In order to complete the CDP, I ask students in introductory cultural anthropology courses to write and perform a fictional dialog based on one ethnographic article from Spradley and McCurdy's *Conformity and Conflict* (2000). Dialogic writing helps students to develop and apply ethnographic imagination, encourages them to think critically about the ethnographic encounter, and pushes them to develop a deeper understanding of the ethnographic text. Students then perform these dialogs, providing a dramatic reading of the script on the day in which the referent reading is assigned. The dramatic reading performances provide an entry point into discussions about the reading.

In addition to the fictionalized dialog, a short process paper is also required that allows students to demonstrate their full understanding of the chosen article through more traditional expository prose. In the process paper, students are required to explain how their plot, characters, and dialog relate to the basic thesis and central concept(s) presented in the article. This reduces anxieties over grading and frees students to take greater risks in writing their fictional dialog. Likewise, the process paper allows the instructor to apply consistent and explicit social science criteria in assessing the project, rather than grading on the artistic merits of the dialog (although an artful dialog will be more successful in dealing with the cultural questions raised in the article).

Together, the dialog and process paper comprise the CDP. The project is developed in four steps: initiation, dialog workshop, writing, and performance. Because the dialog performances are designed to enhance the daily reading discussions, it is best to have the CDP completed during the first few weeks of the term.

Step 1: Introducing and Initiating the Project

On the first day of class each student chooses an ethnographic article from *Conflict and Conformity*. Since they will not have read the articles yet, ask them to go through the reading schedule on the syllabus and choose a set of article titles that catch their eye. Instruct them to read the article abstracts outside of class and come to the next class with two or three options. By asking them to choose more than one option, a broad range of articles can be covered over the course of the term by the class as a whole.

Also on the first day hand out at least one example dialog and process paper. When first starting the project, it is helpful to create your own dialog, both in order to gain a sense of the project first hand and to create an example for students. The first time I assigned this project, I wrote a dialog based on George Gmelch's "Lessons From the Field" (2000), one of the first reading assignments for the term. Exemplary student papers can be given out in future iterations of the course, perhaps by incorporating them into a course reading packet. Providing students with multiple sample dialogs, plots, and premises will help them realize that there are multiple ways to approach the assignment, rather than one ideal type or single expectation on the part of the instructor.

In addition to explaining the general goals of the dialog, explain the process paper as well. Emphasize that they will not be graded on the artistic qualities of the dialog *per se*, but rather will be assessed on how well they do three things: (1) engage important thematic and conceptual elements of the article; (2) summarize the article in the process paper; and (3) explicate the goals of their dialog in relation to the central issues raised in the article.

Step 2: Dialog Workshop

On the second day, model the sample dialog with the aid of a few willing student performers. Read the stage directions while students read the dialog. This will do the double duty of giving students an idea of what the reading performances will look like and, at the same time, provides a point of entry into class discussion concerning the article for that day. In other words, the dialog writing, performances, and workshops are not an "add on" to the course, taking valuable time away from essential course activities, but instead provide an effective means of exploring course readings and concepts.

On the third day, have student groups create plot outlines for the daily reading. I assign Laura Bohannan's "Shakespeare in the Bush" (2000) for this exercise. Each group needs to choose an issue in Bohannan to illustrate. They then decide upon characters and a plot that would engage the thesis and a central issue or concept from the article. The creative genius of collaboration is often evidence in this exercise. Students who would play it fairly safe on their own (e.g., the Bohannan and Tiv dialog, virtually verbatim from the article) will often take greater risks when working collaboratively. For example, more than one group has chosen to present a dialog between the Ghost of Hamlet's Father and the Tiv "Omen." Although not seeming to do so on the surface, the latter premise, if executed well, could meet and exceed the expectations of the assignment. Although that premise does not present a direct representation of the ethnographic encounter, the conceptual misunderstanding between Bohannan and the Tiv is foregrounded nevertheless, as are the key concepts of naïve realism, cultural relativism, and ethnocentrism. Students will not actually write dialogs or perform the plot outlines they develop in the workshop exercise, but they will have started thinking about issues of plot, character, and premise, which they can then apply when they begin writing their own CDP dialogs.

On day four, now that students have read their articles, ask them to discuss their individual CDP dialogs in small groups. Each student should provide the group with a quick summary of the chosen article and identify the conceptual or thematic question to be brought out in the dialog. If the student has plot, character, and dialog ideas, they should be shared with the group as well. The group should then brainstorm and help each other develop dialog ideas.

Step 3: Writing

Students should share their rough drafts with each other. Ideally, the students working on the same article will be able to trade their papers and provide each other with detailed feedback. I ask them to use a copy of the same assessment form (see below) that I will later use to grade the CDPs.

It is useful to require students to turn in drafts of their CDPs to the instructor after receiving peer feedback. They will want to know that they are going in the right direction, or may need a creative jump-start if they have been unable to develop a plot on their own. In order to develop a premise, plot, characters, and dialog ideas, I encourage them to focus on the thesis and major concepts presented in the article. However, I do not require that they

feature the anthropologist and informants found in the article. Recent examples from *Conflict and Conformity* where students used other characters to bring out themes in the reading include: an encounter between Brazilian and U.S. students discussing "race," a U.S. tourist attending a friend's wedding in India, an Islamic student-teacher explaining her clothing to curious kindergartners, Nuer immigrants of different generations colliding over proper codes of behavior, among others. Some choose to enhance scenes that are already present in the ethnographic text, while others add additional scenes in order to further explore issues raised by the ethnographic author.

I tend to "frontload" the course with this project, saving other activities and assignments for later. That way, actual in-class readings can begin fairly early in the term. Also, this is excellent early training if they are going to be conducting ethnographic projects themselves. They will have at least an initial sense of what an ethnographer actually does in the field and will become familiar with the types of research questions that guide anthropological research.

Step 4: Performance

I allow students to choose one of two performance techniques. They may either present a live dramatic reading or a videotaped reading. Naturally, many student authors are nervous about oral presentation, even with a written script. Students for which English is a second language are particularly nervous. I would no more force every student to act than I would require that they sing, dance, or play a musical instrument. I do ask them to find a way to present the dialog that goes beyond simple reading or recitation, however. Those interested in live performance select willing "actors" from the class to perform their roles while the author introduces the dialog and reads the stage directions. Most of the actors in my class are culled from the Performance Group, a small collaborative group of performers who have chosen to undertake a fully memorized intercultural performance in order to fulfill their course research requirements. There are always at least a few students willing to perform in other's dramatic readings.

Video can further reduce performance anxiety by giving students the opportunity to create a presentation in the relative safety of their own homes. They can put trusted friends through multiple takes until the video presentation reaches a presentable state. I grade the presentations based on organization and clarity, not on the artistic merits of the performance itself. However, creativity and quality exceeding these basic expectations is rewarded.

Before students start presenting their dialogs, I have one last presentation workshop. While small groups discuss their upcoming presentations, the Performance Group works on developing a model dramatic reading. I use the first scene from Diane Glancy's "Truth Teller" (1997) for this. It is a narrative about intercultural contact and colonialism in Minnesota. Once again, this does double duty of presenting a model reading and leading into the day's topic.

After prepping and completing the model performance, the class performs a critical review. In order to model this, I ask students to critique a recent lecture. First, I ask them to tell me three things that I did well in the lecture. Next I ask for three areas that I

should work on for the future. If you ask students to start with criticism, only the very bravest among them will participate. Having demonstrated that constructive criticism is to be welcomed by the public performer, and having modeled the process of taking such feedback, I then ask the class to do likewise with the model dialog performers. I supplement this peer feedback with my own suggestions for the upcoming presentations. In addition to assuring clear and useful presentations throughout the term, workshops like this help build student's oral communication skills, an essential set of skills that are too often neglected in the college curriculum.

From that point on, readings are introduced by student dialog performances every day. I designate small groups, on a rotating basis, to generate statements and raise questions based on dialog performance. That facilitates entry into class discussion concerning the basic thesis of the article and moves the class toward consideration of more subtle aspects of the article author's argument. I then ask the day's response group to provide a written peer assessment of the presentation.

The actual assignment guide is presented in the Appendix as it appears in the course syllabus.

Conclusions

Considerable attention has been given to the parallels between fictional and ethnographic narratives in recent decades. It stands to reason that fiction would provide an effective means of exploring ethnographic questions in anthropology courses. Likewise, the discipline's growing interest in performance and body politics makes this exercise timely and useful as a teaching tool. Rather than simply reading and talking about an ethnographic text, the CDP encourages students to creatively and critically engage with the ethnographic text in order to bring the ethnographic encounter back to life in the classroom.

References Cited

Bohannan, L.
  2000. Shakespeare in the Bush. In *Conformity and Conflict*. Spradley, J. and D. McCurdy eds, pp 35-44. Boston MA: Allyn and Bacon.

Glancy, D.
  1997. Truth Teller. In *War Cries*, pp 253-271. Duluth MN: Holy Cow Press.

Gmelch, G.
  2000. Lessons from the Field. *In Conformity and Conflict*, Spradley, J. and D. McCurdy, eds. pp 45-55. Boston MA: Allyn and Bacon.

Rice, P.
  1985. Ethno-Improvisation: A Technique for Teaching Cultural Emotions. *Anthropology and Education Quarterly* 16:280-287.

Spradley, J. and D. McCurdy
  2000 *Conformity and Conflict: Readings in Cultural Anthropology*. Boston MA: Allyn and Bacon.

Turner, V.
  1986. *The Anthropology of Performance*. NY: Performing Arts Journal Publications.

CDP Writing Guide

Read your chosen article during the first two weeks of class and start writing a scene based on an encounter between the author (ethnographer) and an informant or informants. We will develop these plays in class, working on issues of plot development, characterization, and dialog. The goal is to capture a sense of the ethnographic encounter while dealing critically with the central thesis of the article. The entire paper will be at least seven pages long, including a process paper. In your process paper, state the thesis of the article. Explain how your plot, characters, and dialog deal with the author's thesis. List and define the major concepts in the article and explain how at least one of those concepts is presented in your play. The CDP paper will be worth 20% of your final grade. See the CDP Assessment Form for specific grading criteria.

Technical Suggestions and Format Guide

... Start by presenting the characters and a synopsis of the plot.
... Provide a full citation for your article in AAA style. Use the following example:

Gmelch, George
  2000 Lessons From the Field. *In* Conformity and Conflict, Spradley James and David W.
   McCurdy, eds. Pp 45-55. Boston: MA: Allyn and Bacon.

... Always capitalize character names.
... Use regular print for all dialog and italics for background narrative and directions.
... Put italicized direction in parentheses if it is presented inside the dialog section.
... Use this format:

  PRINCIPAL: The award for volunteer services will be given to James Farham.
  MARGARET: (*to the committee*) But, that jerk isn't even eligible!

CDP Assessment Form

I use this form to provide feedback on drafts and their final project. Students also use this form to provide each other with feedback on rough drafts of the dialog.

... Basics: is the paper at least 7 pages long, spell-checked, double-spaced and correctly formatted?

... Does the author deal with the thesis, a major issue, and a key concept or concepts from the article? Does the author provide the reader with critical insights into the subject matter of the article?

... How might the author improve the following: plot, characters, dialog?

... Overall, how effective was the scene and what are its major strengths and weaknesses?

... Does the process paper clearly identify and concisely summarize the argument presented in the ethnographic record?

... Does the process paper clearly identify and concisely summarize the argument presented in the ethnographic article?

... Does the author list and define a major course concept and explain how the concept is represented in the play?

... The main goal of this assignment is to think critically about the encounter between anthropologist and an informant. Overall, how well does this project (the play and the process paper) demonstrate the ethnographic encounter?

Teaching Culture Through Life History: The Spradley Approach

David McCurdy

In the mid 1970s, James Spradley developed a course called "Cultural Life History." The course was distinguished by several features:

... the use of students' own life experiences during childhood (between the ages of 6 and 12 usually) as a source of data;

... a focus on culture, not personality or the ways students personally handled life;

... an approach designed to elicit small, detailed cultural rules, categories, and meanings as well as broader cultural themes in the everyday lives of students;

... a structured set of tasks each of which helped students recall parts of their lives in detail and each of which could be used by itself as part of other courses;

... class presentations of weekly assignments using overhead transparencies;

... and lots of writing.

This account is based on Spradley's course notes, my participation in four class sessions Spradley gave to interested faculty several months before his death in 1982, and what students have said about the method as they experienced it. Most of the specific instructions presented below are paraphrased or taken directly from his course notes. Since there is not room to present the whole course, the emphasis will be on the course structure and a few of the specific "recollection tasks" that occurred as part of the course that can easily be used in introductory or upper division anthropology course settings.

Background

Spradley developed the cultural life history course for several reasons. First, he had written a life history of a Kwakiutl chief and had experience with the approach. Second, the cultural life history method had several teaching advantages. Students could become their own informants, avoiding problems associated with finding informants and checking with Human Subjects Research Committees. Students would know about their own lives and enjoy talking about themselves. They would enjoy the sense of discovery and nostalgia that accompanies recovering the past. They would also discover as they listened to each other discuss class assignments, that many cultural aspects of their earlier lives were similar to those of their classmates, but that there were also cultural differences associated with gender and with regional, ethnic, and class backgrounds.

The method presented two potential difficulties. First, American students are individualistic (a cultural characteristic) and surrounded by psychological explanations for behavior. Would a life history class simply devolve into group therapy sessions for the expression of emotions and the relating of past personal trauma? Spradley tried to counter this tendency by warning students not to let this happen, and by emphasizing the social nature of the concept of culture. He devised weekly recollection tasks that asked students to look for **cultural** categories, rules, and themes in their lives.

Second, there was the problem of recollection. Just as cultural informants may have trouble remembering events and describing their worlds when they are interviewed in ethnographic research, life history students might find it difficult to recall the past in detail as they sought to construct their own past experiences. To deal with this problem, Spradley did two things. He divided his course into "recollection tasks" around particular areas of life, such as space, eating, play, and kinship. The rationale for this structure was that students would remember more detailed information if contexts were defined more specifically. (An added advantage is that class members worked on the same kind of task together each week, which facilitated class discussion and interest.) A second approach was to stimulate recall by having students take "left brained excursions." Spradley had students close their eyes and try to imagine themselves in past contexts, then write notes about what they had remembered.

The Cultural Life History Method

The following, now written in the present tense, are some of the steps used to structure the cultural life history method.

Step 1: Define Culture. Since a goal of the cultural life history method is to discover culture through the analysis of an individual's past, it is first imperative to define culture clearly. The exercises described here use a cognitive definition (you may use any definition you wish) that says culture is a kind of **knowl edge** that is shared, thus social, learned, and that is used by people to generate behavior and interpret experience. It is the system of knowledge people use to classify their worlds and give meaning to them.

The definition implies that there is also something called **personal knowledge**. This is knowledge that is not socially shared, that all of us have as we attach special meanings to categories based on our individual experience.

The cultural life history method seeks to discover the cultural, not the personal, knowledge revealed in individual student experiences, although personal knowledge and strategies surface regularly in the process of relating data.

A second consideration is to describe where shared knowledge is likely to be found in day to day living. One answer is that cultural knowledge is shared by members of groups and/or among participants in particular social settings. For example, students will recall events that happened in their families at home, routines followed by friends at play and in the more structured context of school. All these settings have cultural elements that can be discovered as life history students recall and analyze them.

Step 2: Choose One or More Recollection Tasks. The next step is to assign one or more recollection tasks to students. Recollection tasks are processes that help students remember particular areas of life, such as play and eating. You may want to choose only one for an introductory class or more if cultural life history is a major course goal. The original course listed the following tasks but you can think up others that may be more useful.

... Construct a Life Chart with the major time periods and marker events that structured your life in a designated past period.
... Outline the cultural patterns of summer.
... Draw a primary turf map.
... List your play activities.
... Describe an average day of eating.
... Make a chart of all the groups you belonged to and list your friends.
... Describe your family and kin.
... Describe earning or getting, and spending

money.

... Make a list of all the actions adults used to reward or punish you.

... Describe ritual in your life.

Each of these tasks can be done alone. All have several requirements listed under them in the original course outline although there is only space here to look at two or three. Take **eating practices**, for example. The requirements for this task include the following:

... Make a list of all the regular and special eating times that have occurred during growing up. Use native (folk or inside) terms when possible.

... Select a period of your childhood you remember well and describe in a three to four page paper the eating customs in your family for a typical day. Include types of foods, seating arrangements at the table and food preferences.

... Make a list of cultural rules, both explicit sayings made by your parents and the more tacit do's and don'ts that governed eating behavior in your family. Put the explicit rules in quotation marks.

A second example is the "**turf map**" task above. It asks class members to:

... Make a list of all the places, locations, routes, and other territorial units of which you had a working knowledge. Where did you live? What places did you go to play? What routes did you take?

... Make one or more sketch maps of your primary turf when you were six to twelve years old (or some other period). Identify the main features of the landscape, the places that held significance for you, and locate important events on the map.

... Write a three or four page paper in which you identify some of the cultural themes (with examples) that influenced your use of this primary turf.

A final example is **patterns of play**. Requirements for this task are as follows:

... Make a list of all the play events and activities you have engaged in during the life period you have chosen to recall.

... Write a three or four page paper that identifies and gives examples of cultural themes underlying the patterns of play during your childhood. Tell us how you played as a child. What things did you enjoy? Whom did you play with? What was the meaning of the play?

Step 3: Explain Cultural Themes and Cultural Content. Prepare students to analyze their life history data for cultural content. It is difficult to give a neat formula for spotting cultural information in life history material, but there are often hints about what might be cultural. For example, one student writing about the average day of eating noted that family members could not start eating until "mother lifted her fork." This was a family cultural rule. Another student noted in the kinship task that his father had a special chair. Family rules said that you could sit in the chair if he was not there, but had to vacate it if he came into the room. Other examples included the rules for who cleared the table and who loaded the dishwasher, who took out the garbage, who had to mow the lawn, and how the phone was to be answered.

Students may recall unusual information that is cultural during the course. One student drew a turf map of his neighborhood. He indicated the houses of his friends, the route he took to school (this was before bussing), and a variety of other things. Surprisingly, he also correctly drew maps of every alley in his urban neighborhood. When he labeled each, it turned out that alleys were where he and his friends could ride their bicycles (the parental cultural rule forbad riding in the street), and that each alley had special characteristics that were recognized and shared by his group of friends, including where the good puddles would form after a rain, where you could slide your bike sideways, and where you could set up jumps. These are all examples of cultural knowledge.

Discovering cultural themes is more difficult. Note that a cultural theme must run through and connect the actions, beliefs, and events that students recall. For example, one student attended an open school. A cultural theme that ran through her experience there was the requirement that students had to choose what they wanted to do each day, and that they didn't have to do what anyone else did. The theme was expressed when students had to decide on such things as subjects to study, daily activities, and how to relate to others. It affected teachers by preventing them from directing students. A second theme in the school was equality. No one had the right to tell anyone else what to do. On the other hand, equality was tempered by the theme of cooperation, so students were supposed to go along with what others wanted. Again, these are insights about culture that can easily come out of the life history experience.

Step 4: Have Students Prepare Assignments. Each recollection task involves at least two "product" tasks. One is to prepare a chart or visual device to show in class. For example, students present their turf maps to each other and describe the important areas on them. The second is a three or four page description of some aspect or all, depending on what you ask them to do, of the recollection assignment. These can be read in class and/or handed in to the instructor. If you decide to have students do several recollection tasks, the weekly papers can be connected to form a final, much longer paper.

Step 5: Decide on a Final Product. If your class is asked to do only one recollection task, the final product might be the class presentation and discussion, and the short descriptive paper outlined in the task requirements. Or you might have your own ideas about how to present the task material. If the class is to do more than one recollection task, you can assign a final paper or presentation that asks for a longer paper, or for a paper that looks at the similarities and differences in the life history cultures presented in class.

Final Observations

Experience with the term-long course as it was taught for years yielded several observations. Students came to see that their parents were often acting culturally, not personally, toward them. Several students who had left home actually reconciled with their parents after taking the course. Students also came to see their present lives in cultural terms. They began to realize that they continued to use cultural knowledge to navigate their daily lives. Finally, because they learned so much about each other, classmates tended to form strong social bonds. Students referred to themselves as "lifers" and often came to form the active core of the department anthropology club.

Using Values Orientation to Understand the Role of Culture in Cross-Cultural Communication

Anne E. Campbell

Overview

The values orientations framework and five activity-based strategies discussed below were developed to supplement introductory anthropology courses in the following areas: cross-cultural communication and understanding, language and culture, and contemporary U.S. cultures. In these courses, students examine culture and the ways in which it impacts on inter-ethnic and cross-cultural group relations, as well as institutional structures within the U.S. Students in the classes often have had introductory cultural anthropology, and represent a variety of undergraduate majors. Although the students have studied "culture," many of them tell me that they "don't have a culture." They don't think of themselves as cultural beings. They have never closely examined the complex conceptual frameworks that guide and shape their perceptions of the world and their understandings of how things are "supposed to be." Before they can effectively analyze and understand cross-cultural conflict, for example, I believe they need to understand themselves and the ways in which their values orientations shape how they perceive, understand, and evaluate others.

To get at this understanding, I have found the values orientation taxonomy to be a good beginning. It is comprehensive and has applicability to a variety of areas in which cross-cultural conflict can occur. It is used extensively in cross-cultural psychology, as well as in international training and development programs. Although I have developed the values orientation taxonomy activities for upper division courses, they could be used in small to medium sized introductory cultural anthropology courses, with the activities spread throughout the term.

The activity-based strategies detailed below provide a framework for examining individual, as well as micro and macro group cultures. They also develop students' ability to use the taxonomy as a tool to analyze and understand cross-cultural communication. The first strategy sets the stage for discussions throughout the term. The students work together to develop class definitions for each value orientation and to complete their own values orientation taxonomies. Through in-class sharing, discussion, and comparison of their taxonomies, the students begin to develop a sense of themselves as cultural beings with deeply held values orientations. They realize that they have been shaped by social circumstance, family, community, and life experiences. They begin to understand that individuals, with different experiences, may have different, valid, and just as deeply held orientations. The second and third strategies provide guided practice and develop the students' ability to use the taxonomy as a tool to analyze and compare ways in which values orientations influence individuals in a variety of cross-cultural situations. For the fourth, students work in groups to synthesize data gathered individually and to evaluate the taxonomy as a tool in cross-cultural research. The fifth provides an opportunity to use the taxonomy to research contemporary issues in cross-cultural communication. A final strategy is provided that can be used in an upper division course on language and culture.

139

Conceptual Framework

A major premise underlying the chronological development of these strategies is that culture is not just an important factor influencing an individual's overt patterns of behavior and language use (surface culture). It also influences how an individual perceives and interprets another person's verbal and non-verbal behaviors (deep culture). By understanding the values orientations that comprise one's own cultural system, individuals can learn to identify ways in which those orientations predispose one to perceive, interpret, and evaluate other people's responses in social situations. By understanding one's own value orientations system (deep culture), an individual can then work to understand another's value orientations. In so doing, greater cross-cultural understanding and communication can occur.

The "Values Orientations Worksheet" that students use (see appendix) was developed by Clemens Hallman in 1983. It was based on the taxonomy of cultural value orientations developed by Conden and Yousef (1975) in *An Introduction to Intercultural Communication*. The original taxonomy, based on extensive cross-cultural research, was developed in 1961 by Florence Kluckhohn and Frank Strodtbeck. A series of changes occurred between the original taxonomy and the Hallman worksheet.

The Strategies/Activities

I begin the course where these strategies/activities will be used with a small group activity in which students discuss four questions:

... what is culture?
... what is language?
... what is the relationship between the two?
... how do these two influence cross-cultural communication?

As a result of this discussion, the class develops definitions for key concepts that will be studied during the term. This also provides me with an informal assessment of the students' background knowledge. We then complete Strategy #1 and develop definitions for the values orientations. These activities provide a framework for the rest of the term as students develop and deepen their understandings of course concepts and materials. In parenthesis after each activity is the amount of in-class discussion time I normally allocate. Times vary depending on student background knowledge and course topics, and less time can be assigned for some activities, if needed. I use a total of approximately 15 hours (or one hour a week in a three credit course) during the term for these activities, but they could be done in as little as 10 hours.

#1: Definitions and Individual Taxonomies (4-6 hours). We begin by reading Condon and Yousef and use the "Values Orientations Worksheet" to develop class definitions for each orientation. The worksheet that students actually use for taxonomy assignments has space for writing underneath the categories and is six pages in length. Once students understand the values orientations, I ask them to decide where they would place themselves for each category of the taxonomy. As we discuss their individual taxonomies, we often find that no two people in the class have rated themselves exactly the same way. As we discuss reasons why, we develop a list that invariably includes the multiple factors influencing individual culture discussed by

James Banks (1994): ethnicity, gender, religion, geographical region, disability, social class, and "race."

#2: Chapter Application (2-3 hours). Students are assigned to one of four groups: members in each group read and analyze one of four chapters (4,5,6, or 7) in Stewart and Bennett's *American Cultural Patterns: A Cross-Cultural Perspective* (1991). I chose the book because each of the chapters illustrates different sections of the taxonomy. Stewart's first edition, published in 1971, was developed as a response to the growing need for training materials that would better prepare Peace Corps volunteers and other U.S. foreign service personnel for their overseas assignments. Using Kluckhohn and Strodtbeck's work, the first edition synthesized cross-cultural research and systematically compared "American" cultural patterns with those of other countries. Stewart and Bennett noted that primarily white, middle-and upper-class males were involved in overseas work. As a result, most of the research illustrated the values system of that particular group. That system is considered by cross-cultural training researchers to represent what is called "mainstream American culture."

Each group uses its assigned chapter to develop specific examples for categories on the taxonomy. Once the chapter analyses are completed, students are regrouped, this time so that each student in the new group has read a different chapter. Their task is to share what they learn with the others in the group. By the end of this activity, students have developed a comprehensive understanding of the taxonomy and have examples for all of the categories. Students then discuss ways in which "mainstream American culture" is alike or different from the other cultural groups discussed in the book. Students also compare their individual taxonomies that they completed earlier and identify ways in which their own values orientations are similar to or different from "mainstream American culture."

#3: Book Application. Students identify general cultural and ethnic groups that they would like to learn more about: African American, Native American, Asian American, Southwest Asian, Hispanic/Latino/a, and Eastern European groups, for example. Students then divide into groups. Each student individually selects, reads, and analyzes a book using the taxonomy. The book can be fiction or non-fiction, but it must be written by a member of the chosen group. The book can be representative of any group that falls within a general category. For example, in the Hispanic/Latino/a group, students might read books by Cuban, Puerto Rican, Mexican, Mexican American, or Chicano/a as well as modern Spanish authors. Or, in the Native American group, any number of authors from different tribes or nations could be represented. This activity has also worked well with gang-related studies and literature, gender studies, as well as with books about the deaf community.

Once students in each group have finished their book taxonomies, they discuss and compare them in class. It is here that they begin to see that although there may be many values orientations that are common to the different groups within a general category, there are also differences that are unique to each group because of its collective history and experiences. Additionally, when students read books such as *Migrant Souls* by Arturo Islas (1990) that deal with multiple generations, or when they are in groups where the books read were written at different points in history, students often find within-group changes in value orientations over time. These changes usually indicate either an increase in assimilation into the "American mainstream" or a withdrawal from the mainstream and a maintenance of the heritage cultural values. This activity helps students understand the concept that culture is not static, but changing, and that it is a cultural construct developed by a group as a result of their shared experiences and interactions with the world around them.

#4: Group Presentation (2-3 hours). Students in each group combine their book taxonomies and develop a presentation about what they learned. They develop a chart that compares and contrasts their general group with "mainstream American culture." They may also talk about within-group differences and reasons for those differences, or they may talk about generational shifts over time and the effects on family and community relationships.

#5: Understanding Conflict (2-3 hours). After the cultural group presentations, students usually feel comfortable using the taxonomy. To show the applicability of the taxonomy as a tool for understanding contemporary cultural groups and cross-cultural conflict, I then ask students to read newspapers for the next two weeks and develop a collection of articles that illustrate the cultural values orientations. If students are fluent in another language, I encourage them to read newspapers from other countries. At the end of two weeks the students share what they have found. They then write a reflective paper based on class discussions and readings they have done about the usefulness of the taxonomy for understanding cross-cultural communication and for providing insights into the resolution of cross-cultural conflict.

Additional Strategies: Linking Language and Culture

In a course on language and culture or cross-cultural communication, we examine the concept of language and the relationship between language and culture. We discuss issues of language loss or language maintenance, and the concepts of language as a resource, legal right, or problem. The linguistic histories of various groups within the U.S. are studied briefly.

As part of a final project, students are asked to find a specific example or situation in which cross-cultural miscommunication occurred or is on-going. The situation could be one related to a debate in their major area of study, it could be from their own experience, or from a situation reported in the newspaper. The situation must be researchable and one in which the cultural values and language use of the participants can be documented and analyzed. Movies that illustrate complex cross-cultural relationships can be used with approval from the instructor. The assignment is to analyze how language and culture influenced the ways in which participants understood and interpreted what happened and how their interpretations influenced their responses and proposals to resolve the situation. The students then develop strategies that are designed to improve communication between the participants and to reduce or solve the miscommunication and cross-cultural conflict illustrated in the situation.

References Cited

Banks, J.
   1994. *Multiethnic Education: Theory and Practice*, 3rd edition. Boston MA: Allyn and Bacon.

Condon, J. and F. Yousef
   1975. *An Introduction to Intercultural Communication*. Indianapolis IN: Bobbs-Merrill Educational Publishing.

Hallman, C.L.
   1983. *U.S. American Value Orientations: Cultural Monograph #4*. Gainesville FL: University of Florida Bilingual Multicultural Education Training Project for School Psychologists and Guidance Counselors.

Islas, A.
   1990. *Migrant Souls*. New York: Avon Books.

Kluckhohn, F.R. and F.L. Strodtbeck
   1961. *American Cultural Patterns: A Cross-Cultural Perspective*. Chicago: Intercultural Press.

Steward E.C.
   1972. *American Cultural Patterns: A Cross-Cultural Perspective*. Chicago: Intercultural Press.

Steward E. C. and M. Bennett
   1991. *American Cultural Patterns: A Cross-Cultural Perspective*, 2nd edition. Yarmouth ME: Intercultural Press, Inc.

Values Orientation Worksheet *

Name_____   Chapter # _____   Date _____

I. SELF
    A. **Individualism - Interdependence**
        1. Individualism   2. Individuality   3. Interdependence
    B. **Age**
        1. Youth   2. Middle Years   3. Old Age
    C. **Sex**
        1. Equality of Sexes   2. Female Superiority   3. Male Superiority
    D. **Activity**
        1. Doing   2. Being-in-becoming   3. Being

II. THE FAMILY
    A. **Relational Orientations**
        1. Individualistic   2. Collateral   3. Lineal
    B. **Authority**
        1. Democratic   2. Authority Centered   3. Authorization
    C. **Positional Role Behavior**
        1. Open   2. General   3. Specific
    D. **Mobility**
        1. High   2. Phasic   3. Low

III. SOCIETY
    A. **Social Reciprocity**
        1. Independence   2. Symmetrical-Obligatory   3. Complementary-Obligatory
    B. **Group Membership**
        1. Many Groups   2. Balance of No. 1 and 3   3. Few Groups
    C. **Intermediaries**
        1. No Intermediaries   2. Specialist Intermediaries   3. Essential Intermediaries
    D. **Formality**
        1. Informality   2. Selective Formality   3. Pervasive Formality
    E. **Property**
        1. Private   2. Utilitarian   3. Community

IV. HUMAN NATURE

A. **Rationality**

| 1. Rationality | 2. Intuitive | 3. Irrational |

B. **Good and Evil**

| 1. Good | 2. Good and Evil | 3. Evil |

C. **Happiness and Pleasure**

| 1. Happiness as Goal | 2. Inextricable Bond of Happiness and Sadness | 3. Life is Mostly Sadness |

D. **Mutability**

| 1. Change, Growth, Learning | 2. Some change | 3. Unchanging |

V. NATURE

A. **Relationship of Man and Nature**

| 1. Man Dominates | 2. Man/Nature in Harmony | 3. Nature Dominates |

B. **Ways of Knowing Nature**

| 1. Abstract | 2. Induction/Deduction | 3. Specific |

C. **Structure of Nature**

| 1. Mechanistic | 2. Spiritual | 3. Organic |

D. **Concept of Time**

| 1. Future | 2. Past | 3. Present |

IV. THE SUPERNATURAL

A. **Relationship of Man and Supernatural**

| 1. Man as God | 2. Pantheism | 3. Supernatural in Control |

B. **Meaning of Life**

| 1. Physical, Material Goals | 2. Intellectual Goals | 3. Spiritual Goals |

C. **Providence**

| 1. Good in Life Unlimited | 2. Balance of Good and Misfortune | 3. Good in Life Limited |

D. **Knowledge of Cosmic Order**

| 1. Order Comprehensible | 2. Faith and Reason | 3. Mysterious/Unknowable |

* worksheet based on Hallman (1983).

Teaching as Theatre

Charles F. Urbanowicz

The strategy discussed in this article is about the use of a theatrical device to encourage students to ask questions and raise problems about some aspects of anthropological theory. A few years ago, I decided to appear in class as a theorist, in this case, Charles Darwin, and present his (now my character's) thoughts about his research and theory and his response to some of his critics in a way that would more closely involve students. Appearing as Darwin, in costume (and shaved head) is not a new idea: zoology professor Richard Eakin portrayed great scientists in his classes at Berkeley in the 60s and 70s. (See Eakin1975.) I have presented Darwin in the first person since 1990. Students could listen to Darwin as a person, and ask him questions about his theory and contributions to science. Recently, I converted the presentation to video tape and show several visuals to my classes that demonstrate Darwin's place in 19th century scientific thought. Students seem to like this approach and display increased involvement and enthusiasm about theory. The personal approach takes them beyond the written word.

I believe the theatrical device works well because the theater-like classroom creates an ephemeral sense of intimacy for both the instructor/performer and student audience. Although a theatrical performance lasts only for an afternoon or evening and ends, the classroom theater can create a sense of intimacy that may last for weeks or years, creating a positive atmosphere throughout the rest of a term.

Since different anthropology courses highlight different theories and theorists, you will have to make a choice about whom to portray in front of your class. I suggest you find an appropriate individual, one whose life, career, and theory is important and well known. Remove that individual from the academic pedestal of words and, representing him or her, share with your students the problems and processes of research and scholarship that went into making that person an important contributor to the discipline. I suggest that you stress the "context" within which the person worked, so place your individual in the milieu of the time.

Make sure there is enough information about the individual you intend to portray. For example, I can show that Darwin's work was highly creative. Born into a wealthy family, he was an individual of leisure. With ample time, he wrote a great deal about his life, including the development of his thinking and the impact it had on his life. As I play Darwin, I mention that various people were important in my (his) life: Hooker (the botanist), Huxley (scientist often referred to as "Darwin's Bulldog"), Lyell (geology), Wallace (naturalist), and Wilberforce (theologian). Darwin was also written about extensively, making it easier to see his impact on others during his lifetime. So as I play Darwin, I can also comment on the material that was written about me (him).

When I first became Darwin, I simply wore my academic robe to class (and obtained a typical black "bowler" hat from a local costume shop). As my Darwin evolved, I eventually shaved my head, acquired some professional costumes from the Theatre Arts Department on campus, and became Darwin as an older individual. I've had a beard for thirty years and for the videotape of Darwin I let it grow longer than usual and used gray tint to make me look older. Although you can make yourself up to look older or younger and even change your sex with a lot of make up, it is more difficult to play a five foot tall Margaret Mead if you are six foot tall. It is easier to choose an individual to match your physiognomy and age.

I present Darwin in the first person, maintaining character throughout: the classroom is a theatre setting and one is always in character. I speak of my supportive family, especially my younger and older sisters, how I went to university and graduated, but did not know what I wanted to do with my life, and how I lucked out. Students who are about to graduate are often amazed that Darwin did not have his life picked out for him in advance. In some respects, he "stumbled" into his career, but he faced it with an open and inquisitive mind.

I discuss my marriage to my cousin Ms. Emma Wedgwood (and one can get into some traditional anthropological kinship relationships then), and then I talk about leaving "dirty" London for the bucolic countryside. I discuss my professional papers, my extensive correspondence, and the children than Emma and I had: Emma bore ten children, but only seven survived beyond childhood. I discuss the impact of my various scientific publications, more than twenty-in-all, the reactions of the citizens of the time, and eventually I speak of my death and my burial in Westminster Abbey. In brief, I become Darwin for the day.

Students respond by asking me "how long did it take you to prepare for this?" and "was it a lot of work," and "how did Darwin develop his theory?" I respond by pointing

out that "work can be fun" and it has taken many years to become Darwin, and I am still working at it. I also point out that Darwin developed his theory by building on the work of others and thinking about what he observed in the world of nature. We discuss the communication techniques of the day and students are amazed that so much correspondence is available and that Darwin was such a meticulous note-taker and observer of nature. We discuss the need for research and the importance of "time" in allowing ideas to develop.

To prepare for your performance, read, synthesize, travel, and create your own understanding of the people you are to portray. Where and how did they live and what did they do to become recognized? What was the creative process they experienced as they matured and with whom did they interact during their lifetimes? For example, I have read most of Darwin's publications and correspondence. Indeed I discovered that Darwin was called "Bobby" when he was a young man and "Philos" later by Captain Robert FitzRoy of the HMS Beagle. I really needed to become an expert on this literature. I learned, for example, that there are different editions of *The Origin of Species* and that they vary over time as Darwin reworked them and added to them. I have visited Darwin's home in England and sailed through the Galapagos Islands, which were so important to his scientific insights.

In short, I found that the theatrical approach is a manageable and enjoyable (for both instructor and students) way to introduce and discuss the work of a theorist who is important to our discipline. How you work that performance out, how you involve the audience, and which points you stress will be a matter for you to develop for yourself. But for me, at least, the approach changes the tenor of the classroom and engages students in a way that lecturing, reading, and discussion cannot manage.

Reference Cited

Eakin, R.M.
   1975. *Great Scientists Speak Again.* University of California Press.

"Flags"
The Power of Patriotism and Nationalism
The Arbitrariness of Symbols
And Signification:
A Classroom Exercise that'll Wake'em Up

Dickie Wallace

This is a classroom exercise for introductory level anthropology classes that conveys the importance of symbols in culture and the arbitrariness of their signification by leading students to unwittingly create important symbolic objects. Furthermore, it demonstrates the power of national identification and patriotic loyalty by provoking students to destroy (or almost destroy) what is quite possibly a very cherished symbol to them.

What to Do

Pass out two pieces of 8½ x 11 inch paper that you have recycled from the bin next to your local copier, ideally with some useless text on one side (I once grabbed a handful of paper from my own recycle-paper stash and realized that I was passing around parts of a draft of my Master's thesis). If you forget to get paper ahead of time, just ask your students to take two sheets of blank paper out of their notebooks without anything important on the other side.

Ask the students to hold one piece of paper horizontally in front of them (i.e., "landscape", as opposed to "portrait") and then to draw a large circle in the middle of the paper. Next, tell everyone to take the paper and put it on the floor. As they look at you queryingly, ask them to step on their paper, shuffle their feet back and forth and rip up the paper into tiny bits in the process. Some

people will do this with abandon, but a few will only do so reservedly, as they try to figure out what is really going on.

With the ripped papers left on the floor, ask them to take the second sheet of paper and to hold it as they did before and in the upper left quadrant, draw as many stars of fairly uniform size as fast as they can, filling in that whole quadrant. Walk around the room and encourage them to scribble them in quickly. Tell them if they never learned how to do five-pointed stars in grade school, they can just do asterixes or some star-like squiggles as fast as possible. I usually make some comments about this, like, "Dang, did you come to college for this?" and "Isn't kindergarten fun," anything to get a light, silly atmosphere.

After a half-minute or so of this, hopefully most of the students will have some scrawls filling up that quarter of the paper, so then ask them then to draw a bunch of parallel lines horizontally as fast as possible in the remaining three quadrants. Move quickly now, because by this time most of the class will have figured out that you've had them drawing what looks like a hasty sketch of an American flag. After a few seconds of horizontal line drawing, ask them quickly, yet with gravitas, if they would please put this paper on the floor, stomp on it, and rip it up.

Some students will tend to put the paper to the floor rather slowly and with some deliberation, while others will suddenly look resolved in their decision not to do it at all. In the confusion of this sometimes angry/tense/nervous moment, I recommend blowing the whistle on the whole thing abruptly and to tell your students that they can stop, or they can do what they want. Keep the excercise in their hands, let them decide what to do, and don't force anything.

Then discuss what you've just had them do (or almost do). Ask why some students hesitated. Depending on your comfort level in the classroom, ask individuals why they are still holding their papers. Ask them what was holding them back. Usually, some will say that they can't do it, that they just can't do it. Ask, what it is they think they were doing or why they can't do what you asked. And someone will usually say, it's the American flag, that's why.

I particularly like it when I can get my students to tell me that it is an American flag that they have created so I can explain that I didn't have them draw an American flag – I only asked them to hurriedly draw some lines and scribble some stars or asterixes or whatever. I ask them, by what process did this paper suddenly become something that they did not want to stomp on and rip up? I point out that it was just scrap paper with some useless words on the other side just a minute ago. What made this scrap suddenly so valuable, so sacred that they can't rip it up now? I ask them what they plan to do with this paper. Are they going to throw it out in private? Keep it in their notebooks for all eternity? When will it be something they can crinkle up and throw away?

As you talk about this with the students, pick up someone's ripped and dirty page from the floor. Ask them ask how it is that so many hesitated to stomp on an American flag, yet how is it that no one seems to have had any compunction about trashing a Japanese flag or a Bangladeshi flag? From this point, I discuss the emotions we attach to symbols and how some things as simple as

lines on paper can be interpreted in different contexts.

I usually am told by at least one person that I have been unfair and manipulative with this exercise and I don't deny it. I ask if anyone had an inkling that they were making a Japanese flag when they ripped it up and if it dawned on them as to what I was up to when they were scribbling stars. I make sure that we have time to discuss their concerns and in doing so, my discussants usually end up restating the power of American national/patriotic symbols which we then can deconstruct.

Ethnicity, Nationalism, Patriotism

I will have already set my students up for the idea of flags as national/nationalist symbols because in the immediately preceding class period, I talked about my world area of research, East Central Europe, and about the war in the former Yugoslavia. Among other things, I will have told them about Croat pride in the "ancient" symbols of their flag and how some Croats saw it as a symbol of resistance to the oppression of "Greater Serbia" symbolized by the Yugoslav flag. Conversely, I will have talked about how Serbs saw the Croatian flag as provocation because for them it evoked the Croat's Nazi-puppet ustaše regime during the second world war when Croats had fought Serbs. I often show the film *We Are All Neighbors* from the British *Disappearing World* film series. This film powerfully documents the coming of the war to a Bosnian village where a Norwegian anthropologist, Tone Bringa, had been doing ethnographic fieldwork. While students are usually deeply saddened by the distressing final scenes of *We Are All Neighbors*, the reasons behind the war are utterly incomprehensible to them and it seems that the power of patriotism and national identity is lost on them until their own national values are insulted by the "Flags" exercise. This, of course, is not to say that this exercise can be equated with the horrors of the war in the former Yugoslavia; but the "Flags" exercise helps illuminate the ideas from the prior class discussion because it hits closer to home.

I do not know the original source of this "flags" idea. Someone once told me about a professor who asked students to rip up little American paper flags, but I feel I have improved the impact of the exercise by asking students not to draw an American flag, but instead to scrawl squiggly stars and then lines. In other words, I don't ask the students to draw a symbol, but instead I encourage them to hastily and sloppily scribble on scrap paper. Then, in this "useless" mess, I let them find the symbol; I let them make the meaning for themselves. Additionally, I have added the "control" of the Japanese or Bangladeshi flag. I believe it helps drive home the point all the more effectively as students see how their perspective created meaning in the scribbling.

After you finish talking about "Flags," be sure to clean up the classroom since you don't want to leave ripped up paper for the next class or for the custodial staff to clean up. I exploit one more point from the exercise as I walk around with the bin asking everybody to pick up the paper: it's nice to get the word to one's students that we shouldn't take the Buildings and Grounds people for granted, and that it is good to be friends with people who clean your building.

Handle "Flags" with Care

Part of the effectiveness of "Flags" is, frankly, in its gimmickry and shock value. Students are actively doing something and then they are confronted with a moral/civic dilemma upon which they are expected to act (or not act) in an instant. Any emotions invested in their country and flag are suddenly exposed; it's a deliberate attempt to hit a raw nerve. I calculatingly try to create an innocent, childish atmosphere, before hitting them with the idea of ripping up a (possibly) cherished symbol. Obviously, I'm being manipulative and some theatricality is necessary to pull this off effectively.

It may not be something that every teacher should try. I would never recommend doing "Flags" until you are fairly comfortable with your class, since some people may find this exercise offensive. Don't do this with a class in the first few weeks of a semester or until you're pretty sure you have a good enough rapport with your students.

Think about how the "Flags" exercise could go wrong. Envision a student who lost a sibling in a U.S. military action who could start crying. Maybe some students could be infuriated enough to call home to complain that flag desecration is being taught at this school, and then how are you going to explain this to the dean?

For me, "Flags" has been well worth the risk, but just a few people let me know that they "didn't like it one bit." It ticked off one student, a retired worker who was coming back to school to work on an undergraduate degree, to the point that I ended up inviting him for coffee afterward to further explain what I had been trying to do in the classroom.

He was willing to concede that the exercise made the points that I was trying to get across much more alive and personal. He said he respected my effort, but I think he still came away from our conversation feeling rather ambivalent.

Another time I was teaching a very small continuing education class in which I happened to have in the same class, an older veteran, a native Japanese student, and a born-again Christian who was having a lot of trouble understanding the concept of ethnocentrism. In this case, I simply decided not to do "Flags" at all — I judged the risks of alienating any of these three people greater than the demonstrative power for the rest of the class members. Nonetheless, in the classes where I have done this exercise, most students have found this illustrative action and the ensuing discussion to be a very memorable way to think about symbols and nation.

Taking Students on a *Walkabout*

Michael J. Oldani

It was into my third year of teaching when it dawned on me that I was at my best when I was able to sell students on the merits of incorporating an anthropological perspective toward their views of other cultures and societies as well as into their own individual lives.

As all instructors of introductory anthropology know, there is a lot of material to cover in the course. In order to keep things fresh and the students engaged, one strategy I employ is to mix film with lectures and class discussions. I am fortunate to have access to both *National Geographic* films (for evolution and archaeology) and the *Faces of Culture* series (for culture and linguistics) as well as some current documentary films such as *Amazon Journal*. All of these films go over quite well. However, it is the showing of the feature film, the *Walkabout*, where most students are forced to confront a very ethnographically rich and critically engaged commentary concerning the "west" and the "other."

The *Walkabout* was filmed in 1971 by Nicolas Roeg. It has been hailed by critics as a "masterpiece" for many reasons. The setting is Australia and the film begins with scenes of a modern city. A father is at work, goes home, and while having a cocktail and waiting for his wife to make dinner, he watches his children swim in their pool. Shortly after, the scene switches to the Australian outback, where the same father is taking his daughter and son on a presumed picnic. As the daughter begins to display their picnic lunch and her younger brother plays in the distance, the father begins to *shoot* at both of his children with a gun. After failing to kill his children, he burns his automobile and turns the gun on himself. (You may want to warn your students of this initial violent scene.) The children are thus left on their own in the Australian outback to begin their own walkabout. As they wander, they only have a battery-operated radio, some toys, a few bits of food, and a bottle of water, and are quickly near starvation and dehydration. Unfortunately, after finding an oasis which literally dries up while they are there, they are again facing near death conditions, when over the horizon a figure emerges. At first he seems to be dancing and then we realize he is hunting iguanas, and that he too is on his walkabout. This young aboriginal boy approaches the "whites" as they desperately try to communicate to him that they need water. Finally, by gesturing to him, the aboriginal understands and shows them how to find water in the ground and suck it up through a reed. The three of them leave the oasis together and this begins the major narrative of the film – a journey through the outback and back to "civilization."

Throughout the rest of the film we come to realize that the aboriginal boy does understand and speak English, but chooses to communicate only in his language. We realize he could deliver the children back to their "European" world, but he chooses to wait. We also come to realize the aboriginal boy and the "white" girl are attracted to each other, yet this attraction can never be fulfilled. Slowly, steadily, and uneasily, we begin to understand that this film can only end as it began – in tragedy.

The *Walkabout* is a rare and unique film that allows for very stimulating (at times intense) discussion after its viewing.

Important anthropological topics, such as western notions of civilization, "primitive," nature, and "race," as well as concepts of cultural relativism and modernization (and post-modernization) are discussed. An especially powerful scene in the movie where a "cheap-labor" force of young aborigines is depicted making plaster casts of their own cultural artifacts inevitably leads to discussions concerning enculturation/ deculturation, and occasionally (and to my delight) indigenous rights, colonialism, post-colonialism, and ecotourism. Finally, depending on the class and previous discussions, "orientalist" discourse is discussed as well as bourgeois notions of utopia (both natural and civilized). After a long term of anthropological theory and terms, the *Walkabout* in a timeless fashion allows for a visible rendering of issues and concerns that anthropology is confronting today.

I usually require students to write a brief essay of their interpretations and critical insights regarding the film, but not a mere summary. Many students were "blown away," others found it "sad," "depressing," or "weird." However, a large majority of students felt the movie had caused them to "see things differently," giving them a "different perspective" on life and the lives of others. By complimenting the film in this way, one of my goals as a teacher was achieved – an anthropological way of thinking had seeped into their consciousness. Introductory courses in anthropology are themselves a journey and the *Walkabout* can help make it memorable.

Note:

The *Walkabout* is available large video stores.

Building Student Interest, Input, and Engagement: Organizing Small Group Projects in Large Classes

Marilynne Diggs-Thompson

The Problem

Some departmental faculty said it couldn't be done, or shouldn't be done, that the logistics were just too complex to ultimately be feasible. If one wanted to conserve time and preserve sanity, then using small groups, giving two exams, **and** assigning two written papers is simply out of the question. My teaching experiences elsewhere were with class size set at a maximum of 50 students. At Hunter, with a combined enrollment of 380 students in two introductory sections of cultural anthropology, it would seem that common sense and crowd management would mandate multiple choice exams, straightforward, and relatively simple assignments. Yet, given the tendency for large classes to be sterile, uninspiring, and often confusing to first year and even upper level students, I felt the need for a different approach.

Without engagement and personal connection with the instructor and with each other, the drop out rate (both on a temporary and permanent basis) for large enrollment courses can be quite high. And when I first developed this more intensive, interactive approach, I had the additional complication of teaching two different sections at opposite times of the academic day. In the early section (9-10 am), students were just waking up, if they made it to class at all. The later section (3:45-5) fell at the end of the day for most day students and often the temptation was to cut that last late class and start the evening or weekend a little early. Thus the challenges (in addition to the obvious ones) became how to keep the masses awake, impart knowledge, engage their interest, get to know them at least a little, and encourage directed dialogue among each other. Given a New York City location, the student body is one of the most culturally and ethnically diverse in the country. Additionally, student activism and extracurricular involvement continues to reach new heights, I felt that this was an ideal setting for my experiment.

A Solution

My first tasks were to select a relatively straightforward user-friendly but comprehensive text and to construct a clear, direct yet flexible, syllabus to keep us all on track. I use Haviland's *Cultural Anthropology*, 9th ed. (2000). It also seemed important to distribute a separate one-page summary of guidelines for writing assignments that included the due dates and the expectations for each specific assignment. The text, covering traditional introductory cultural anthropology material, is supplemented with two small contemporary studies of ethnic groups (from the Allyn and Bacon *New Immigrant* series) to be tackled at the end of the term. The syllabus mandates the reading of the *New York Times* at least three times a week with the specific charge that the first written assignment would be a one page summary of a newspaper article that discusses a contemporary social, cultural, economic, or scientific issue. This assignment is designed to drive home the fact that anthropology is not just the study of ancient, extinct, primitive, or remote peoples. The secondary purpose of this assignment is to identify group project topics that are related to specific topics in the assigned text. The other one page assignment requires that students provide follow-up on the initial topic and critique the way the article is presented. Both papers also serve the purpose of getting students accustomed to writing academic papers early in the term; this in turn serves my own covert agenda which is to get students to develop the habit of reading a "national focused" newspaper.

Ultimately, I select approximately 60 topics and then classify them into 20-22 broad themes that correspond roughly to chapters in the basic text. Next, I randomly divide the class into 20-22 groups; in order to achieve maximum participation and to prevent some students from being left out or overlooked, I refuse to allow them to pick their own group or topic. (In a class of 190 students, this makes the groups of 9-10 students quite manageable.) Each group selects one of the 20-22 topics (a representative from each group randomly draws a topic from a hat) for which they are to give group presentations at the end of the term. Members of each group are encouraged to exchange telephone numbers, and in addition to the fifteen minute get-together allowed in class each week, are encouraged to meet informally whenever possible. The group project is worth 10% of their final grade and students are told that an evaluation will be made of their final presentation and the demonstrable level of involvement of each group member. Predictably, the endeavor is not a bed of roses and requires a certain amount of time, patience, and persistence on the part of all. Complaints and problems are expected: for example, some students complain that other students fail to appear for group meetings, or do not contribute to discussion or preparation. However, in the end, a clear division of labor did emerge and each group finally settled into a regular working pattern.

Results

I have used this approach for four semesters and am happy to report that the process gets easier and the logistics now run fairly smoothly. Because it is interactive, I find that both morning and evening students respond well to this approach. The process of preparation animates the morning students and keeps the late-afternoon students awake and involved. More importantly, the results have been astounding and certainly have surpassed my expectations. My students and I have enjoyed imaginative, insightful, thoughtful, and thought-provoking, highly creative presentations on topics such as: prevention and treatment of HIV and AIDS; the declining effectiveness of antibiotics (biological anthropology); gay and lesbian marriage and parenthood, arranged marriage versus "romantic" marriage (sex and marriage); bilingualism and linguistic nationalism (language and communication); homelessness and "street people" (patterns of subsistence); global capital, global music, the power and abuses of multinational corporations, computer technology and its discriminatory effects, sweat-shop labor (globalism and culture change); welfare and workfare, unemployment and underemployment, Russian capitalism, dismantling the U.S. welfare system, and a topic that we are locally fond of, the socio-economic foundations of anti-CUNY attacks (economics).

To date, students have been attentive, involved, and more importantly, responsive and supportive of each other's presentations. They have utilized poster formats as well as video and audio-taped media to make their points. This allows students who are extremely shy, uncomfortable with English, and/or creatively talented to showcase their

157

contributions. Despite the size of the groups, students have divided the labor so that each member is able to demonstrate a specific participatory task. For example, some students have introduced the presentations while others have summarized their group's presentation in a concluding statement. When students within a group have found themselves at opposites ends of an issue, they have taken sides and presented the material in the form of a debate. Some students have prepared class handouts, while others have created slides, transparencies, or charts. Certainly students have added to their body of knowledge well beyond the boundaries of introductory course materials. They have connected anthropology with real and contemporary local and world issues and have added their own interdisciplinary dimension to the subject.

Three other tactics prove to be helpful and supportive of the end of term group project approach:

... the "mid-term" and "final" exams are replaced by "Exam 1" and "Exam 2," each covering different material, the latter taking place at the end of the completion of the textbook assignments, approximately three weeks before the end of term;

... the final 3-4 page final take-home essay/ paper is based on the short ethnographies of particular ethnic groups and due the last week of class;

... while several groups (approximately half) who select projects corresponding to "formal anthropological" topics make their fifteen minute group presentations during the week in which the "formal" topic is covered in class, the final three

weeks of class are given over to the remaining presentations.

Students are instructed that their group presentations must in some way enhance, expand, or debate material obtained from their reading of the *New York Times* and/or issues covered formally in the text. For example, I notice that many groups introduce their presentations with either the formal definition of a term or concept, or with "ethnographic" examples cited in the textbook. They then proceed to elaborate or to debate the text readings with information they have assembled from library and Internet sources and with information that they have obtained from the *New York Times*.

The timing of exams and student's preoccupation with preparing for the final presentation are tactics that combine to significantly reduce stress. In addition, the elimination of the traditional end-of-semester final has resulted in a significant reduction (about 80%) in the number of students who are absent from exams. The reduction of exam-associated stress allows students to concentrate on writing final papers and to become actively involved in preparing for the final group presentation. I am rigorous about taking attendance during the final three weeks of presentations (by way of sign-in sheets), particularly since I have told students that grading of their final presentation is also contingent upon their attending the presentations of other groups.

Granted, not all colleges and universities around the country have as culturally diverse a student body as Hunter College, nor is the *New York Times* easily available in large numbers outside of New York City. However, you could either make a deal with your local newspaper stand to get multiple copies of the *Times* for the term and place them in an established place (such as at the reserve desk in the library and/or in folders placed in your departmental office) or assign another "national focused" newspaper that is more readily available.

Conclusions

What about those skeptical faculty who said it couldn't be done? Some faculty argue that the process involves too much grading and is too time consuming; I certainly won't argue with that. But this approach lends itself very nicely to the excellent use of a teaching assistant to help in grading the writing assignments and in organizing the group topics. And I must admit that I derive a great deal of pleasure from watching students (mostly nervous freshmen) who start the semester as disconnected strangers begin to enter and exit class animatedly chattering in groups. Another advantage of using small groups is that they provide a venue for students to pose at least some questions and/or queries to each other, exchange missed lecture notes and materials, and build support for informal study groups. In short, using the small group approach in large classes allows me to turn a demanding teaching situation into a process of mutual learning, personal satisfaction, and to generate excitement among initially resistant student participants.

Reference Cited

Haviland, William
    2000. *Cultural Anthropology*, 9th ed. Ft. Worth TX: Harcourt Brace.

Nacirema Writing

John M. Coggeshall

"OK -- everybody take out a piece of paper and put your name and social security number on it." Twelve times a semester, these words stimulate first a groan and then a rush of creative thinking in undergraduate students enrolled in my introduction to anthropology course because the command signals a forthcoming essay on an article due to be discussed that day. Those who have read the assignment listen carefully for the imminent question they will have to answer, pens in hand, prepared to start writing. Those unprepared nervously search the faces of their classmates for some clue as to the content of the reading they now regret "blowing off." After 10 minutes, the students pass in their answers and class formally begins -- with a discussion of the article assigned for the day.

The purpose of these in-class essays is to fulfill several important pedagogical purposes: to supplement text assignments, to improve student writing, to enliven class discussions, and to guarantee student compliance. While many students may not consciously recognize an improvement in writing skills during the semester, students receive ample practice in summarizing complex information within a concise and coherent paragraph or two. Secondly, the essays enliven and enrich in-class discussion. It is often difficult to get students to talk, particularly in large classes, and the essays guarantee that they will have ideas to share. Finally, the writing assignments help guarantee that students will have actually read the article and the instructor can be relatively assured of a base level of knowledge for the entire class, providing a springboard for launching additional lecture or discussion material. Most students, anticipating a potential essay with every reading, will have read each article before class. This assumption is theoretical, of course, but it seems to work.

Through trial and error, I have learned to address the essays in the course outline and to offer hints to students for reading. In the "course mechanics," I write "Note: appropriate article preparation requires that you read carefully the assigned article well before class begins. Hints: (1) take notes on the main ideas of the article; (2) summarize the main points, and (3) think about how those points relate to class information. Do not substitute highlighting for note taking. Remember that I am not interested in, nor will I test you on, definitions and/or terms from the readings; rather I am interested in your ability to relate what you are reading to a larger context." Students typically highlight what they consider to be important points from articles. Note-taking, on the other hand, requires that students not only read but translate the important points into their own words, reinforcing the learning process even more by the act of recopying.

The articles that students read for these timed writings are taken from *Applying Anthropology* (Podolefsky and Brown 2001), but could as well be taken from any typical undergraduate collection or from articles gathered from instructor-selected sources. The questions I ask are not summaries; rather, students must draw upon information from the article in order to answer a related question. After the essays are turned in, we have a class discussion on the question upon which they had just finished writing.

At the next class session, I often read an essay example (anonymously) to the class to illustrate what a well-reasoned argument sounds like. This is an oral follow-up to a statement in the course outline that clearly tells students how their essays are to be evaluated. Under "grades and assignments," I write "Essays -- in order to enhance analytical and writing skills, brief essays will be assigned in class, usually based on the assigned articles in the reader. At the beginning of class, you will be asked to write for about 10 minutes on a question relating to the assigned reading or video for that day. Notes cannot be used as memory aides. Thus it is imperative to have done the readings carefully before coming to class. Essays will be evaluated on a 10-point scale as follows:

10 pts = clear and detailed; insightful
 9 pts = clear and detailed
 8 pts = details need elaborating but
         generally answered question
 7 pts = too much unnecessary information
 6 pts = too vague
 4 pts = absent for essay

Writing experts often argue that in-class writings should not be graded because to do so might inhibit free expression; students can get overanxious about spelling to the point of missing the point of the essay. I tell students that I do not evaluate their essays in terms of grammar or spelling but evaluate them solely for their content. This allows students who have carefully read the articles and thought through their answers to be rewarded. In turn, students need not worry about grammar and free-write instead.

Here is a specific example: for Horace Miner's classic "Nacirema" article, I ask students to explain what the basic Nacirema value or attitude is and whether or not it differs from our own. Those students who have not read the article generally either admit their lack of preparation or guess at an answer. Those who have glanced at the article generally write about the Nacirema concern for health as their answer to the basic value question, while those who have read it more carefully recall the Nacirema concern about the body. Even better students make the connection that the Nacirema consider the body to be unclean and degenerating, and thus undergo painful rituals. I award the maximum amount of points for original thought or good organization, regardless of whether the writer actually recognized themselves as Nacirema.

Similar essay assignments could be given in any upper-division anthropology class, even those that might at first not appear structured enough to utilize a collection of articles. Students in methods classes, for example, could read and critique the methodology from journal articles. They could also develop their own research project using the same or an alternative methodology. Likewise, students in a theory class could explain the underlying assumptions by the author of an article, and perhaps critique those ideas against another theory already mastered in class. Regardless of the topic, students can be asked to write and to think critically, and can do so effectively. And, as a bonus, the instructor has a class that is prepared to discuss the day's topic.

Reference Cited

A. Podolefsky and P. Brown, eds.
    2001. *Applying Anthropology, 6th edition.* Mountain View CA: Mayfield Publishing Company.

Familiarizing the Exotic in Ethnographic Film

Sam Pack

The Problem

Ethnographic films are now a common component of many introductory anthropology courses. Since most students enrolled in these courses are not anthropology majors, but rather are taking the course because it fulfills general education requirements, this is the one and only chance most students have to see the cultural "other." Generations of students have become acquainted with people from all over the world through such classic ethnographic films as Robert Flaherty's *Nanook of the North* (1922), John Marshall's *The Hunters* (1958), Robert Gardner's *Dead Birds* (1963), and the Timothy Asch/ Napoleon Chagnon corpus on the Yanomamo. Although for some instructors, films provide a needed respite from lecturing duties, for the vast majority, films are shown in a serious attempt to convey anthropological knowledge in a way not possible through a written medium.

In a highly heralded project, Wilton Martinez conducted a reception study of ethnographic films among undergraduate anthropology students at the University of Southern California and found that instead of challenging stereotypic perceptions, these films confirmed and reinforced prejudices that audience members held toward foreign cultures (1990, 1992, 1994, 1995). Martinez's study has sounded a panic alarm in anthropological circles because of its subversive implications: "These 'symptomatic' readings indicate more than a pedagogical problem; they suggest that the use of film has powerfully catalyzed the crisis of representation in the classroom" (1992:132). His conclusions suggest that anthropology instructors may be unintentionally perpetuating the devaluing of other cultures by screening ethnographic films to their students.

Martinez calls the interpretive gap between the intentions of the film makers and student responses "aberrant readings" (1992:132). However, a key weakness of Martinez's study is that he does not address where these so-called "aberrant readings" come from, presents no explanations for their causes, and offers no suggestions for solving the problem.

Why do ethnographic film representations reinforce negative stereotypes? Once we begin to understand the answer to this question, we might be able to help solve the problem. I contend that negative stereotypes of the "primitive" are inherited by and perpetuated through popular media representations. After a lifetime of exposure to television programs, feature films, music videos, video games, and the like, how can consumers of the electronic age view the "exotic other" in any way other than negatively? Based on the breadth and depth of this inculcation, there is nothing "aberrant" about these readings at all. They are, in fact, perfectly normal readings.

So it should not be surprising that students watch ethnographic films from an inherently ethnocentric perspective. One of the students I interviewed in my own reception study (Pack 1997) eloquently states:

> We're going to watch the things and look out for the important things to us. That's the most fundamental problem about learning things when

it comes to different cultures. We, through media, through television, through advertising, through personal experience, through what we learn from our parents, we grow up our entire lives looking at – and I'll be real general – the world in a very certain way, other people in a very certain way. And to suddenly alter things that have been ingrained in our brains for our whole lives is exceptionally difficult. (Male senior, age 25.)

What a picture means to the viewer is strongly dependent on his or her past experience and knowledge. The reading of an image, like the reception of any other text, is dependent on a prior knowledge of possibilities. As anthropologist and film maker, Allison Jablonko points out, "people only 'see' what they already have in mind" (1988:175). In this interpretive setting, viewers construct their own meaning of images based on previously acquired knowledge.

Invariably, the viewer will interpret a film according to existing stereotypes from his or her own culture. Despite a film maker's best intentions, ingrained viewing habits encourage viewers to attribute to footage whatever stereotypic explanations they may believe to be accurate (Biella 1995:243). Research indicates that when the intended message conflicts with viewers' world view, the viewers' attributions will likely dominate (Ruby 1994:195). In the contested space between the power of the film maker and the power of the viewer, the latter will always win.

Different kinds of visual texts require different strategies of interpretation. Unfortunately, these are lacking for the majority of the viewing population. Most of our viewing socialization has resulted in a rather narrow or restricted set of viewing instructions and habits that have produced a meager repertoire of interpretive skills (Chalfen 1988:179). It is my contention that viewers of ethnographic film rely on viewing habits and interpretive strategies more appropriate to popular modes of representation. Simply stated, most viewers attribute to these films what they already know, or think they know, regardless of what the producer intended (Ruby 1994:195).

Indeed, both negative and positive stereotypes of the "primitive" are shaped by mass mediated images that influence how viewers interpret ethnographic films. But the reverse is also true: ethnographic, or that which purports to be ethnographic, representations reinforce popular ones. Thus, the process is circular rather than linear as the "reel" and the "real" are mutually perpetuating. To the undiscerning eye, the antics of the "Uta Bagee" (Professor Krippendorf's penis sheath-clad alter ego in *Krippendorf's Tribe)* is given credibility because of his similarity to a Yanomamo headman on "The Discovery Channel" or to Tim Asch and Napoleon Chagnon's portrayal of another Yanomamo headman in *The Ax Fight.* All of these images meld together into a homogenous, nameless, indistinguishable mass called "the primitive."

Solving the Problem: Pedagogical Pointers

Devising ways to combat ethnocentrism in film spectatorship in introductory level anthropology courses is certainly a formidable challenge. Ruby wonders how many instructors even recognize the need to deal with students' visual naivete:

"In order to teach anthropology with film, teachers have to first instruct students on how to critically examine what they see" (1995:28).

The majority of introductory anthropology courses survey a wide variety of cultures around the world. This form of "ethnic snacking" is hazardous to the goals of cultural understanding. One week it is the Dani, next the Yanomamo, followed by the Kayapo, and so on. Ethnographic film maker John Marshall asserts that "we shouldn't be surprised to hear that after a quick trip on the ethnographic Love Boat most students remain ethnocentric, oblivious and self satisfied" (1993:129). Even the most serious student has trouble remembering all of the exotic names, much less anything substantive about the culture of the given week.

As a pedagogical model to remedy some of these deficiencies, I offer my own experiences in teaching cultural anthropology through film. The introductory course I teach operates from an underlying premise that most students bring certain preconceived notions of "primitive" peoples that have been shaped by media representations of alien cultures. I designed the course to explore this relationship between ethnographic and popular constructions of the "exotic other" with the ultimate goal of utilizing the former to help dispel the latter. Therefore, I show *Krippendorf's Tribe*, a feature film starring Richard Dreyfus as anthropologist James Krippendorf in conjunction with *A Man Called "Bee,"* an ethnographic film about anthropologist Napoleon Chagnon, to compare and contrast the depiction of anthropology and its practitioners. In a similar capacity, we, as a class, juxtapose the African villagers in *The Hunters* with their fictional counterpart in *Ace Ventura 2*. This can be accomplished with any feature film that depicts "exotic" people in tandem with an ethnographic film about a comparable "looking" culture.

The class assignments further compel students into confronting their own ethnocentrisms. For their final papers, students select a feature film that describes some component of their own culture and relate its treatment by an ethnographic film. Paper topics include investigating kinship in *The Brothers McMullen* and *Jaguar*, culture change in *Hoosiers* and *Trobriand Cricket*, warfare in *Braveheart* and *Dead Birds*, and social control in *Good Fellas* and *The Ax Fight*. Feature films provide a wonderful spring board for class discussion and paper writing precisely because students feel a sense of competence and expertise when asked to comment on mass mediated forms of information that are so familiar to their media-saturated visual environment (Chalfen and Pack 1998:104).

In order for this assignment to be successful, the instructor must possess some degree of familiarity with a variety of ethnographic films to make adequate suggestions. Either in the absence of such knowledge or as a supplement to limited knowledge, I highly recommend *Films for Anthropological Teaching* (Heider and Hermer 1995). The book organizes anthropologically relevant films and videos alphabetically as well as by topic and geographical area. It also provides brief summaries of each entry and includes the necessary distribution information in the event that the college/university where the instructor teaches does not own a copy of the desired film or video.

164

Another assignment that I have found to work extremely well is asking students to analyze one of their home movies as if it were an ethnographic film about a culture different from their own. In a style similar to Horace Miner's Nacirema work, one of my students described a video of her wedding from a surprisingly detached perspective while another commented in detail about all of the exotic rituals involved in footage of a friend's 21st birthday party. By turning the tables, students were able to see and feel what it is like to be on the other side of the anthropological gaze. In the process, the us/them dichotomy begins to blur. Thus, one path to familiarizing the exotic – which is the expressed goal of all ethnographic films – is by first exoticizing the familiar.

References Cited

Biella, P.
1995. Academic Hypermedia: A Reply and Update. In *Visual Anthropology* 7(3):240-248.

Chalfen, R.
1988. Navajo Filmmaking Revisited: Problematic Interactions. In *Native North American Interaction Patterns*, R. Darnell and M. K. Foster, eds. Quebec: Canadian Museum of Civilization, pp. 168-185.

Chalfen, R. and S. Pack
1998. Why Krippendorf's Tribe is Good for Teaching Anthropology. In *Visual Anthropology Review* 14(1):103-105.
Heider, K. and C. Hermer
1995. *Films for Anthropological Teaching*, 8th ed. Arlington VA: American Anthropological Association.

Jablonko, A.
1988. New Guinea in Italy: An Analysis of the Making of an Italian Television Series from Research Footage of the Maring People of Papua New Guinea. In *Anthropological Filmmaking: Anthropological Perspectives on the Production of Film and Video for General Public Audiences*, Jack Rollwagen, ed. Chur, Switzerland: Harwood Academic Press, pp. 169-196.

Marshall, J.
1993. Filming and Learning. In *The Cinema of John Marshall*, Jay Ruby, ed. Chur, Switzerland: Harwood Academic Press, pp. 1-133.

Martinez, W.
1990. The Ethnographic Film Spectator and the Crisis of Representation in Visual Anthropology. MA Thesis, University of Southern California.

Martinez, W.
1992. Who Constructs Anthropological Knowledge? Toward a Theory of Ethnographic Film Spectatorship. In *Film as Ethnography*, P. Crawford and D. Turton, eds. Manchester: University of Manchester Press, pp. 130-161.

Martinez, W.
1994. Deconstructing the 'Viewer:' From Ethnography of the Visual to Critique of the Occult. In *The Construction of the Viewer*, P. Crawford and S. B. Hafsteinsson, eds. Aarhus: Intervention Press, pp. 69-100.

Martinez, W.
1995. The Challenges of a Pioneer: Tim Asch, Otherness, and Film Reception. In *Visual Anthropology Review* 11(1): 53- 82.

Pack, S.

1997.   Beauty and the Beast: Imagining the Primitive in Ethnographic Film and Indigenous Media.   Temple University. Unpublished paper.

Ruby, J.

1994.   The Viewer Viewed: The Reception of Ethnographic Films. In *The Construction 0f the Viewer*, P. Crawford and S. B. Hafsteinsson, eds. Aarhus: Intervention Press, pp. 193-206

Ruby, J.

1995. Out of Sinc: The Cinema of Tim Asch. In *Visual Anthropology Review* 11(1): 19-35.

Pre-Class Fieldwork:
Ethnographic Introductions

Dickie Wallace

For the first class meeting of every cultural anthropology course I have taught, I always begin with my "doing ethnography" demonstration. I find it to be a novel way to introduce both myself and the idea of ethnography to a classroom full of students who are accustomed to having a boring first class session. Although this "trick" may be more suitable for cultural anthropology courses, it could be used at the beginning of a four-field introductory level course as well. Class size is no obstacle as it works equally well in small or large classes. It does not work well in upper-division classes, however, if students know you from a previous experience. And, given the nature of the "trick," at a certain age, the instructor will probably not be able to "get away with it."

For each first class meeting, I come to the classroom well ahead of time. I leave a pile of syllabi on the front desk and a few notes on the chalkboard. One note asks students to take a syllabus and to read through it.

Then I sit in the back of the classroom as if I am a student, usually with the college newspaper in front of me or some innocuous reading material. I always have a copy of the syllabus with me. Then I wait and watch as the students come in. I take "field notes" during this time, observing seating patterns, interactions, mode of dress, cognizance of my syllabus note on the chalkboard or whatever occurs at that time and place. I record the passing time, "map" the classroom, and generally record the type of things I would record in the "field."

After a minute or two into official class time, a few people start getting edgy as they begin wondering if the teacher is going to show up. At that point I get up and walk to the front of the classroom. I quickly make it plain that I am the instructor and immediately launch into an explanation about participant observation and qualitative social science research. (I like to watch students come to realize that I am already teaching in the first five minutes and that they should be taking notes instead of sleeping through the usual introductory spiel and syllabus overview.)

I explain that I was doing an "ethnographic experiment" as they were coming into the room. I tell them that this has been the one point in the semester when I am able to see what my classroom might look like before the instructor has entered the room; once the presence of the teacher is known, the classroom power dynamic changes and students are likely to act differently. As I explain this, I summarize some of my "field notes" and pull out interesting details. Usually I can find some pattern in student seating: for instance, students who do not know each other will not sit next to each other until the class is more than half full. Or female students are more likely to read the chalkboard instructions and take a syllabus than are male students. And if the males take the syllabus, they usually don't read it. Unacquainted students are likely to speak to each other only if they sit next to each other in the five minutes immediately preceding class. Sometimes I can use the field notes to put the class at ease, inject some humor, and tease the males who didn't take a syllabus.

I ask students to compare the participant observation method with a questionnaire or an interview: "If I had asked you what students do before the instructor arrives, would you have been able to give me those details? Would you have observed these different behaviors? Would direct questions have elicited as full a picture as an ethnographic method?"

We also question whether my participant observation was ethical. Was I not spying by "misrepresenting" myself as students walked in? Could my data now be used against anyone? I mention, teasingly, that the best students are the ones who read the syllabus right away (as I hand out syllabi to the students who did not heed my chalkboard instructions). I talk about the second time that I did this pre-class fieldwork and how, just as I was about to identify myself, two students, who happened to know each other vaguely, sat down on either side of me and proceeded to talk about how they hoped the "instructor in this class wouldn't suck." I explain that if I were truly doing ethnographic research, that for ethical reasons, I would have had to introduce myself at the beginning of the observation. Doing pre-class fieldwork allows me to discuss participant observation and ethics in an ethnographic context beyond the classroom situation, one that all field anthropologists find themselves in at one time or another. I conclude this subject, for the first session anyway, by talking about the difficulties of doing research when one is up front about research objectives.

Only later in the first session do I worry about attendance and rosters, the syllabus, and where to buy the textbooks. At the end of the class period, I hand out the first assignment, in which students must work together to write "mini-ethnographies."

I have often worn a baseball cap and a baggy T-shirt the first day of class in order to blend in with students, though to be honest, as I get further away from the "traditional student" age, I am not sure how much longer I will be able to use this "trick." Most recently, I have had two students insist that they found me very suspicious because I did not "look right" and I was "way too busy writing stuff" to even be a non-traditional student!

Hopefully, however, I will be able to continue doing some form of this "Pre-class Fieldwork" because it catches student attention and helps establish rapport quickly. And, best of all, it shows students that ethnographic methods are really part of our everyday world, making cultural anthropology immediately relevant.

Potlatching Classroom Participation: Using "Prestige" and "Shame" to Encourage Student Involvement

Daniel M. Goldstein

The Problem

"How can I get my students to participate in class?" I had been teaching anthropology for only a few months, but I had found myself voicing this question on more than one occasion. In my first forays into the college classroom, I was shocked to encounter what one colleague referred to as "the wall of silence," the refusal by students to participate in classroom discussion. When I tried to engage students, they would only stare mutely, lips pursed, blinking at me like fish inside a glass tank. I wondered if there was a conspiracy of silence among the members of the group. Most students steadfastly rejected every invitation to participate in a dialogue about the course material, with only a few individuals willing to verbalize their ideas in the classroom.

Despite assurances from other instructors that this was a common problem in middle-sized undergraduate classes, I immediately blamed myself for the problem; perhaps I was not sufficiently firing the interest of my students, and so they remained mute. A better teacher could surely get some reaction from them. My second inclination was to blame the material: perhaps the ins and outs of Boasian historical particularism or Durkheimian conceptions of social solidarity were just too inherently dry to instigate much conversation. Finally, I blamed the students: maybe they were just too "dumb," or too unprepared, or so apathetic that I could not possibly hope they would respond to my urgings to participate in classroom discussions.

Ultimately, I rejected all of these hypotheses, and began to look for the solution to this problem in the complexity of classroom dynamics: perhaps there is something about public speaking that freezes the undergraduate tongue, such that only the bravest and most self-assured among them feel comfortable in voicing ideas or venturing questions. In conversations with students outside of the classroom, my suspicions were confirmed. It was not that I was an uninspiring teacher, or that the material on the history of theory in anthropology was inherently boring. Rather for many of them, the experience of voicing their ideas (as opposed to their opinions) was completely unprecedented. For undergraduates with limited experience discussing (or even thinking about) ideas and theories, speaking publicly on such topics can be a daunting prospect. Even students who have done the assigned readings for a particular class session and who have definite opinions about the material covered may hesitate to participate in classroom discussion out of a quite understandable disinclination to make fools of themselves before their teacher and fellow students. Embarrassment-avoidance behavior is practiced to ensure that situations do not arise in which they might be exposed to ridicule. In the particular class discussed here, this was compounded by the fact that classroom participation had not been explicitly factored into the semester grade, and many of the students were loath to speak in the absence of a tangible incentive. As a result, the majority of the class preferred to sit silently, allowing those braver, more articulate, and more experienced public speakers in the group to represent the majority when the classroom activity turned to discussion.

Student reluctance to participate in the classroom can have significant repercussions for student learning. The reluctance to speak impacts students' willingness not only to contribute comments in discussion, but also to ask questions on points of the lecture or reading that they find confusing or particularly interesting. Not wanting to ask a question that might appear "stupid" can be paralyzing, and many students would rather not risk seeming foolish even if it means they remain confused on a particular subject. Guarantees from the instructor that "There are no stupid questions" do not seem to help, nor do assurances that "if you are confused about something, many others in the class probably are as well." As questions go unanswered, the instructor, assuming that all is well with student comprehension, proceeds on to new material. Meanwhile, previous failure to understand goes uncorrected, impacting the student's ability to follow subsequent lectures, resulting in poorer test scores. Frustrated, the student "checks out," becoming even more reticent to voice an idea in an arena in which he or she "obviously" knows nothing, contributing to a downward spiral of incomprehension and resentment. The student may even retaliate on the instructor evaluation form at the conclusion of the course, giving the instructor low marks for, ironically, failing to encourage student participation or engage student interest.

For the instructor who wants to get away from a pure lecture format by incorporating classroom discussion and debate of issues into the lesson plan, the refusal on the part of many students to participate can be extremely frustrating as well. Though we recognize that student learning occurs via multiple avenues, of which passive absorption through lecture is but one, we are often at a loss as to how to encourage classroom participation so as to broaden our pedagogical effectiveness. Faced with student silence, it is quite tempting simply to blame the students, and to lapse back into pure lecture mode. This seems to be what students expect, after all, and it seems to require less effort on everyone's part.

A Solution

However, classroom participation can be encouraged and promoted through a simple trick that I call "potlatching" student participation in the classroom. It is a technique that I invented off the cuff in response to this problem of engaging student voices. The beauty of this trick is that it is easy, effective, and need only be done once or twice in a semester. Potlatching provides a brief but powerful impetus to students to participate in class, requiring each of them to offer at least one comment or question in the course of a class period (or two, depending on the size of the class). As a result, each student has the experience of speaking publicly on a topic in anthropology, of having taken the risk of actually venturing a thought or posing a question before peers and instructor. The outcome is that, at last for a few of them, this experience mitigates their personal reluctance enough that on future occasions they are more willing to speak in class. For particularly reticent classes, the potlatch game can be repeated many times during a term. The activity is most effective with classes of around 20 to 25 students, though a group as large as 40 could realistically benefit from it.

Potlatching student participation is based on the classic studies of the potlatch institution of the tribes of the northwest coast of North America, described in the work of such scholars as Franz Boas and Marcel Mauss. It is a particularly effective trick to use in courses such as the History of Theory in Cultural Anthropology, or in an advanced course in cultural anthropology, because the form of the method so neatly fits the content under discussion. In the description that follows, I will make reference to using the trick in courses I teach, but the technique can be applied to many other course situations. For example, since all introductory level courses (four- field or cultural) are apt to have a section on potlatching, it would not be out of line to have students read the "four pages" in the text that describe the classic potlatch at the beginning of the term with subsequent in-class use of the potlatch idea for discussion rewards. Just because potlatching is usually discussed as a topic under economics does not mean it can't be used earlier.

I begin the potlatch game by lecturing on Mauss (1954) and his analysis of the great feast of the potlatch (based in part on Boas's [1897] original fieldwork) as a "total social phenomenon," one in which many different "spheres" of the social world come together (e.g., the economic, the political, the religious, etc.). Mauss uses the potlatch as a central example of his theory of the gift. According to Mauss, though gifts purport to demonstrate the spontaneous generosity of the giver, they in fact must be understood as reciprocations of previous gifts, where the return is given under duress and extreme social obligation. Failure to reciprocate a gift (such as a potlatch feast and its attendant material and symbolic exchanges) leads to shame on the part of the individual or group unable to pay back the original gift. I also lecture on the creation of prestige through potlatching, that is, the ways in which individual and group status differentials are produced by means of ever-increasing potlatches. In the next class session, students see the film *Ongka's Big Moka* (Granada Television International 1990), that depicts the efforts of a "big man" among the Kawelka people of New Guinea to organize a big feast of reciprocity (*moka*) to avoid shame and curry personal prestige. Viewing this film juxtaposed with the readings on the potlatch provides some cross-cultural comparisons on the subjects of gift-giving and the maintenance of reciprocal obligations.

The third day begins the classroom potlatch. The trick here is that the instructor gives students an individual proxy "gift," and then requires that they pay it back in the form of classroom participation. Before class I print each student's name on a 3" x 5" note card. I then hand these cards out to the students in the class, each receiving the card bearing his or her name. (Many instructors begin the semester by having students fill out personal data cards, which could also be used effectively for this purpose.) Once these cards are given to each student, I inform them that they have just been "gifted," i.e., I explain they have received a gift from me, and now they are under obligation to pay me back. The only way they can pay back this gift is by returning the card to me, and the only way to do that is by attempting to answer a question posed to them. (In this way, their gift to me would be greater than my gift had been to them, a classic element of the potlatch obligation to always reciprocate with a larger amount than originally given.) After the gift giving, I review terms and ideas from the preceding few class periods, during which I had lectured on issues related to gifts and to the Durkheimian social theory at their foundation. Each student who answers a question pertaining to these terms and ideas can return his or her card to me, thus completing their potlatch obligation.

As a result, I inform them, they receive "prestige." (Although some instructors may wish to reinforce this prestige graphically with a gold star applied to the student's forehead or with a piece of candy, I am partial to maintaining the immateriality of prestige.) Inability or refusal on the part of some students to answer a question results in their being left holding their card, a marker of "shame" for having failed to reciprocate. Further, a student who makes a correct response then has the power to select the next student to have the opportunity to answer a question and thus discharge their potlatch obligation. This little twist injects an element of politics into the game, as students immediately begin trying to solicit the attention of successful question respondents. A dimension of nepotism also enters at this point, with students passing the favor of answering a question (how quickly it ceases to be a burden!) to their buddies in the class.

After this brief question-and-answer review period (lasting perhaps ten minutes, but depending on class size), I inform the students that we will now proceed with the day's lecture, wrapping up the analysis of the gift and beginning on other varieties of functionalism to have emerged from the Durkheimian foundation. Those students who have not yet been able to discharge their potlatch obligation are not permanently shamed, however, as I inform the students that they can still pay back their debt by participating in class in some way, either by asking a question, answering a question, or offering a comment. Then I begin my lecture for the day.

The effectiveness of this technique is immediately apparent. Students who previously sat stone-faced for the entire semester suddenly begin actively looking for opportunities to participate in the class. Students race to answer questions that I pose during the course of the lecture; this intensifies as the period nears its close and those who are still holding their cards begin to feel the weight of "shame" bearing down on them. Others raise their hands to offer comments on the material being discussed, or to ask questions from the readings they had done the night before. It really is amazing; previously, these same students had remained silent, refusing to pose what turned out to be really excellent questions. Throughout the class, a level of humor and high spirits is maintained, as those who have already achieved "prestige" laugh along with those still struggling with their "shame," sometimes stepping in to answer questions, gratuitously robbing those unfortunates of their waning opportunities. By the end of the class, all but a few students manage to discharge their potlatch obligation, and leave feeling relieved and rewarded. The positive emotion registers visibly on their faces. As for those unfortunate few left holding their cards at the end of the activity, I playfully wag my finger and pronounce shame upon them. They seem to take it in stride. I have repeated the game on other occasions and have found it to be effective in increasing student involvement in class even when the topic is not specifically the potlatch or the gift.

Potlatching student participation, it must be pointed out, is very overt and entertaining. From the outset, students recognize that it is a blatant attempt to force them to participate in class. Nevertheless, this recognition does not in any way hinder their willingness to get involved and play along. In fact, they do so with abandon: many of them seem to have been craving just such an excuse to put aside their inhibitions and express themselves; others vent their confusion over and frustration with the difficult material. An additional benefit of the activity is that it drives home for students the principles of the ethnographic potlatch and the experiences of shame and prestige that accompany it.

References Cited

Boas, Franz
  1897. *The Social Organization and the Secret Societies of the Kwakiutl Indians.* Washington DC: Report of the U.S. National Museum, 1895.

Granada Television International
  1990 (1976). *Ongka's Big Moka.* Chicago: Films Incorporated.

Mauss, Marcel
  1954. *The Gift.* London: The Free Press.

How to Teach Self Ethnography

John L. Caughey

Introduction

Anthropology shows us how culture influences the lives of people in other societies; turned back on ourselves, it also sheds light on the cultural dimensions of our own experience. A useful teaching trick is to take ethnographic techniques for studying others and systematically apply them to our own lives. Techniques of "autoethnography" or "self ethnography" are effective tools for engaging students' interest in introductory anthropology courses, in special topics courses, and in advanced fieldwork courses. Here, I will briefly discuss the theory of self ethnography and then show how its perspectives and practices can be used in conjunction with other teaching methods.

The Theory of Self Ethnography

Ethnography has always been oriented toward the study of "other cultures" but the idea of self ethnography lurks just below the surface. As Agar (1986, 1994) and others suggest, the paradigmatic ethnographic situation has been understood as the encounter between an ethnographer operating with one cultural tradition and a set of informants operating with an alternative tradition -- a different system for thinking, feeling, and acting in the world. As Agar suggests, it is the creative tension between the ethnographer's tradition and that of his or her subjects that provides the medium for understanding. One sees the other culture through contrast, because its beliefs and practices differ in multiple ways from the tradition the ethnographer thinks with. A key opening

involves "breakdowns" or "rich points," moments when our own expectations are violated. When your informant mentions that "sharks are people," that "the world is flat," or that a particular young person is "obviously more attractive" than another, one is alerted to the fact that the informant classifies sea creatures, understands cosmology, and operates with standards of beauty drastically different from your own. Instead of glossing over such statements, we need to cultivate them as key entry points into the orientations of other cultures. Awareness of difference reveals cultural construction that can then be systematically explored through interviews, observations, and the analysis of conceptual domains.

But rich points are not only entry points into the **other** culture, they are also the moments that raise our consciousness of our own cultural conditioning. To learn how others orient differently to animals, cosmology, and attractiveness raises all sorts of interesting questions about how these previously taken for granted matters are conceptualized in our own culture. Called to awareness these cultural domains can now be investigated carefully. Providing students with this "ah hah" experience about their own cultural conditioning forms the basis for teaching self ethnography.

Turning the systematic questioning and analysis of ethnography back on ourselves requires another modification of ordinary procedure. Many anthropologists still speak as if people operate with one single culture or cultural tradition. This is not useful in getting students to think about the cultural dimensions of their own lives. Most students, like other contemporary humans, are multicultural. They operate with a diverse and often conflicting set of cultural traditions. This is obviously true of "halfies" and other classically bicultural individuals but even students who have never left the United States are still likely to be influenced by a diverse set of religious traditions, work traditions, leisure traditions, music traditions, or political traditions. Often people know a minority tradition, a dominant tradition, and more than one ethnic, religious, or class tradition. It is also useful to get students thinking about the particular **relationship** they have with each tradition; ask them: "Do you have a dominant relation with the tradition, generally accepting its beliefs and practices? Do you have an oppositional relationship with the tradition, resisting and seeking to evade its orientation? Or do you have a 'negotiated' or critical relationship with the tradition, selectively accepting some aspects but modifying, resisting, or evading others?" Much more than a mono-cultural approach, such questions can productively fuel the use of self ethnography in anthropology courses.

Because the issues of self ethnography are clearest in fieldwork courses, I will begin with a discussion of how self ethnographic techniques can be used in teaching ethnography and then move to how they can be adapted for exercises in special topics and introductory courses.

Using Self Ethnography in the Fieldwork Course

The undergraduate field work course is the best way to give students a feel for the interest and power of the ethnographic experience including its self ethnographic dimension. While useful in many ways, guides to teaching this course do not adequately address self ethnography. However, this dimension can be added by getting students to turn the methods presented back on

themselves as well as on their informants. What follows is a way to do this.

Teach the fieldwork course as a life history class and require students to locate an individual whose cultural background is significantly different from their own. Tell students it is to be a dual or double life history since it is about the other's cultural experience in comparison with the student's own. The student's main assignment is to:

... identify the student's own and the other person's several cultural traditions;

... determine each person's "relationship" to each tradition;

... discover how each manages or juggles multiple traditions;

... consider how all of this has shaped past and current experience.

Ask students to keep this general inquiry in mind but direct them to focus on a particular theme or issue, such as how an individual's diverse traditions affect his or her experience of family or work or leisure or how the person negotiates two particularly contradictory traditions, such as evolutionary biology and fundamentalist Christianity, or how each person constructs a meaningful sense of life from disparate traditions. Suggest that all of an individual's traditions are likely to impinge on such focal issues, though some more than others.

The following exercises are useful in self ethnography. Before the students ask their informants about a given area of life, have them ask the question of themselves and write out the answers. Then, after interviewing the other person, have students reanalyze their own initial answers in light of and in contrast with the informant's responses. Usually they will find that the responses of the other, used as leverage for self inquiry, reveal new aspects of their own cultural conditioning and deepen self understanding.

Exercise 1: "Chapters of Your Life." The first task is to get an overview of each individual's life and to seek to identify how and in what context the person learned the various cultural traditions that were influential. Ask students: " If you were going to write your own autobiography, what would be the chapters or phases of your life so far? Label each chapter and then explore what was going on in each phase, particularly what cultural traditions you encountered and learned. For example, in a given phase were you introduced to a new occupational tradition, switched to a new school, or more deeply involved in a religious tradition?" Use class discussion of student self ethnographic exercises to show how people are introduced to new traditions at many different stages of life and how they incorporate them in relation to other traditions.

Exercise 2: "Who am I?" Ask students to think about the question "Who am I?" or "What kind of a person am I?" and write out a series of words and phrases as answers: " I am.....," I am a person who...." Locate each response in its particular language concept system. Is it a term from a work tradition ("waitress"), a psychological tradition ("adult child of an alcoholic"), a religious tradition ("lapsed Catholic"), a media tradition ("a John Wayne Fan"), a large bureaucratic tradition (224-55-9867)? Use class discussion of self ethnographic responses to help students see how their very sense of self is constituted by the concepts for kinds of persons available in the traditions they have learned to think with.

Exercise 3: Roles, Dramas, and Social Worlds. Ask students: "What social scenes, institutions, or groups do you move through over the course of a given day, week, month, and year? What are the work worlds, school worlds, clubs, commercial establishments, religious institutions, and entertainment worlds you move through? Take one or more of these worlds and explore it further. What is the dominant cultural tradition at play here? What role do you play here in relation to what set of others playing complementary roles? What expectations and obligations do you have as an actor in this role? What are the problems, strains, and successes in role play? Discuss the cultural structure of a current drama, a particular story about social interaction in this world." Use class discussion of self ethnograhic exercises to help students see how each of us moves through different roles with different cultures and different expectations. Help them learn to analyze their own and other people's worlds as culturally constructed dramas.

Special Topics Courses

In virtually any special topics anthropology course, self-ethnography assignments can be developed that require students to systematically map out their own cultural experience with the topic at hand. Since teaching self ethnography is especially effective when used in conjunction with interviews, consider having students pair up and do a series of interviews with each other while they are also doing self ethnography. If this is not feasible, you can still set up self ethnography exercises by using class readings about other cultures, including case studies of individual experience, as comparative leverage to get students to defamiliarize and then systematically investigate how religion or economics or aspects of social organization, such as gender or kinship or friendship or courtship, work in the cultural traditions they operate with.

Anthropology of the Mass Media

Since contemporary students are extremely involved in mass media, it is useful to tap this interest as part of such courses. A good format is to use readings that illustrate other cultural constructions of mass media and then to ask students to use this as a starting point for exploring the cultural dimensions of their own experience.

Exercise 4: Relationships with media figures. Give students the following assignment: "make a list of at least 20 figures (e.g. actors, sports figures, politicians, musicians, fictional characters) you know about through the mass media (television, film, radio, books, magazines, newspapers) and describe in a sentence or two how you feel about them. Pick one figure who has been significant to you. Consider how you conceptualize and emotionally orient to this figure. Do you like them or not? What real relationship would you say is most analogous to the imaginal mediated relationship you have to this figure (do you see the person as a hero, a role model, a friend, a lover, an enemy)? Through what media do you relate to the individual and what are these experiences like? How and to what extent does the person affect your consciousness, do you dream about him or her, recall past performances, or construct daydreams? How and to what extent does the individual affect your actual interactions (e.g. do you discuss the person with others, participate in fan clubs or listservs, use the individual as a model or anti model in deciding how to behave)? How and

to what extent does your interest in this figure connect to your particular social and cultural location in contemporary American society?"

Using this exercise helps students see how media figures are a pervasive and powerful part of our social experience. In class discussion, compare American orientations to mass media with those of other societies, or with traditional cultural orientations to spirits and gods, and show how a person's social location (age, class, gender, race, ethnic or sexual orientation, including complex aspects of individual and group acceptance of and resistance to these cultural categories) affects orientations to mass media figures.

Psychological Anthropology

Many aspects of such courses including the study of emotions, ethnopsychology, identity, deviance, and dreams lend themselves to self ethnographic exercises.

Exercise 5: The Culture of Dreams. Tell students about their assignment: "For the next ten days, keep a pencil and paper by your bedside and try to record a dream or two immediately upon awakening. Try to record the narrative of the dream from the inside as exactly as possible. Pick one (or more) dreams for cultural analysis. What was the dream like as an alternative world? What were the characteristics of the dream self, dream settings, other dream figures, and dream action? How is the dream world similar to and different from your culturally constructed experience in the waking world? How does the dream reflect your particular mix of cultural traditions and roles? Can it be read as a commentary on the stresses and strains of your waking social world? How might the dream be interpreted in the culture we read about last week? What meaning do you see in it? In our dominant American culture, dreams are often dismissed as meaningless, yet there is a lurking suspicion that they may be significant, e.g. psychologically revealing or even premonitions of the future. How do you read your dreams given these prevailing notions? How have dreams been interpreted in the religious, ethnic, or psychological traditions you know? To what extent do you use such traditions in thinking about your own dreams?"

Use class discussion to show how dreams are composed of culturally relative materials available in the individual's waking experience and how types of dreams can be systematically linked to the strains of particular roles (e.g. student dreams, waitress dreams, nurse's dreams) and how variously dreams have been interpreted in the multicultural traditions that prevail in different sectors of American society.

Introductory Anthropology Courses

In introductory classes, self ethnography helps students realize that the cultural perspectives, analytic concepts, and methods being introduced can not only illuminate other cultures but that they can also help us understand our own cultural conditioning. Simplified versions of all the above exercises are suitable for introductory courses as well as other relatively less complex exercises, such as the following.

Exercise 6. Greeting Rituals. Tell students: "As you walk around campus tomorrow try the following exercise. What thought process do you use as you see someone you know approaching you on a campus sidewalk? What are the cultural categories you use to classify different kinds of persons on campus. What kinds of options do you have as you approach the other person

(greet, avoid, or wait and see what the other person does) and how do you decide which option to use? What would happen if you chose to violate these rules, such as looking at a person you know but not greeting them?"

Use class discussion to describe how different cultures use different kinds of greeting rituals and how our rules reflect the pervasive power of our own culturally constituted system for social interaction. Discussion can help students see the struggles we all go through in accepting and resisting the ways our cultures sort people out into kinds of persons and the profound influence this has on our social experience.

Conclusions

Self ethnography helps students understand the cultural structuring of human experience and it helps them grasp the tools we anthropologists use for investigating cultures. Self ethnography raises students' interest in anthropology because they find that learning more about their own cultural conditioning is an engaging as well as important part of anthropological education.

Self ethnography works for us as teachers too. First, there are several ethical aspects to teaching self ethnography. To ask students to discuss their own lives and cultures in class or in homework papers is not a typical practice and may be initially strange or even threatening to a few students. Clearly we do not want to push people into making revelations they are uncomfortable with. We need to make sure students know that they have permission to avoid areas of life that they do not want to reveal and we need to create a classroom climate that is accepting and respectful of difference. It is also important for us as teachers to model self ethnography for the students. If we are asking students to analyze and discuss their own cultural experience we need to offer examples of **our** experience and to model ways of talking about them in class. It is useful to adopt a perspective of curious, interested self inquiry, to show amusement with one's self, to be critical of aspects of traditions one uses but feels critical of, but also to show respect for one's own sense of the value of cultural traditions one believes in whether these be anthropological traditions, ethnic traditions, or religious traditions. I think it is good to be relativistic about one's own beliefs but not cynical about them.

Finally, in my experience, teaching self ethnography is not only good for students, it is good for the instructor. For me it makes the effort to teach more interesting because it is more like collaborative ethnographic research than "just" teaching. To ask myself and my students to use self ethnography to dig into the ways cultures influence some aspect of our experience -- whether this be friendship, dreams, or greeting rituals -- and then to come together in class to discuss our efforts and compare our findings is surprisingly satisfying. By doing this together, students always teach me something new and interesting about how cultures structure our individual lives.

Notes

Behar (1996) provides a good review of the issues involved in investigating our own "intellectual and emotional baggage" as these have developed in the reflexive tradition of anthropological writing.

This approach to different "relationships" to cultural traditions has been adapted from a formulation on different "readings" of media ideologies as developed in British cultural studies (Fiske 1987:260).

How-to-do-it texts like Spradley (1979) or Emerson, et al (1995) typically advocate keeping a fieldwork journal and discuss the importance of being wary about the influence of one's own cultural perspectives in doing fieldwork -- but these directives are typically presented as methodological suggestions for studying others; they are not developed as ways of systematically raising one's consciousness of one's own cultural conditioning.

While a few instructors seem to fear that asking students to investigate their own cultural traditions risks jeopardizing their faith or loyalty in them, I have not found this to be the case. To know that something we do is culturally constructed and relative does not mean it is not valuable and important.

References Cited

Agar, M.
   1986. *Speaking of Ethnography*. Beverly Hills: Sage.

   1994. *Language Shock*. New York: Morrow.

Behar, R.
   1996. *The Vulnerable Observer*. Boston: Beacon Press.

Emerson, R. M., R.I. Fretz, and L. L. Shaw
   1995. *Writing Ethnographic Fieldnotes.*
Chicago: University of Chicago Press.

Fiske, J.
   1987.   British Cultural Studies and
Television. In *Channels of Discourse*. Robert
C. Allen, ed. Chapel Hill NC: University of
North Carolina Press.

Spradley, J. P.
   1979. *The Ethnographic Interview.* New
York: Holt, Rinehart and Winston.

Additional Reading

Caughey, J. L.
   1982. Ethnography, Introspection, and
Reflexive Culture Studies. *Prospects: An
Annual of American Culture Studies* 7:116-
139.

      1985. *On The Anthropology of America.
Epilogue to Symbolizing America*, Herve
Varenne, ed. Lincoln, Nebraska: University of
Nebraska Press.

   1994.   Gina as Steven: The Social and
Cultural   Dimensions   of   a   Media
Relationship. *Visual Anthropology Review*
10(1):126-136.

   1999. *American Selves: A Life History
Approach to the Study of Identity. Scholarly*
Resources Press, forthcoming.

Ellis, C. and A. P. Bochner, eds.
   1996. *Composing Ethnography: Alternative Forms of Qualitative Writing.* Walnut
Creek, CA: Altamira Press.

Grounding the Culture Concept, or Pulling the Rug Out From Students

Brent Metz

The meanings of "culture" in and outside anthropology have multiplied and undergone dramatic shifts in usage over the past century, leaving students lost among myriad versions. Even the best students often explain culture with incoherent combinations of "a(n Other) people," "an ethnic group," "customs," "a system," "adaptation," "heritage," "beliefs," "education," and even the occasional "art, literature, and opera." Some of the confusion reflects a popular equation of culture with "peoples," societies, or ethnic groups, thereby essentializing or racializing characteristics of "peoples" (Kottak 1997:20-21; Turner 1993:411-15). As a corollary, those who celebrate their ethnic ancestry (or imagined ancestry) often equate Culture with "high" Civilization by proclaiming "our culture (or ancestors) had great accomplishments too," like monumental architecture, literature, music, and art (Turner 1993:416-17). Multiculturalism can mislead "Whites" in particular to regard culture as something only Others have or are, whereas Whites are thought to have "lost" **their** cultures. Anthropology curriculums that overemphasize indigenous and tribal cultures compound the linkage of culture with Others. One student essay I read while writing this article used "people of race" and "people of culture" interchangeably to specify Latin Americans with African heritage.

Within anthropology, there continues to be as many definitions of culture as there are textbooks (cf. Kroeber and Kluckhohn 1952). Students in the same department may learn that culture is quintessentially about hominid adaptation, production, worldview,

ethos, patterned behavior, social cohesion, function, reproductive fitness, or power. More definitions for memorization are not the answer, nor is excising the concept from anthropological pedagogy. The challenge is to operationalize the concept for students by identifying competing versions, specifying where anthropological versions diverge and overlap, and demonstrating through personal and immediate examples as well as cross-cultural ethnographies the cultures in students' lives, thereby defamiliarizing them from their own mental and physical routines. Though students may be interested more in anthropological certainties than critical self-reflection (cf. Haviland 1997), learning to question one's cultures is a key function of anthropology, and operationalizing "culture" is pivotal for developing such a metacultural perspective. The following strategies for teaching culture have emerged from my trial and error teaching introductory cultural anthropology at seven universities and colleges and the discipline's changing approaches.

(1) Eliciting Student Versions of "Culture"

Even when a course has a derivative of "culture" in the title (e.g., Intro to Cultural Anthropology, Cultures of Africa, Gender in Cross-Cultural Perspective), it is tempting for teachers and students to take its meaning for granted. Directly addressing the concept from the start is key, and a brief discussion (**not** a definition) of culture is optimal. But before elaborating on your approach to "culture," it is useful to elicit student understandings of the term. You might preface your elicitation by explaining that varying versions are not "wrong" but must be distinguished from the course's usage, so that students do not feel you are setting them up for public humiliation. Some will likely confuse culture with an ethnic group, ethnicity, identity, civilization, or a society, but if they do not, it is still important to ask them directly how culture differs from but relates to these. A one-page paper in class on this theme is sometimes helpful to identify points for further clarification.

(2) Culture as Social Construction

Varying anthropological approaches to culture must also be confronted and consolidated. Rather than ignoring the variability and providing students with my authoritative definition to memorize, I emphasize the common denominators. Most discussions of culture include:

... learning as opposed to instinct;
... symbolic communication enhancing shared conscious and embodied, routinized knowledge;
... dialectical interplay with physical surroundings;
... power.

A helpful metaphor for cultural dynamism is "construction" because it infers an ongoing interplay and reminds us that cultures are forged or reproduced in social interaction rather than existing as primordial, discrete "things" or coherent self-regulating "systems" (Harris 1997). Power is also worth discussing, as many anthropologists are increasingly exploring how social construction often involves some people having greater negotiating power than others to popularize some understandings, routines, and settings and enforce the abandonment of others. Many anthropologists feel it is anthropology's role to uncover specifically how powerful constructors of global consumer cultures have enforced and obscured the extinction of local and regional cultures (e.g., Turner 1993).

(3) Microcultures: Grounding the Culture Concept in Students' Lives

I follow social construction with examples familiar and immediately relevant to students, challenging the "common sense" of their everyday lives. To convey that culture is about the construction of knowledge and routines in particular historical and physical contexts , I ask them to reflect on the unique understandings, jokes, and routines that they build with their roommates, fraternity brothers and sorority sisters, families, and work mates. We discuss these groups' communication styles and specialized vocabulary and their potential power. For example, we discuss what they learned in order to be a functioning waitress, roommate, or family member, and what they themselves have contributed to these cultures. Here, we are reflecting on the construction of microcultures internested within broader regional, national, and global cultural arenas (McCurdy 1994). In this way students realize not only that culture precedes them, but that they reproduce and construct culture everyday in their kitchens, work places, and classrooms. In fact, are we not creating unique understandings and practices in our course? Are we not constructing shared expectations, ethos, routines, and anthropological knowledge?

(4) How General Can a Culture Be?

Obviously, students bring pre-existing cultural knowledge, including some longstanding traditions, to the construction microcultures, such as language, recognized symbols for respect, and recreational tastes. To what extent is this knowledge shared with others? Can a general United States culture be said to exist? Students might offer such examples as shared symbols, understandings and practices regarding driving, economic exchange, television programming, consumer brands, or fashions. To what extent can a global culture be said to exist? Those with foreign travel (or internet) experience often relate the surprising ubiquity of even new technologies, consumerism (e.g., Coca Cola, music), and the English language. I emphasize, though, that while people may share general knowledge and practices, local contexts, meanings, and applications can vary widely. People in the United States and Bolivia may share general understandings about money, but meanings and practices regarding monetary exchange may vary dramatically.

Cultures, then, be they micro or macro, are overlapping and crosscutting because social relations are, and students soon comprehend that everyone is a unique, shifting cultural locus. Because people co-produce knowledge and routines in different social spheres, they can practice cultures that can contradict each other. To exemplify this, I ask them how they reconcile anthropological explanations of biological evolution with their religions. Most who share both a religious subculture and evolutionary understandings exhibit tension here, revealing that they have not yet done so. We may also turn to ethics to demonstrate the contradictions between values of cooperation, democracy, and equality versus the celebration of competition, leadership, and individual achievement.

(5) Knowing How? Knowing Why: Embodiment, Forgetting, and Power

To de-emphasize conscious thought, I remind students that culture involves subconscious bodily routines like walking in a particular fashion, the proverbial distances between partners in conversation, learned exclamations (like "ouch"), distinctive conversational rhythms, and narrative styles. We tend to be unaware of how or why we learned these practices, which exemplifies that culture is as much about forgetting and unreflective convention as it is about remembering. I ask them to ponder the origins of the buttons, zippers, and collars on their clothing, of eating some edible organisms and not others, of watching television over socializing in public places, and of attending universities versus on-the-job training. To call into question everything we do, however, such as calling barking four-legged creatures [dawg], tying our shoes, or eating with spoons is inefficient and irritating. When exposure to other cultures challenges our routines, we have a tendency to be defensive and ethnocentric, even though our routines may be no more rational than anyone else's.

It is the taken-for-granted character of embodied knowledge that makes culture especially potent. Without reflecting, questioning, and self-awareness, we are unable to imagine alternatives. Power thrives on ignorance, forgetting, and the inability to imagine alternatives just as much or more than it does on conscious ideology.

(6) Metaculture: Toward an Ideal Scientific Perspective

In this sense, both the information our courses provide about other cultures (demystification) and the culture of questioning toward our own cultures that it foments (defamiliarization) empower students to be more informed participants in social construction (Marcus and Fisher 1986). The class culture we are constructing entails understandings about understandings, a culture about cultures, a metaculture. I point out that a key contribution anthropologists make to the scientific community is their striving to build metacultures by which cultural bias can be identified. For most students, the meaning of science is as ambiguous as culture, and this issue is worth discussing despite some students' inevitable surrender to the "all is subjective; therefore, nothing is certain" argument. We discuss the fact that in one sense, science is an ideal quest for expanding unbiased, metacultural information by questioning one's data collection, testing and re-testing one's conclusions, and making them transparent for intersubjective scrutiny by others. This means anyone can engage in science, not just professionals, and innumerable scientific traditions exist around the world that complement Western ones. In another sense, the actual practices of professional scientists involve culturally specific languages, unproductive competition for personal gain, funding skewed by political, economic, religious or other interests, authority based on elitism, and privileged information, to identify just a few problems. Our school itself is subject to such influences. I always emphasize, though, that it is better to confront these challenges anthropologically and strive for metacultural science than do nothing at all.

(7) Applying "Culture" Throughout a Course

I find it necessary to revisit the concept throughout the course whenever possible. If It useful to assign a final paper that challenges the ability to demystify other cultures while defamiliarizing students from their own cultures. Sometimes I ask them to critique commercials aired during Sunday morning news programs that represent foreign Others to promote global capital investment.

we discuss fieldwork, I stress that ethnographers create cultures with informants more than they study them as laboratory specimens. Are they not participating in a joint construction of knowledge, engaged in others' understandings and routines as well as their own? With examples from my own fieldwork and through the imagined fieldwork of an ethnographer in their homes, I highlight how difficult it is for a professional stranger to pry information from others without reciprocating information about themselves, whether the exchange is equal or not. If we discuss Whorfian linguistics and the tendency by speakers of European languages to objectify or "thingify" abstract concepts and phenomena, I remind the students that the popular use of "culture" involves the same cultural process. To view certain groups of people as if they have inherent characteristics or traditions is the error of essentialism, to which lack of knowledge and our language make us susceptible. When addressing "race" and IQ tests, social construction and scientific improvability are again emphasized. When treating identity, I turn to the students themselves and point out that as much as some do their best to accentuate their individuality, they often do so within subcultural traditions, such that piercing, tattooing, and "alternative" music, for example, are not unique to themselves alone. When we discuss relativism and indigenous cultural rights, I emphasize that the struggle is not over timeless, static cultures, but the degree of social control over the construction of culture.

Likewise, I may call on them to respond to a subtly essentialist treatment of Other cultures in a popular magazine article, newspaper article, or TV show. Another popular exercise is to have students read an ethnography, preferably in the style of a personal ethnographic narrative or confessional, and then write a first-person ethnographic narrative from the perspective of a cultural Other from the book visiting a U.S. campus.

Some students meet the challenge of cultural self-application better than others, but all leave the course with more uncertainty as to the inevitability and rationality of the cultures they practice.

Note: I capitalize Whites and Blacks not to reify the distinction, but to accentuate that they have been reified or socially constructed, like Indians, Asians, Latinos, or African Americans for that matter. In my opinion, leaving Whites and Blacks un-capitalized naturalizes the distinction by conflating it with the spectral colors "white" and "black."

References Cited

Harris, M.
1997. Anthropology Needs Holism; Holism Needs Anthropology. In The Teaching of Anthropology: Problems, Issues, and Decisions. C. P. Kottak, J. J. White, R. H. Furlow, and P. C. Rice, eds. Mountain View, CA: Mayfield Publishing Company, pp 22-28.

Haviland, W. A.
1997. Cleansing Young Minds, or What Should We Be Doing in Introductory Anthropology? In The Teaching of Anthropology: Problems, Issues, and Decisions. C. P. Kottak, J. J. White, R. H. Furlow, and P.C. Rice, eds. Mountain View, CA: Mayfield Publishing Company, pp.34-38.

Kottak, C. P.
1997. Teaching the Introductory Course. In The Teaching of Anthropology: Problems, Issues, and Decisions. C. P. Kottak, J. J. White, R. H. Furlow, and P. C. Rice, eds. Mountain View, CA: Mayfield Publishing Company, pp.13-21.

Kroeber, A. L. and C. Kluckhohn
1952. Culture: A Critical Review of Concepts and Definitions. Cambridge, MA: Harvard University Press, Papers of the Peabody Museum, 47.

Marcus, G. E. and M. M. J. Fisher
1986. Anthropology as Cultural Critique: An Experimental Moment in the Human Sciences. Chicago: University of Chicago Press.

McCurdy, D.W.
1994. Using Anthropology. In Conformity and Conflict: Readings in Cultural Anthropology. J. P. Spradley and D. W. McCurdy, eds. New York: Harper Collins, pp.419-430.

Turner, T.
1993. Anthropology and Multiculturalism: What Is Anthropology That Multiculturalists Should Be Mindful of It? Cultural Anthropology 8(4): 411-429.